Enduring Schools:
Problems and Possibilities

Enduring Schools:
Problems and Possibilities

Rita S. Brause

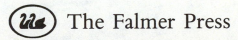 The Falmer Press

(A member of the Taylor & Francis Group)
Washington, D.C. • London

UK   The Falmer Press, 4 John St., London, WC1N 2ET
USA   The Falmer Press, Taylor & Francis Inc., 1900 Frost Road, Suite 101,
        Bristol, PA 19007

LA337
.B73
1992

© Rita S. Brause 1992

First published 1992

A catalogue record for this book is available from the British

Library of Congress Cataloging-in-Publication Data

Brause, Rita S.
    Enduring schools: Problems and possibilities/Rita S. Brause.
        p.   cm.
    Includes bibliographical references (p.   ) and index.
    ISBN 0-7507-0012-2 — ISBN 0-7507-0013-0 (pbk.)
    1. Education — New York (State) — Case studies.   2. Learning —
Case studies.   I. Title.
LA337.B73   1992
370'.9747 — dc20   91-44381
                                                                        CIP

ISBN 0 75070 012 2 cased
ISBN 0 75070 013 0 paperback

Set in 10/12pt Bembo by Graphicraft Typesetters Ltd., Hong Kong
Cover design by Caroline Archer

*Printed in Great Britain by Burgess Science Press, Basingstoke
on paper which has a specified pH value on final paper
manufacture of not less than 7·5 and is therefore 'acid free'.*

Contents

Contents

List of Tables and Figure

Acknowledgments

Now that I've finished writing 'the text' I face the most daunting task of all — that of expressing very personal feelings in a public forum. The professional documentation within the text identifies traditional information sources. But many others are responsible in large measure for my writing this book. They deserve public recognition as well.

From my early school days, my prime teachers were my parents, Ruth and Jack Brause, my sister, Roberta, my brothers Louis and Barry, as well as Jane Godfrey, Elizabeth Repath, Bertha Laufer, and Henry Mazur. Individually they inspired confidence in me and helped me envision more ideal worlds. As a young teacher I received much encouragement from Pearl O. Shutman, Edna Morgan, Bebe Calder, and Anita Dore. They privileged me to work with enthusiastic youngsters and neophyte teachers.

A whole new world opened up to me when I became a teacher-educator. At Richmond College (now the College of Staten Island of CUNY) my visions were enriched as I 'rapped' with Fran Silvernail, Peter Babcock, Judy McCoy, Donna Jeffrey, and Frieda Rosner. Bernard Walker's invitation to base the secondary teacher education courses in his newly opened junior high school, sustained my belief in the possibility of change.

John Mayher, colleague, collaborator and friend, has been the most influential person in the development of my understanding of schools and learning and a constant inspiration. Our conversations and projects over the past 20 years encouraged my pursuit of an 'uncommon-sense' perspective. In many respects this book is as much his as it is mine because so many of our collaborative projects provided important data on the complexity of the teaching-learning process and schools. Despite his hectic schedule he critically responded to every draft, enabling me to clarify my interpretations as well as my presentation. In a very real sense, without him, this book would not exist.

Josephine Bruno's concern for improving schools, particularly making school a place where students eagerly come, continues to challenge me. As the principal of a New York City bilingual elementary school she allowed me to talk with her teachers, parents and students. I met some dedicated teachers at Jo's school, particularly Don Murphy, who invited me to literally live in his classroom. We've had many challenging discussions trying to envision classrooms which engage students' interests while preparing them to participate in the larger society.

When I arrived at Fordham University, Dean Jonathan Messerli (now president at Muhlenberg College) encouraged me to make a difference. Max Weiner, the dean during most of my years there, has been most enthusiastic in his support of my work. In addition, I have benefitted from extended conversations with Bryant Fillion (now at Wichita State University), Fred McDonald, and Jerry Starratt. I have received two faculty fellowships which enabled me to devote intensive time to this project. During one of these, Paul Ylvisaker, then dean at Harvard's Graduate School of Education, invited me to luxuriate in the Cambridge community. His promise that it would be a 'memorable' year was certainly realized; I remember the exhilaration of that time with great fondness.

Many of my current and former students and other professional colleagues have also influenced me. Some participated in research studies, namely Dorothy Feola, Sandra Lanzone, and Greg Hodge. Others read drafts, providing insightful criticism along with encouragement to get it done, namely Kathy Malu, Arlene Moliterno, Sandra Lanzone again, Maxine Weiss, and Kathryn Smerling. Still others freely shared their activities and concerns, including Laura Miraglia, Sallyanne Waldinger, Susan Holt, Denise Levine, Fran Gilkenson, Sheila Rosenberg, Dorothy Kirshenberg, Cara Mulqueen, Maureen Clark, and Maria Radford-Fragoso. Ed Levine's graphics clarify complex presentations.

Judith Orasanu, when at the US Department of Education's National Institute of Education, encouraged the study of classrooms through financial support and personal involvement. Ray McDermott shared his careful procedures for analyzing classroom settings, as well as his concern for improving our schools. Those discussions influenced my own research as well as much of my current practice.

Conferences sponsored by the National Council of Teachers of English, the Conference on English Education, New York University, the International Federation for the Teaching of English, and LEARN provided important forums for contemplating these issues. Colleagues at these events, including Garth Boomer and Gordon Pradl, shared their concerns. Gordon gave freely of his time in reading an earlier draft. His critical comments contributed to a more clearly focused document. Others whose sharing of stories have contributed to this project include Ruth, Louis, Barry, Michelle and Ruth A. Brause, Angel Fragoso, Michael Lobel, Michael Preston, Cecilia Kingston and Hank Mayers.

Debbie Brause volunteered to read a very early draft of this book. Her inquiry into my reasons for taking certain positions helped me to rethink some of my ideas. Julie and Melissa Brause have been sharing their school stories, knowing they had a sympathetic listener. I greatly value their trust. David Brause's insistent probing as to how my book was coming along put just the right amount of pressure on me to get this done (and almost on time).

The person in my family who has been with me through it all — from my early days as a neophyte teacher — straight through the last draft of this book, is my sister, Roberta Brause. As beginning teachers we had daily conversations driving to and from our separate school assignments, sharing insights, strategies and stories. She is as committed as I to improving schools.

Jackie Brause's experiences (many elaborated on by Gerry Brause) have given me great hope that things can be different. I have learned much in the process and am deeply grateful. I consider myself blessed to have had the assistance of so many wonderful friends. I am sure all are as happy as I that this day has finally arrived.

Rita S. Brause
December 1991
New York City

The author and the publishers would like to thank the following.

Permissions

The author gratefully acknowledges permission to reprint the following materials:

pages 49–50   From *The Chomsky Reader* by Noam Chomsky, edited by James Peck. Compilation and interview copyright (c) 1987 by Noam Chomsky. Intro. copyright (c) 1987 by James Peck. Reprinted by permission of Pantheon Books, a division of Random House, Inc.

page 129   From *Life in Schools*: *An Introduction to Critical Pedagogy in the Foundations of Education*, by Peter McLaren. Copyright (c) 1988 by Longman Publishing Group. Reprinted with permission from Longman Publishing Group.

pages 153–4   From *Sonnets for Athena*, dissertation by James Hercules Sutton, 1988, (University Microfilms Order No. 8815143), with permission of the author.

pages 180–3   From *The English Coalition Conference: Democracy through Language*, edited by Richard Lloyd-Jones and Andrea A. Lunsford, NCTE, 1989. Copyright 1989 by the National Council of Teachers of English. Reprinted with permission.

Prologue: Learning — Process, Settings and Outcomes

As Benjamin Franklin wrote (probably drawing upon a proverbial expression), 'in this world nothing can be said to be certain, except death and taxes'. Schooling should be added to these two inevitabilities since parents enroll their children in school with the same resignation as they file tax returns, and students' disaffection with schools is legendary. Lucky children have one or two good teachers during their schooling.[1] As we enroll our children and bring them to school, we must do more than what a school principal recalls her mother telling her, 'I left you at the door and prayed you'd be educated.'[2] We must wonder:

- Why are so many students bored?
- Why are so many unhappy?
- Why do so many inspired teachers leave?
- Why do so many teachers get 'burned out'?
- Why don't schools reform themselves?

Schools[3] have failed not only those 20–50 per cent[4] of students who drop out without receiving a high school diploma, but also those who have graduated despite their limited understanding of the world, or of themselves. When left to their own resources, 44 per cent of high school graduates avoid reading books.[5]

Why do students and educators endure schools? Some find their happiness in perverse ways:

- By starting with low expectations from school, and supplementing school experiences with extensive enrichment, they are pleased that *anything* good happens in school;
- Those from homes which isolate or abuse, find school a refuge;
- Many defer happiness believing that once they get their high school diploma they will have increased employment opportunities, a chance for higher education and increased freedom to live the good life.

These outcomes are far removed from our implicit goals for schools: *to promote student understanding of society; to enable their active participation in advancing society; and to increase each individual's confidence and ability to learn and survive independently within that society*. It is the unusual student who becomes intellectually challenged and nurtured in our schools. Educators — teachers and principals, and society in general — want students to learn and to become excited about learning, but many practices limit the realization of our ideals.

Why Am I Writing *Enduring Schools*?

The thesis of *Enduring Schools* is that, despite the good intentions of all involved, there are dangerous consequences for allowing schools to endure and for rewarding those who endure it. This book helps us understand that our well-intentioned plans have gone awry, and how school practices need to change to achieve our democratic ideals. The complexities inherent in reform efforts become apparent in this process.

The findings presented here resulted from numerous studies over an extended time period, utilizing a combination of research techniques, principally critical ethnography and case study.[6] Most of the schools studied are in the New York City area. New York City schools are much like those across the rest of the United States with high drop-out rates, bored students, graduates unprepared to accept adult responsibilities, and high teacher turnover.[7] Perhaps the magnitude of the problem becomes more pronounced in New York City schools, especially the publicly financed schools, but the problems I address are pervasive, and not restricted to urban areas or public schools.

Although I could identify exceptionally brilliant teachers (or demoralizing ones), in the main, these are exceptions. Instead, I focus on typical teachers and students — much like Kidder (1988) and Sizer (1984).

This book documents my recognition of how the goals of democratic schooling are subverted, and how I, along with my professional colleagues, unwittingly become so caught up in the daily activities of schooling that we unconsciously perpetuate poor educational practices. This realization has evolved over a couple of decades, particularly from my opportunity to step back from daily responsibilities to reflect on the broader contexts which are influencing these practices. I find expediency and efficiency replace concerns for educational excellence. We have lost sight of learning in schools, despite our rhetoric. My perspective differs from previous critiques in two ways:

- it takes a holistic stance, considering the daily, six-hour experience which extends over a thirteen year time span; and
- it presents a professional educator's viewpoint on some of the effects of current schooling practices.

This book looks seriously at schools from a broad perspective, noting the interdependencies which influence much of what happens to most students in most classrooms. I hope that by providing a better set of lenses through which to see schools, the total community will engage in open discussions, where professional educators can become less defensive and where our collaborations can result in the establishment of more effective educational settings.

Like other reports starting with the National Commission on Excellence in Education (1983), *Enduring Schools* calls urgently for dramatic change.[8] By 'going public' rather than keeping this book within the educational community, I believe it is more likely that there will be the drastic reforms essential to create schools which are educationally sound. Adults working in schools devote little time to conceptualizing alternatives. Silence on the part of concerned professional educators deceives the students, the parents, the community and the profession-at-large. Most professional educators avoid addressing these real problems both in their own settings and with outsiders. In contrast, I am compelled to share my understanding of the major problems we have and offer strategies for improving education. We need everyone's help; none of us can do it alone.

The need for educational reform is clear. For example Goodlad (1984) and Sizer (1984) identify major problems particularly focusing on the limited achievement of students in schools. John Mayher (1990) provides an *Uncommon-Sense* perspective, giving us new lenses for understanding why schools have failed to educate students. He focuses on the content and form of classroom activities in the main, providing a penetrating analysis of classroom practices. In this process he presents a coherent and consistent theoretical perspective for reflecting on educational practice and creating classes which are centers for learning. But there are major institutional and societal obstacles to accomplishing these revisions of classroom practice. The magnitude of these barriers became apparent to me in the process of writing this book.

I endured my years in school with the goal of changing what was going on in the classrooms. I wanted to be a teacher, not like most of the ones I had, but more like the ones I had read about and dreamed were possible. I endured school, but I wasted so much time. Retrospectively I consider that my intellectual inquisitiveness was on stand-by for most of my school years. I believe, despite our rhetoric about the importance of schools, schooling currently is a waste of time for most students, inconsequential for some, while for a select few, it is highly beneficial. And the practices which allow this to continue are clear. We need to make major changes so that schools are excellent for all and that school success sets the stage for success in life. The magnitude of change will become clear as we look at the layers of practice which influence what happens to each learner while enduring school.

Enduring Schools?

I am not despairing about a decline in our schools, I agree with John Mayher (1990) that schools have probably never been good for most students — while our expectations for school accomplishments have increased over this century. Schools need to take on new roles which result from two concurrent forces: the dramatic transformation of our society from an industrial workplace to an information-rich, service society; and our expanded knowledge of the way people learn. These changes have not penetrated most schools; our schools have not changed for the past hundred years. They are the one aspect of our society our grandparents would find quite comfortable (Mayher and Brause, 1986; Cuban, 1984).[9]

In addition to these intellectual and societal concerns, a clear indication of the need for change is evident when we consider how few students seem to be committed to their schooling. We observe children involved in their ballet or basketball practice, yet who are remote in school situations. We see that children's interest in school diminishes as years go by. As students, we remember being denigrated or ignored. Our memories, when jolted, focus on many negative experiences. Why do these school practices endure? We know schools need to be better. We need to understand schools so that we may improve them. *Enduring Schools* addresses two crucial issues: Why have schools been so impervious to change? How can schools be organized to enhance student learning?

Learning and Schooling

Student learning is assumed to be at the heart of schooling, but the implicit focus on learning is replaced by a concern for social conformity. To understand this phenomenon, we need to understand current perspectives on what learning is and what types of settings nurture learning. Campbell (1982, 1989), Bruner (1987), Chomsky (1972), Kagan (1989), Kegan (1982), Kelly (1955), Mayher (1990), Smith (1986, 1990) and Vygotsky (1978, 1986) provide us with rich theoretical and empirical bases.

Learning, especially academic learning, is what we expect students to engage in at school. Oftentimes, people consider teaching and learning as synonymous activities. But this perspective is inconsistent with our personal experience and current knowledge of how learning happens. As adults we know we have learned about the seeming inevitability of war, for example, when we read historical accounts and current news stories. We may arrive at new insights through trial and error, careful experimentation, brainstorming, inventing, speculating, and the like, but as students we had few such experiences as we 'learned' the curriculum.[10]

Like many students today, I memorized vocabulary lists, historical dates, scientific formulae, and mathematical proofs for the frequent tests which my schools encouraged (even mandated). Yet I cannot tell you what the Spanish American War was about, although I know 'the date is 1898'. Why was that date so important? Understanding the event would provide important understanding of people's values and how these affect social conditions, but

4

these concepts are elusive. I could easily find this information out now, but that misses the point. The pervasive focus on dates trivializes the important concepts students need to learn.

Although my conscientious teachers transmitted information, and I read many pages in textbooks, my mind did not make any real connections with this information. I evidently stored facts briefly and probably in isolated, now irretrievable chunks. I never *really* learned that information. It never became part of my knowledge — although my test grades were good enough — superlative in some unusual cases. When education is equated with teaching, we dismiss the reality that the student/learner must be an active participant. What I engaged in and what many students still do is pseudo-learning — learning which evaporates when we turn in our papers. *Real* learning is very different and rarely accomplished in schools as currently organized.

This absence of consequential learning becomes a major issue, particularly for students whose lives outside of school exclude experiences which are commonplace for children living in homes which prepare them to participate in 'mainstream' activities. Frequently these underprepared students are considered representatives of a 'minority', despite current demographic information which identifies the majority of students nationwide as living in such settings (Brause and Mayher, 1991 b). The label itself, however, serves to diminish attention to the issue.

Our current understanding of the learning process reveals a highly complex phenomenon, one that cannot be simplistically translated into teachers telling us information and tests which assess our memory. In fact, the act of 'teaching' from this sterile stand-point does not necessarily promote learning. Learning is very complex. Each individual knows a great deal to survive in her own setting[11] — knowledge which has been gradually acquired since birth. Our survival reflects our successful adaptation to and learning of implicit rules and traditions. Learning occurs simultaneously as we intentionally and naturally engage in activities which we share with others. Learning does not occur in a vacuum. As we engage in an activity our minds inquire, wonder, speculate — all of which are aspects of thinking. Unconsciously, and continuously we all learn, and we do so privately, in our minds, but within an active social context. (When more experienced individuals share their understandings with us, we learn from their stories — an indirect method of teaching.) Although we cannot actually see learning happening, we know we have learned when we have enriched perceptions and used more diverse strategies. And we unconsciously learn to engage in activities with people we respect. We reshape or reorganize our understanding and our visions to be consistent with others in our community. This learning can occur anywhere — a school building, a grocery store, the theatre, or the beach. Our learning is apparent as we interact socially, use language, create art works, and hone physical feats. Although only some of these dimensions of learning are rewarded in schools, all can be invaluable in life.[12]

Our schools need to replace practices based on now-rejected theories of learning, specifically those which advocated isolated drill and the atomistic presentation and memorization of information. These need to give way to our current knowledge that learning occurs when individuals are actively involved in purposeful, collaborative tasks.[13] Schools traditionally value only a small subset of the vast repertoire of knowledge successful individuals acquire. Both the process of schooling and the content of schooling need to be consciously studied. Recent advances in psychology, psycholinguistics, anthropology and sociolinguistics provide educators with important new models to design educational experiences. Our schools have not changed despite the dramatic revisions in our understanding of how people learn. (See the Coda to this chapter, Learning: Process, Settings and Processes for an elaboration on the characteristics of settings which promote learning and the evidence which documents that learning.)

Schools need to become places where our children make meaningful connections, enabling them to respond spontaneously to unpredictable demands in the twenty-first century. We need to consider:

- What are our students learning from their participation and attendance at school?
- Why are our students bored so often?[14]
- Are schools organized as settings which promote consequential, lifelong learning?
- Are these the best schools we can have?

A Guide for Reading *Enduring Schools*

Enduring Schools is filled with stories which exemplify school practices. These stories are accurate accounts representing typical tales accumulated over more than a quarter-century. To be consistent with representing typical situations, I have identified most teachers as female and most administrators as male. Most names have been changed to respect individuals' privacy. Artifacts from schools in the form of typical comments and signs, serve as chapter dividers. Documentation within the text has been kept to a minimum, but extended citations are provided in the notes and references.

Early chapters focus on individual students, with later chapters taking increasingly broader aspects of the school community, constantly mindful of the effects of this larger community on each student. The goal is to understand why schools are so ineffective in promoting student learning while considering issues needing major reforms. An additional issue to consider is the consistency between our democratic philosophy which values equality, freedom, excitement, and variety, and our practice (Giroux, 1991, Goleman, 1990b; Dewey, 1963). Readers are encouraged to adopt multiple critical perspectives on these issues in the process of visualizing how things might be improved.

To Begin

To start us in the process of questioning and reflecting, I'd like you to reflect on your own experiences, creating several sketches.

Draw a picture of yourself as a student in your fourth grade classroom.

Draw a picture of one of your typical teachers as s/he typically instructed your class.

Draw a floor plan of a typical classroom when you were a student — including the arrangement of the furniture.

Draw a map of the entire school building — or at least the first floor.

Draw a map of the neighborhood where the school was located, including the proximity of your home to the school and local museums.

Now that your memories of school have been recalled, we will use these in sequence to understand the effects of enduring school on student learning.

Learning is implicitly at the heart of compulsory schooling. Although 'learning' occurs frequently in our daily conversations, educators use this word to refer to two complex phenomena. These focus on the *conditions which promote learning*, and *authentic evidence which documents learning*. The next section provides an overview of these professional issues.

Coda: Learning — Process, Settings and Outcomes

Learning is an activity which is characteristic of all human beings, resulting from our innate biological endowment. From birth, our minds are figuring out what is happening in the environment in which we find ourselves, and our role(s) in that setting. Learning has multiple meanings. This ambiguity in our language is consistent with John Dewey's observation (1934) that terms such as ' "building", "construction", and "work" designate both a process and its finished product. Without the meaning of the verb the noun remains blank' (p. 51). Specifically learning refers to two phenomena, namely: a *process* in which we engage, which I will call Learning-how-to-learn, and an *outcome* of that process which I will call knowledge.[15]

Learning is a lifelong process of making sense of situations and activities. Learning is a mental process, which we are unable to see, understand or realize as it happens, but we can note its occurrence retrospectively as we reflect on actions and insights. Learning involves mentally construing similar personal experiences and understanding in new contexts. We may visualize, read, write, experiment, pantomime, talk, or engage in an infinite variety of activities, as we go about learning. Mature learners, enhance our understanding

9

of ourselves, our world, and our visions of a better world. Learning is a complex process which learning theorists are working at understanding, describing and explaining (e.g., Britton, 1970, 1982; Britton, *et al.,* 1975; Bruner, 1990; Kelly, 1955; Mayher, 1990; Smith, 1986, 1990; Vygotsky, 1978, 1986; Wertsch, 1991). Many of its mysteries are unclear to date, but there is sufficient knowledge about language learning to guide us in understanding the nature of learning and the conditions which encourage learning.

Knowledge is evidenced by insights and understandings. It is acquired as we Learn-how-to-learn. Knowledge is comprised of both conscious and unconscious understandings and proficiencies. Knowledge is derived from reflecting on our personal experiences. We do not forget our learnings because connections are made with previous understandings, and therefore are not isolated in our minds. Learning is distinguished from studying information which we do for tests and forgetting those definitions on leaving the test. Recall studying definitions for many vocabulary words. The case I'm trying to make is that true learning is a redundant term and pseudo-learning is an oxymoron.)

Characteristics of Settings Which Promote Learning-How-to-Learn

Individuals learn all the time, but some settings are particularly conducive to learning. There are many factors in the setting which contribute to learners' success, namely:

- Predictability;
- Activity-based;
- Socially situated;
- Success-oriented;
- Learner-controlled;
- Intellectually challenging;
- Respectful.

When learners successfully *predict* what will happen or how their actions will be responded to, they gain confidence in their ability to make inferences about rules, and to understand what is happening. They also gain confidence in their ability to learn. Predictable settings enact one consistent philosophy. This consistency enables learners to predict how people are likely to respond to their actions, and results in increased learner-confidence of success in their interactions. Confident learners willingly try new tasks, and take on new challenges, essential stances to advancing personal knowledge. [Polanyi (1958, 1966) makes a case for all learning being personal.] George Kelly's (1955) theory of human development which is based on prediction believes learning so pervades our lives that it is impossible to separate learning from living.

Learners implicitly seek to discover the tacit rules for accomplishing specific *activities* by sub-consciously speculating, experimenting, reflecting, confirming, and revising their understandings based on their personal experiences. All of these activities assist in learning unstated principles.

Those learners who access extensive resources learn more easily than those with fewer resources. People in settings which promote learning *collaborate* by responding to spontaneous questions and events at the 'teachable moment', and scaffolding understanding within the 'zone of proximal development'.

Direct teaching does not ensure learning. In fact, there is no necessary connection between what is taught and what each individual learns. Although many people try to establish time schedules for learning, there is no evidence to support the success of that programming. Each individual, in collaboration with a guide controls the rate at which personal learning occurs.

Effective guides expect success, and convey this confidence subtly or explicitly to the learner: 'I'm here to help you learn and to make sure you succeed' is the prevailing atmosphere. The learner expects to learn, investing the activity with intensive energy.

Learning happens while individuals are engaged in *learner controlled*, personally meaningful tasks and challenges for which the learner has clear responsibility and intentions of success. These challenges derive from our personal inquisitiveness as well as externally from our social interactions. Contexts which support inquiry and exploration encourage learners to adopt alternative perspectives on problems and issues. Our minds seek challenge and stimulation from new experiences.

Learners *trust* selected others to help them to learn by sharing their knowledge, experiences, questions and problems. Each individual learner's experiences and motivations are respected. In sharing, the individual becomes more conscious of personal strategies, and has access to increased information about personal learning processes. Individuals located in settings with these characteristics are likely to learn.

What Does the Learner Bring to the Learning Process?

Each person learns individually. Some learning results from a learner's conscious decision. Other learning occurs incidentally as an individual engages in a variety of activities. Learners can contribute to this process in diverse ways, namely by:

- being self-motivated;
- searching, exploring, questioning;
- having self-confidence that they can and do learn;
- accepting a long-term commitment to learning;
- trusting their guides;
- reflecting upon and celebrating their own learning.

Learners are self-motivated
Learners unconsciously or consciously decide to belong to particular 'club's — of readers, writers, singers, gymnasts, athletes, artists, as well as a family,

a gang, a class, a neighborhood, or a religious group. These decisions are influenced by the implicit invitations the learners are sent in the process of engaging in these activities. Learners who are included in the club of their choice (of readers, for example), are personally and intensely motivated to do what the others in the group are doing. As learners engage in personally motivated activities for an extended time period (in the company of more experienced club members), they become increasingly proficient at these tasks.

Learners are actively engaged
Learning results from active engagement in projects. The projects may be serious, or they may be humorous. The projects may be individual or collaborative, or a combination of the two. All contexts are potential settings for learning.

Learners have self-confidence that they can and do learn
Learners tackle new challenges by adopting strategies and perspectives which draw on their experiences as well as trying new tactics when confused. They are resourceful at finding ways to work through ambiguous and conflicting situations.

Learners accept a long-term commitment to learning
Recognizing the complex and lengthy process of learning, learners subconsciously discipline themselves to defer immediate gratification. They expect future personal fulfillment and patiently and diligently work to achieve their goals.

Learners trust their guides
Learners rely on their guides to share their personal knowledge and their personal support to enable the learner to be more independent.

Learners reflect upon and celebrate their own learning
Learners realize retrospectively that they have learned and willingly share their new knowledge and strategies for accomplishing this learning with others.

Equity and Learning

Each learner has an infinite capacity to learn. There is never a time when our brain cells are filled to capacity. Research in language development (Brown, 1975; Halliday, 1990; Mayher, 1990) highlights the similarities in our learning across age, gender, wealth, and ethnicity. Yet, in our culture, there is a common-sense belief that there are innate and immutable differences in intelligence. This is evident in statements such as 'He must have been behind the door when brains were handed out' or 'They must have run out of brains by the time they got to her!' This troubling belief is far-reaching, with predictable gender, ethnic, and social class differences. [For example, using this belief system, we hear predictions that boys will excel at math, that Japanese students will be conscientious, and that students of color will have difficulty reading.] Binet, the father of IQ testing, sought to 'identify inferior intelligence, not inferior schooling, as the source of the children's scholastic problems' (Mensch and Mensch, 1991, p. 45). And his legacy lives on in most school tests and school practices.

Although differences are frequently realized, the causes for their appearance are not questioned; rarely do we ask how our society is contributing to some excelling in math while others are designated as needing remedial reading or special education. We know that these same children, prior to entering school were successful in negotiating their social settings, and particularly adept at learning the complex rules which govern their understanding and production of language at home. So we know they are proficient learners. Despite this knowledge, they are sorted for selected *differences* when they come to school. Those who enter school as readers, for example, are placed in classrooms where they are spurred to great heights, in contrast to students who excel in chess or other atypical school activities, for example, who are designated for reading remediation.

Perhaps most importantly, those who do not read when they enter school will be subjected to a program of study which isolates reading from all other activities. This denies an understanding of the features of texts within a specific context as essential to becoming a proficient reader.

When students enter school they have markedly different experiences. Despite these differences, an expectation of similar outcomes after 12 years is pervasive in our society. The differences are devalued, despite the rhetoric of our larger society and our technological progress which depends on diverse perspectives to create increasingly more complex machines and processes. In fact, these differences can also be perceived of as a unifying or centripetal characteristic.

Schools need to establish a balance between the centrifugal elements in our society which focus on our student differences and the centripetal elements which focus on commonalities. We need to value our similarities and celebrate and share our differences. To establish a cohesive and productive society we need to understand and respect each other's proficiencies, as represented in Figure 0.1 where the similarities (the centripetal forces) are in the center and the differences (driven by the centrifugal forces) balance on the outer circle. The goal is to increase the centripetal force — expand our understanding of each other to recognize our common culture, on a non-exclusionary, integrative basis, enlarging our view of how we fit into the center in the process.

Flexible, independent people search for new experiences and look at the world in new ways. This stance typifies an educated person. As an information society, we need multiple strategies to interpret information. Schools which promote mental flexibility will prepare students for their real world needs.

The boredom and mediocrity which pervade schools deny such flexibility.

Figure 0.1: *Visualizing our society's complexities with a centrifuge*

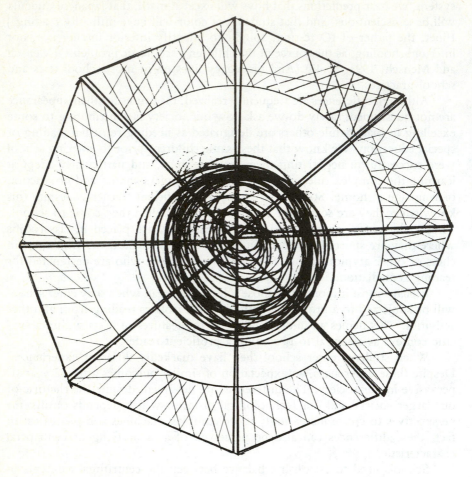

Students' potentials are untapped in most school settings which restrict the range of abilities and talents which are rewarded. By valuing only a small subset of accomplishments, schools become sorting centers, valuing an arbitrary elite group, while denying the accomplishments of genius level achievement by the likes of Mozart, Ballanchine, Bobby Fischer, and Marie Curie. Equitable settings for learning sponsor each individual's interests.

Documenting Knowledge

Knowledge is apparent as individuals participate in activities. From experiences, learners make conjectures about the chaotic world. With time, learners establish a rich repertoire of strategies for obtaining, evaluating, and comparing information. Learners read, write, discuss, interview, laugh, investigate,

Figure 0.2: *Increasing complexity of a concept from Daddy to society*

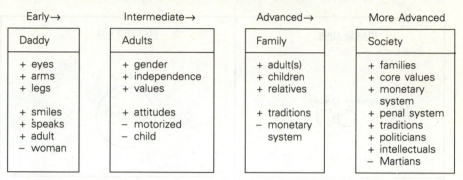

Early→	Intermediate→	Advanced→	More Advanced
Daddy	**Adults**	**Family**	**Society**
+ eyes	+ gender	+ adult(s)	+ families
+ arms	+ independence	+ children	+ core values
+ legs	+ values	+ relatives	+ monetary system
+ smiles	+ attitudes	+ traditions	+ penal system
+ speaks	– motorized	– monetary system	+ traditions
+ adult	– child		+ politicians
– woman			+ intellectuals
			– Martians

+ = concept includes this characteristic
– = concept excludes this characteristic

reflect, dramatize, speculate, imagine, argue, draw, paint, dance, and enact to obtain this information. Each individual has a rich repertoire of experiences comprising her personal knowledge. Each individual uses different strategies for learning and draws on different experiences. Common to us all, however, is the evolving sense of self, of the world around us, and our roles in it. This evolving sense is stored as mental constructs or mental models which are constantly subjected to revision as we add to or reinterpret our experiences. These models are in our minds, and therefore only accessible to others from observing our performances. Thus it is not unusual to hear a learner remark, 'I didn't realize how strongly I felt about that subject until I started to talk and write about it.' Other evidence of learning is apparent in a prediction of how to succeed in accomplishing new tasks. Educators seek to bring the process of understanding to a level of consciousness so that the learner can use this personal knowledge as a basis for continued exploration.

Sophisticated learners have highly elaborated and integrated mental constructs of the world. Less experienced learners have fewer constructs, each of which is relatively sketchy and less highly integrated. The goal of integrating these constructs into a more cohesive and efficient model, drives us to connect events in our society and across history, seeking to determine universal patterns and themes. Initial concepts focus on isolated elements, using superficial criteria such as distinguishing who Daddy is, as noted in Figure 0.2.

These early concepts become more precise and more elaborated, incorporating superficial as well as more comprehensive elements, as for example recognizing that Daddy is one of many adults in the intermediate stage of the evolving construct. As this individual continues to experience life, her knowledge about Daddy and adults in general is incorporated into an understanding of how these individuals contribute to the composition of a family. With additional time, and new insights, new concepts emerge, including how a society is comprised of many families. Each concept is richer than the earlier

Figure 0.3: Sample evolution of concept from Daddy to society

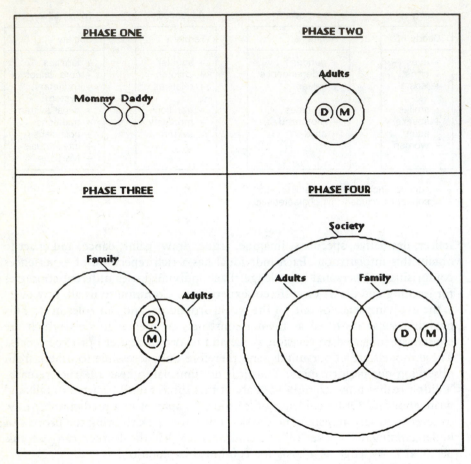

ones, incorporating the concepts from the previous ones, and expanding the purview to larger segments of the world in which we live. Thus, *knowledge* represents an individual's current understanding of disparate elements and how these are interdependent. A less sophisticated learner will have multiple constructs, for example, one for Daddy, one for Mommy, and one for relatives/friends. With time and additional learning, those constructs will overlap, and the similarities will be used to establish more holistic understandings of how people contribute to society, while recognizing each individual's unique contribution. These growing concepts or constructs are evidence of learning. What we should be seeking from schooling is increased conceptual growth, such as sketched in this progression. (See Figure 0.3.)

An individual's knowledge may become apparent in a variety of supportive settings particularly in their writings and their verbal contributions. The crucial contribution of consequential reading, writing, and speaking activities is realized when comparing learners' portfolios. By comparing these displays over an extended time period, we can note where previously isolated knowledge has become integrated. For each individual learner we would expect to see both common constructs and unique constructs. We would also seek to enhance her learning strategies and her resources for understanding and participating in society.

Educators' Responsibilities for Learning

Educators are responsible for providing stimulating, supportive and challenging settings for learning to occur, promoting and documenting student learning. Recognizing that students have lives outside of school which have dramatic impact on their life in school, educators need to draw on the learners' experiences out of school to enhance the likelihood of learning. We want our students to learn concepts which will help them lead successful lives, including learning how to continue learning throughout life. Concurrent with ensuring that our students learn, educators are charged with increasing our personal under-standings in three domains, namely: Learning-how-to-learn; Interdisiplinary Knowledge; and the Topics which interest students. Thus, professional educators, as participants in a true learning community continue to learn as reflective-practitioners (Schön, 1983, 1990). This overview of the conditions which promote learning and evidence which documents learning needs to inform our consideration of the relationship between the schools which endure and the opportunities for student learning at these institutions. Readers are encouraged to consider the relationship between contemporary theories of learning as presented in the foregoing section and the vignettes of school life presented in the next several chapters.

Notes

1   Fred Hechinger, 1987.
2   Cited by Berger (1990) reflecting on the roles of parents in the new school-based management/shared decision-making programs.
3   The intent of this book is to look at typical schools — recognizing that there are many schools which will not be presented here, but these tend to be atypical. The most basic issues prevailing in most schools are reflected in this book, thus the use of the term 'schools' represents most institutions.
    There are an increasing number of alternative schools and programs which are popping up across the country. These places are atypical. They are, however, helping us to see how schools can be exciting centers for learning.
4   See for example, Rita S. Brause and John S. Mayher (1991b) and US Bureau of the Census (1983).
5   Cited in a survey funded by the National Endowment for the Arts, reported by Nicholas Zill and Marianne Winglee (1990).

6   Critical ethnography is explained by Anderson (1989), Marcus and Fischer (1986) and Erickson (1989). The intent of this type of research is to understand the situation from the participants' perspectives. Much educational research of late has been conducted using this methodology, but focusing on microethnographic phenomena, particularly in isolated classrooms (as in Mehan, 1979; and Green, 1983). To understand why classrooms function as they do, a broader perspective is required, consistent with macroethnographic perspectives obtained herein. These macroethnographic perspectives are complemented by case studies which are explained by Brause and Mayher (1991a).

   My experiences as a classroom teacher and teacher educator have provided essential data for this analysis. Much of the research was sponsored by funds from the US Department of Education, the Ford Foundation and Fordham University: Mayher and Brause, 1976, 1977, 1980, 1983, 1984, 1985, 1986; Brause, Mayher and Bruno, 1982; Brause and Mayher, 1982, 1983, 1984, 1985, 1986, 1989; Brause, 1987; Fillion and Brause, 1987; Brause and Hodge, 1987; Brause and Brause, 1989; and Lanzone and Brause, 1990.

7   These characteristics are explained by Cuban (1984) and Goodlad (1984).

8   Much has been written urging reform. Reports from governmentally constituted groups and critical analyses by professionals highlight specific issues: Aronowitz and Giroux, 1985; Bennett, 1988; Chira, 1989a,b; Chubb and Moe, 1990; Coleman and Hoffer, 1987; Commission on the Skills of the American Workforce, 1990; Corcoran, *et al.*, 1988; Carnegie Foundation for the Advancement of Teaching, 1988a,b; Darling-Hammond, 1990; deVise, 1989; Educational Testing Service, 1990; Fiske, 1990; Holmes Group, 1986, 1990; Kaplan, 1989; Lambert, 1989; Lester and Onore, 1990; Lounsberry and Clark, 1990; Maeroff, 1991; Maharidge and Williamson, 1989; Marion, 1989; Mayher, 1990; Metropolitan Life Survey, 1990; Mullis, 1990; National Center for Educational Statistics, 1990; National Commission on Excellence in Education, 1983; *New York Times*, 1989, 1990a,b; Oakes, 1985; Olson and Rodman, 1988; Osborn, 1989; Polner, 1990; Rasell, 1990; Rutter, *et al.*, 1979; Shanker, 1990; Shulman, 1987; Stanley, 1989; *Sunday World Herald*, 1984; Tinto, 1987.

9   Even the Federal Government's sponsored research conducted by the National Assessment for Educational Progress found that over the past twenty years (the extent of their research), 'Little seems to have changed in how students are taught.

   • Despite much research suggesting better alternatives, classrooms still appeared to be dominated by textbooks, teacher lectures, and short-answer activity sheets.
   • Throughout the two-decade span, students spent little time reading at school or at home.
   • They spent little time discussing or writing about what they read.
   • They received little writing instruction, and they rarely worked on independent and group projects' (Educational Testing Service, 1990).

10 Many critics have identified strategies and issues in curricular reform, including Bernstein, 1975; Brady, 1989; Britton, 1982; Britton, *et al.*, 1975; Bruner and Haste, 1987; Clarke, 1987; Duckworth, 1987; Durkin 1978–9; Hanley, 1989; Jensen, 1988; Lee, 1989; Mayher, 1990; Moffett, 1988; Porter, 1989; Rosow, 1989; Rothman, 1991; Sheffield and Frankel, 1989; Tompkins, 1990; Williams, 1988; Verhovek, 1990; Zill and Winglee, 1990.

11 When referring to anonymous individuals, I have decided to use the gender term which refers to the majority at this time. Thus, since there are more females than males in the general population, I will use 'she' when referring to unidentified

individuals. This choice will emphasize that schools are predominantly female institutions in terms of students as well as staff, although they continue to be administrated almost exclusively by males.

12 See Howard Gardner (1983) for a persuasive discussion on this issue.

13 See for example, Jerome Bruner, 1990; John Mayher, 1990, and Frank Smith, 1990 for expansive explanations of this phenomenon.

14 Nearly half of US eighth graders report being bored in school at least half of the day according to an extensive 'shadow' study conducted by Lounsbury and Clark, 1990.

School 'fails all children some of the time and most children all of the time.'

William Ayers, 1990

Chapter 1

Introducing the Learning Community

'Schools aren't good enough', a cry we frequently hear (Rothman, 1991, p. 5), does not inform us specifically about the sources of peoples' unhappiness. By looking at our schools more systematically, we easily identify many troubling issues. In this section we hear from several parents about their school experiences with their children. As we analyze the different perspectives in these stories we will begin to understand why schools are so impervious to change. And we will also see some opportunities for productive collaboration and the creation of real learning communities in school.

Betty's Story

**Register All Children
Born in 1984
For Kindergarten Now!**

With some excitement, Betty noticed the announcement on the bulletin board outside PS 86. She decided to check out the registration procedures, guiding Carol along the path lined with a high metal fence. The first door she tried was locked. Despairing at the prospect of hunting for an open one among the many entrance ways, she systematically walked around the building and eventually found an unmarked door which opened as she pulled the handle.

Once inside, Betty's eyes needed to adjust to the soft lighting. After a tense few seconds, she noticed a second set of doors beyond which a seated woman was reading a newspaper. Betty approached and asked, 'Excuse me. Where do I go to register my Carol?'

'Sign here first. Then go upstairs to the Main Office', was the reply.

Betty picked up the pencil stub on the stack of hand lined papers. Immobilized by the sudden flashback to her own student days, she had difficulty forming the letters in her name. 'What do I write here?' She pointed to the column marked 'Destination'.

'Don't worry about that. I'll fill it in. Just go right up here.' The woman indicated the staircase five feet away. 'Then go into the office and tell them you want to register.'

'Come on Carol,' whispered Betty, somewhat reassured. Awed by the majesty of the marble staircase and high ceilings, Carol walked with great care.

Once upstairs they faced a bulletin board with many students' drawings. Betty turned left and right, quickly surveying the hallway to determine where the office might be. She recognized the room on the right as the auditorium. Walking on, she saw through a windowed-door a brightly lit, large office. Finding the door locked, she knocked at the window. No one inside seemed to hear her. An adult walking down the hall called to her, 'You have to go to the other door,' and pointed to a second door for the same room. Once inside Betty wanted to explain to Carol that they were in the main office, but she was afraid of making too much noise. Glancing at the signs on the teachers' bulletin board she heard a voice from behind the long counter, 'May I help you?'

'I want to register my Carol. She was born in 1984.'

'Do you have her birth certificate?'

'Yes.'

'May I see it?'

'I don't have it with me. It's at home.'

'You can't register her without the birth certificate. In fact, you'll need to bring several documents. . . .'

After a brief conversation, Betty realized that registration was a very complex process. She needed to prove that Carol was eligible to enroll in school based on her birth date, her residence, and her inoculation history. She took out paper and noted the list of documents as a reminder. Then she retraced her earlier steps.

Two weeks later with documents in hand, Betty returned. After intensive scrutiny of the papers, the woman asked Betty personal questions about her husband's occupation and Carol's siblings. Betty was a little disturbed at this seeming intrusion into her private life, particularly since she did not see why the school should know that Carol's father did not live with them. In concluding the interview, she said, 'Carol is now enrolled and must report here on Monday, September 11 at 8:10.' Betty was a little confused since there seemed to be no inquiry about Carol's experiences or her interests. Nor was she given any information to prepare Carol for her first day — or the years to follow.

In anticipation of the first day of school, Betty talked with other parents at the park to find out what they knew about how the school ran, and what they were doing to prepare their children. Most said they were buying special 'school' clothes. Some were reviewing the alphabet song. Most were reading regularly to their children. Betty tried to reconstruct in her own mind what school might be like for Carol, to help her prepare for that first day. She created a list of expectations consistent with her experiences twenty years ago:

- Never question the teacher's statements;
- Do not talk without permission;
- Follow the teacher's rules.

She was unhappy with her memories, noting a conflict between her excitement that Carol was old enough to enter school and the prospects of what that experience might involve. School might not be a happy experience, but it was something she had to endure.

Betty wanted her to succeed because she was convinced it would make a difference in Carol's adult life. She believed the maxims, 'Stay in school and get a good job' and 'College graduates earn more dollars'. She attributed her problems in getting good jobs and getting started in life to the fact that she never graduated from high school. She wanted Carol to have better opportunities than she did. She believed the phrases without really questioning their accuracy. On closer inspection she might have seen people who graduated from high school, who were homeless and dependent on society; high school dropouts sporting heavy gold chains around their necks, rewards from their participation in the local drug trade; and high school dropouts who owned large businesses. Betty had conflicting thoughts, but she quickly dismissed the depressing ones, to give Carol a more positive perspective on an activity which was to take up a major portion of her days for thirteen years.

The First Day of School

In September, Betty walked with Carol, along with her playmates and their mothers. They sought comfort from the presence of friends and hoped they would all be assigned to the same class. Betty remembered being told 'report here' and assumed she was to return to the main office. Arriving at the entrance she used previously she saw no other children. They all went around to where the school yard gates opened. A man with a large clipboard greeted them. 'Do you know what class you're in?'

Betty responded, 'Kindergarten'.

Looking at Carol, he stated, 'Well we have four kindergarten classes. What's *your* name?'

'Carol.'

'Let me see. . . . Carol Gonzalez?'

'No. Carol Miranda.'

'OK. You're in Ms. Martino's class. They're lining up over here.' He pointed to an area where a small group of students had assembled. Then, turning to the others, he asked, 'What about the rest of you? What's your name?'

'I'm Doris Martin.'

'OK Doris. You're in Ms. Stark's class. They're lining up over there', and he pointed to a different section of the large yard.

'I want to be in Carol's class', she protested.

'Well you're assigned to different classes. You'll meet new friends.'

Carol and her mother walked towards the designated area. Betty was holding Carol's hand tightly. Carol was walking slowly. Seeing that there were no other parents there, Betty said, 'Carol, I think I have to go now. You are going to have a fine time. I'll meet you here at the end of school and you'll tell me about all the wonderful things that happen.' Carol gave her a quick kiss and walked over to the growing group of new students. Betty took a deep breath and walked out of the school yard to where other parents were waiting. They all watched through the high fence as their children, forgetting their parents, lined up and entered the building in double file. Betty asked the others, 'When does school end?' One mother said, 'I'm going to be here by 2:30. I'm sure they won't be out before then.'

Carol's teacher led the class to their second floor room. The children were amazed at the building's size. The halls seemed so large and the classroom had such a high ceiling! As they entered their room, Ms. Martino assigned each child to a seat. She gave them each three crayons and one sheet of paper with the instructions, 'Draw a picture about school.' When Carol looked at Julia's work, Ms. Martino told her, 'Watch what's happening on your own paper.' When she wanted to use colors that Julia had, Ms. Martino told her, 'Use only the three colors I gave you. You will have a chance to use other colors another time.'

As the morning progressed, Ms. Martino invited them to 'story time on the rug'. Some children, mindful that they were wearing new clothes, reluctantly sat on the rug while Ms. Martino sat in a low chair. At the end of the day, Ms. Martino gave each student a paper to bring home. Carol ran to meet her mother at the school gate, handing her the paper from Ms. Martino. (See Figure 1.1.)

An Analysis of Betty's Story

There are many perspectives to consider as we analyze Betty's experiences. We will focus on the school administrator's and Betty's perspectives.

The School Administrator's Perspective

Schools are responsible for protecting all students. We are careful to keep strangers out of the building. Only those children who live in the district may enroll. Sometimes parents hear wonderful stories about a school, and use a relative's or friend's address, but such practices could overload the enrollment in our school. The enrollment procedures are efficient and fair.

Figure 1.1: Letter to parents

Dear Parents,

Your child has been assigned to class **K-M**. The
teacher's name is **Ms. Martino**. Please make sure
this information is marked on all his/her materials.

ADDITIONAL COMMENTS FROM THE TEACHER:

I'll agree to believe only 10% of what your child tells me about what's going on at home, if you agree to do the same with the stories you hear about school.

Ms. Martino

    Parents bring their children to school and we are responsible for educating them. We, as professional educators are responsible for designing the educational program. We do not tell the parents how to run their homes and we expect the parents to let us run the school. There will be time for talking with parents, but first we must establish that the students are responsible to us. They must obey our rules and become good citizens in our school building. We establish explicit procedures to accomplish this from the moment students arrive at school.

Betty's Perspective

I feel isolated and helpless. I really want to know what Carol is learning and what she is doing. The man at the gate only spoke with the children, ignoring the parents. There was no consultation with us or our children about their class placement. Ms. Martino's note clearly established mistrust for anything the children might state.

    I really want Carol to do well in school — that means she needs to do what the teachers tell her. She must follow all the rules. By following these rules, she will succeed in school — and in life. The teachers and administrators know what's best for Carol and for all children. I just wish they'd share some of that knowledge with me.

The supervisors and teachers are in total control. They tell our children what to do, where to go and where to sit. Our children are isolated from their friends in some mysterious process. Not only are they likely to be sent to different classes, never having been asked if they would like to be in the same class as another, but once they get into their class, they cannot share their projects with new friends.

Parents are isolated from what children are experiencing in school. We are not advised about what to expect or how we might participate during the school day or at home with our child to continue developing school learnings. By leaving us uninformed about how to help our children, we are officially excluded from our child's education and encouraged to mistrust our children.

No one has ever invited me to any program of parent education. I learned how to be a parent by watching my relatives and neighbors, in the main. And the school has been off-limits until I documented that Carol was eligible to attend. Now that she is enrolled, there have not been any parent meetings to discuss parent goals or school goals — or which goals Carol would be helped to achieve. The isolation, dependency and suspicion suggested in these school practices make me very uneasy.

Ed's Story

In contrast to Betty who was intimidated by the schools, we have Ed who challenged the school's practices. Although the stories start from different vantage points, their outcomes are similar, particularly in the isolation of the parents and the school.

Robert, a third grader, is in a 'gifted program' in the local public school. As the teacher assigned to the class, Ms. Gray feels responsible for 'covering the curriculum' for third grade and enriching it because these are 'gifted' children. Ms. Gray, an experienced teacher with some twenty-two years in the school, remembers previous years when these students would have been considered 'average' but with much middle-class flight in the neighborhood, families with less educational experience have moved in, and most kindergarten children have fewer traditional academic proficiencies than in previous years.

The middle-class families which remain in the community have ambivalent feelings about the public schools. While many parents graduated from the public schools, they want to protect their children from the rumored attacks and robberies at the local school. The administration has created a 'gifted program' to encourage the middle-class families to enroll their children in the school, guaranteeing to keep these children together from kindergarten through sixth grade. These students typically raise the average reading scores in the school and the district. These scores are very important to both the principal and the superintendent since these numbers are printed in the local newspaper and are common knowledge in the community.

Ms. Gray takes great pride in her students' demeanor in school and outside, conveying her clear standards of discipline, and her beliefs about learning. She has many strategies to discourage talking, including placing boys in the 'girls' line' when they misbehave. She marches students parade-style as they go to the neighborhood library.

Robert, the first born, receives considerable attention at home where his parents encourage his reading, writing, and questioning. These intensive one-on-one interactions, however, are not sustained in Ms. Gray's class. Ms. Gray organizes the class mainly in whole-group lessons, moving from spelling to vocabulary, to reading and then to social studies, for example. Robert remembers he while Ms. Gray reviewed spelling words knew, he concealed his reading of a book about dinosaurs under his desk. She considered this behavior a major transgression since Robert was not participating in the review.

On Robert's first report card Ms. Gray noted that he 'needs improvement' in two categories: reading interest and language proficiency. The highest mark Robert received was Satisfactory. Ed expected him to receive mostly grades of Outstanding, consistent with his placement in a gifted class. As far as Ed could determine, Robert was interested in reading and had no trouble communicating. He thought Ms. Gray did not recognize Robert's accomplishments. He did not understand how Ms. Gray 'says nothing nice about him!'

Protocol for report cards includes returning the signed card on the day following their distribution. Robert's mother, Judy, refused to sign it. Ed signed to enable Robert to return his report card on time, but not before jotting a remark to Ms. Gray in the small space designated for parent comments: 'I am sorry that you failed to see Robert's thirst for knowledge, his extensive experience with books, or any good quality at all.' The word 'failed' was consciously chosen. Ed wanted to let Ms. Gray know he was distressed with her evaluation! Robert, embarrassed by his father's comments, concealed his report card on his way to school and placed it in the middle of the pile when he got to class.

Two weeks later was designated as 'Open School' time. Ed, disappointed at receiving no response to his report card comments, went to see Ms. Gray. Ms. Gray complained that Robert did not cooperate with her; he was not supposed to read during class, and he was not supposed to walk around the room during class. Ed agreed how these infractions could be distracting to her and asked if it would be possible for Robert to get other assignments when he knew the work that she was teaching. She said, 'No. . . . he needs to learn to do what everyone else is doing. He is part of a class and there can be no exceptions.'

Ms. Gray sought assurances that she could count on cooperation from Ed and his wife concerning her rules. Ed quickly promised their help but wondered aloud, since Robert is only 8 years old, 'Can you accommodate for differences — at least part of the day?' Her response was 'No!' She followed this refusal with an inquiry, 'Have you visited with the guidance counselor, Ms. Goodman, yet?'

'No. Who is she? . . . Does she know Robert?'

'Yes, She's had some meetings with him. Why don't you stop by her office? It's Room 408.'

Ed found his way to 408 and introduced himself. Ms. Goodman greeted him, 'I'm so happy you've stopped by. Let me get my files on Robert. . . . A few days ago I ran a session with Robert's class discussing physical and sexual abuse. I asked students to share stories about when they hurt. Three children volunteered including Robert who explained' (she read from her notes) ' "my father grabs me by the arm and tells me to go to the dining room for 'time out'. It hurts when he grabs me." ' Then, looking up from her notes, she calmly stated, 'I am concerned that Robert is being physically abused.'

'It seems to me Robert's reflecting more an emotional hurt than a physical one. Did you have time to pursue this issue in class? . . . And anyway, if you *really* believe this, why didn't you call me immediately on hearing Robert's story? . . . Why did you wait for Ms. Gray to refer me to you? . . . Does Ms. Gray have any suspicions from her daily experiences with Robert that he's an abused child?'

Ms. Goodman responded with a suggestion, 'Why don't you set an appointment for family counselling with the school psychologist to talk about this? In the meantime, would you please sign this form which documents our talk?'

Ed went home to relay this series of events to Judy. When they both calmed down, they asked Robert about the session with the guidance counselor. He explained that he thought he was following what the teacher asked them to do and that everybody would tell a story. There was only time for a few students to tell their stories before they returned to Ms. Gray. Crying, he said, 'I didn't want to get you in trouble, Dad!' Ed suggested that Robert try to talk with Ms. Goodman as soon as possible to explain his real feelings about these situations and what happens, for example, when he tries to push his younger brother down the stairs. Robert reluctantly agreed.

Ed and Judy decided to arrange an appointment with the principal, Mr. Winter, to talk about Robert's experiences with Ms. Gray. At the designated time, Mr. Winter who rarely acted alone, called in the assistant principal explaining, 'Although Ms. Gray is rigid, she is not crazy. I inherited Ms. Gray when I came to the school, in contrast to others I have been able to hand pick.' This information confirmed in Ed's and Judy's minds that Ms. Gray was a real problem but not likely to go away. Robert would have to deal with her if he was to remain in the gifted program, a placement which was important to Ed and Judy.

An Analysis of Ed's Story

This story allows us to consider the conflicting perspectives on schooling reflected in the actions and priorities of the teacher, the parents, the administration, and the student.

Teacher's Perspective

I need to establish my authority in this class of gifted students. Students need to do as I tell them. They must follow my directions. I've heard stories about students in gifted classes who think they know it all. I know I need to get the upper hand early so students know I am in control of the class. Robert will try to undermine my authority if I allow him to disobey my rules. I need to stop his transgressions early in the year. If I don't, things will only get worse with time. I'll have this kid until June 30th and he needs to do as I say.

Robert's parents want him to be catered to in school the way they sometimes do at home. But that's impossible considering I have thirty students, not one or two — and they're with me all day long for six-and-a-half hours. His parents think they know how class should be run. They have no respect for my experience or my professional expertise.

I think it's particularly important that Robert learns to be part of a group and to wait for others to catch up with him at times. In fact, he can even learn from the others! They all must go through the class lessons together. They are all expected to participate in class discussions. I make these expectations explicit at the beginning of the school year. These seem simple enough to follow.

Robert's reading is very disrespectful since he's not paying attention to what I and his classmates are saying. I know Robert does well on the tests, but that's true of most of the students in the class. I am offended by his lack of class participation. He's isolating himself from the class. He is not participating as a member of the class. He's potentially a trouble maker or at least a spoiled brat who is accustomed to getting total attention and his way. In this class, that demeanor is not tolerated. I want Robert to be like everyone else and I'll treat him just like everyone else. I know I must have discipline before I can expect students to learn.

I am considered conscientious and reliable, a reputation established with hard work over the past twenty-two years. I must be a good teacher or Mr. Winter would not have assigned me to teach the gifted class. I must fulfill his expectations which, although unstated, I assume are concerned with handling the class in an organized manner. He's commended me and my class frequently on our good discipline.

In all my years of teaching, Ed is the only parent to write a nasty comment on a report card. This home interference must be discouraged. I must let Robert and his friends know I will not be pushed around by Robert's parents. Robert must fit in like all the other students. There can be no exceptions. That's what being in a class and going to school is all about. I am not going to let parents or 8 year old students tell me how to run my class.

Parents' Perspectives

We were pleased at Robert's placement in the gifted program on enrolling him in kindergarten. This confirmed our view of Robert's superior intelligence.

Our pre-school reading time and drilling of Robert on the days of the week and the letters of the alphabet, paid off. We were relieved when his friends from pre-school days became his classmates for we had some qualms about the school. We heard there are many fights after school and some children get mugged for their lunch money. We thought that placing Robert in the gifted class would exclude his mixing with most of the students in the school. This placement will save us considerable dollars eliminating, for the next six years, the need to pay for private schools.

Instead of spanking Robert, we send him to another room to think about his behavior when he is overly aggressive with his younger brother. We are neither abusive, nor spoiling. We encourage Robert to learn and be independent.

We know what's best for Robert, particularly for his education. As long as Robert does not stop others from learning, Robert should be allowed to choose any 'regular' activity. Ms. Gray is too inhibiting and too demanding.

School Administration's Perspective

We school administrators support Ms. Gray's decisions as a state certified, tenured, experienced teacher as long as she does not physically harm students. We believe we know what's best for the students and plan programs which support these concerns. We believe students must learn to get along with all types of people. Discipline is at the heart of the issue. It precedes learning. Robert must resolve himself to the reality that he cannot always do what *he* finds exciting. Although we don't really want him to feel bored, we hope he will become more patient and willing to wait while others catch up with his understanding. We have little time in our busy days to deal with parental inquiries. We need to appease parents and then send them on their way. We insiders (Ms. Gray, Mr. Winter and Ms. Goodman) need to band together to protect each other against the outsiders (Ed, Judy and Robert).

Robert's had two 'open classroom' teachers — one in kindergarten and one in first grade. All teachers are not going to be like them. He needs to learn to get along in all settings. Ed and Judy were real happy when Robert was placed in the gifted program. What more do they expect from us? We've got 900 students to deal with every day. Most of them have serious problems catching up in their reading and math. We need to assign them to some of the good teachers, too. Robert's reading and math are fine. His test scores are good. Why is there such a ruckus about a report card?

Student's Perspective

I don't understand why Ms. Gray is picking on me. I'm not making any noise. I'm not stopping the lesson. I got 100 per cent on my pre-test. I know how to spell all these words. Why do I need to repeat them again and again?

31

Doesn't Ms. Gray realize I understand this? She saw my pre-test. She knows I really don't need any more practice. I'm not calling out how stupid Frank is when he gives the wrong answer, like Bruce keeps doing. I'm listening to what's happening while I'm reading this great dinosaur book. My parents keep reminding me to stay out of trouble which is what I'm trying to do. I don't understand why I can't read when I understand what's being discussed. Once I have the right answer, I don't see what I will learn by repeating the words.

Ms. Gray told us to always have books to read. At home, if I'm watching TV, I sometimes read a book or a magazine during the commercials or at half-time. My Mom and Dad seem to find that OK. I don't understand why Ms. Gray wants me to stop reading.

I like to talk to Eddie sometimes, but Ms. Gray always wants us to be quiet. Her rules are so hard to obey but I really try very hard. I wish I were not in this tense situation. There is a major conflict here between my parents' wishes and my school activities.

Isolation, Arrogance, and Intimidation

Ed and Betty have different implicit theories about how their children should act in school, derived from different experiences and interpretations of learning. Yet these pervasive differences are not discussed openly. By silencing this discussion, the seeds for conflict grow. The school's strategy is to isolate the parents and avoid the discussion. Betty is intimidated, believing the schools are supposed to be independent of the home and that the schools know best. Robert's parents are arrogant, believing they should tell the school how to conduct their responsibilities. The school personnel are similarly arrogant, believing parents should not attempt to influence their professional judgment. The problem is twofold: the school's personnel neither communicate their professional knowledge, nor do they solicit any opportunity for sharing ideas and concerns with parents. The ultimate loser in this confrontation is the student. There is no discussion of conflicting theories of how students learn — or what theory or theories are implemented in the school.

When parents and teachers happen to be in the same setting they may nod in recognition. Any dialogue tends to be superficial, impersonal and brief. Students attempt to bridge two worlds when their parents and their teachers are in the same room. While there are whispered dissatisfactions with our schools,[1] and with home support of schooling, there is no forum for discussing these issues.

In real communities, however, people share stories and experiences which serve to create and perpetuate common goals, social roles and relations.[2] These stories become major components of the 'culture' of the community, establishing traditions and values. Although parents, teachers and students will share stories within their groups, such sharing does not happen frequently between parents and teachers, teachers and students, or parents and students. So, schools become artificial communities. There is no real communing about goals, for example.

There seems to be a tacit agreement between the school and the community-at-large to live and let live. When parents enroll their children, they implicitly accept what goes on in school. A classic educational sociology text[3] notes 'Both [parents and teachers] wish the child well, but it is such a different kind of well that conflict must inevitably arise over it.' Perhaps if this basic conflict were discussed we could come to some understanding on the apparently conflicting expectation in home and school. Admittedly these discussions would be lengthy and time consuming. But they are essential if the tension is to be replaced with meaningful communication and mutual support. We can no longer trivialize education. As a start, we must establish consensus on the goals of schooling.

School Goals

Schools are established to educate students. They are complex organizations, with very complex responsibilities. These include:

- enrolling the students to be educated,
- designing effective educational programs,
- challenging and nurturing student learning, so graduates participate actively in the community-at-large,
- accommodating student needs,
- accessing appropriate resources (including human resources),
- funding the education program,
- designing and maintaining appropriate settings for learning,
- recruiting and developing effective professional staff members,
- encouraging lifelong learning in the community,
- evaluating the effectiveness of educational programs,
- publicizing outcomes.

The primary responsibility of schools is the education of students. There are many influences upon schools concerning this responsibility, however. Some of the individuals and groups which influence our schooling practices are listed in Figure 1.2. People who are at school on a daily basis are listed in Group I. Others serve in advisory capacities in the main, and are in Group II. A third group provides materials, employs graduates and publicizes school actions. Although people represented in Groups II and III potentially influence much of what goes on in school, they rarely enter a school building.

Within each group there is virtually no communication. For example, parents rarely talk with other parents, local school boards or administrators. Decisions made by each group, have profound effects on students, however.

Figure 1.2: The pervasive education-community

Group I	Group II	Group III
Students	Parents	Book Publishers
Teachers	Neighborhood Residents	Legislators
Administrators	Teacher Educators	Politicians
Custodians	Local School Board	Academics
Nutritionists	District Superintendent	Public-at-large
Office Staff		Test publishers
Food Service Staff		Architects
Teacher Aides		Business Community
Counselors		External Evaluators
Nurse		Media
Security Guards		

For example, book publishers influence the content of what teachers teach, as do test publishers. But even though teachers are influenced by the content of the textbooks and the tests, they are rarely asked to work with publishers or educational or academic authorities to determine curriculum content, or to select materials or practices to be used with their students. Similarly, the tests which students take are frequently created by psychologists who are unfamiliar with classroom activities, and then selected by similarly uninformed legislators and school super-intendents without consulting teachers, students, educational authorities, or parents. The expertise available in these different, separate groups does not get shared in the educational community. Ideally, these groups would work together (as shown in Figure 1.3). But in reality, they usually each work in isolation (as noted in Figure 1.2), with chasms separating them from each other. This strategy keeps the system moving, but chaos is inevitable when individuals who operate in isolation, make decisions which effect others. Such practices are particularly objectionable because they are disrespectful, denying expertise which could usefully inform much decision-making.

Many people are represented in Figure 1.2, and consultations with so many people are likely to be time-consuming. Time is a critical factor as many decisions need to be made immediately, leaving no time to consult with others. In addition, time is a rare commodity in most schools. The financial budgets and the established schedules leave little time to meet with others. In the name of expediency, decisions are made which quickly become established tradition and practice. Instead of educational issues being resolved in informed educational settings involving all three groups, individuals make decisions independently of others. Reviews of the effectiveness of specific practices in promoting student learning are rarely conducted. The autonomy expedites decision-making. What is expedient and efficient for the short term, however, frequently proves to be detrimental for the long term, particularly when decision-makers lose sight of the school's primary goal, namely, promoting student learning.

There is little opportunity for analysis and reflection in the current

Figure 1.3: *Alternative interactions within educational communities*

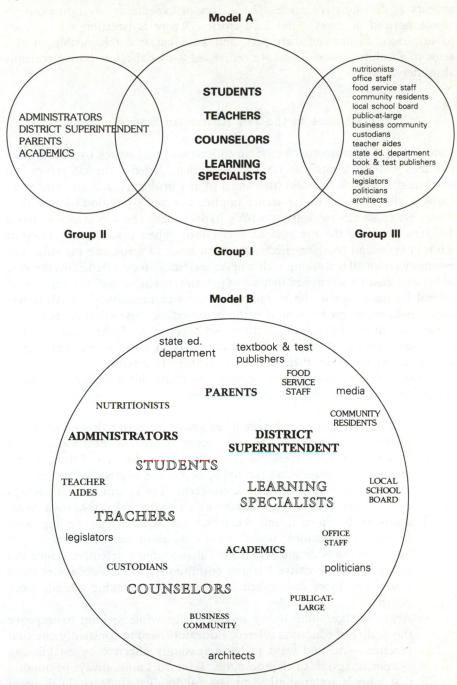

Model A

Group II   Group I   Group III

ADMINISTRATORS
DISTRICT SUPERINTENDENT
PARENTS
ACADEMICS

STUDENTS

TEACHERS

COUNSELORS

LEARNING SPECIALISTS

nutritionists
office staff
food service staff
community residents
local school board
public-at-large
business community
custodians
teacher aides
state ed. department
book & test publishers
media
legislators
politicians
architects

Model B

state ed. department

textbook & test publishers

FOOD SERVICE STAFF

PARENTS

media

NUTRITIONISTS

COMMUNITY RESIDENTS

ADMINISTRATORS

DISTRICT SUPERINTENDENT

STUDENTS

TEACHER AIDES

LEARNING SPECIALISTS

LOCAL SCHOOL BOARD

TEACHERS

legislators

OFFICE STAFF

ACADEMICS

CUSTODIANS

politicians

COUNSELORS

PUBLIC-AT-LARGE

BUSINESS COMMUNITY

architects

Order of importance: FIRST SECOND THIRD FOURTH fifth

organization of educational institutions. The concern for excellence rarely appears as decisions are made. The effects of expediency are numerous — as we noticed in Betty's and Ed's stories. There is isolation which leads to suspicion, alienation, disrespect, and an adversarial relationship. It also leads to absolute power — and we realize anew that absolute power corrupts absolutely.

The US Stance vs the The Australian Stance

Listening to Australian and American educators, I was struck by two distinct attitudes which I identify as US and Australian. Briefly, the US stance is a combination of defensiveness (the denial of any problems) and arrogance (we know it all!). The Australian stance implies insecurity (we don't know anything, we're so far away from what's happening). The US stance enacts a different position: the Pretense of Perfection. When practices are accepted without reflection on their effects, a certain sense of arrogance prevails. The assumption that all is working well is never seriously investigated. This pretense of perfection, an unexamined defense of practice, is philosophically antithetical to real learning, but is rife in our educational community. The Australian stance assumes others know best without subjecting these experiences to systematic scrutiny, while devaluing their own experiences. Either stance inhibits continued learning. [Although these stands may be taken in any geographic setting, I was struck by their frequency in these two settings.]

Educators need to reject both stances and establish a cohesive educational community with two major agendas, namely:

- Identify knowledge and share it. Educators need to reflect on extensive professional theories and practice, contemplate new ideas and consider alternative perspectives. No one knows everything, and there are no uncontroversial answers to complex issues. The educational community would benefit by sharing these concerns. The community of learners needs to get a better sense of who knows what, what is known, what needs to be known, and where to get assistance in dealing with important educational issues. Educators must learn to respect each other's knowledge and experience, abandoning a defensive stance and creating a collaborative learning community, to consider issues more clearly and more comprehensively, ultimately making schools more effective.
- Acknowledge vulnerability and fallibility while seeking to improve the quality of education offered. Educators need to constantly question practice — to find ways to be increasingly effective by establishing systematic review of all procedures. Educators must always be mindful that schools are established to serve individual students. In the next chapter we consider the students' perspectives on schooling.

Notes

1 *Education Week*, September 20, 1989, p. 2.
2 Johnstone, 1990.
3 Waller, 1932, p. 68.

We are shut up in schools and college recitation rooms for ten or fifteen years, and come out at last with a bellyful of words and do not know a thing.

Ralph Waldo Emerson,
Journals, 1839.

Chapter 2

Students

Observing pre-school children at play, we are struck by how much they know: how to get information; how to convince others to follow their lead; how to get attention from different people; how to survive and flourish in their homes and community settings. They were not born knowing all these things; rather they have accumulated a wealth of knowledge in a relatively short time period. We also know that this rapid learning is likely to slow down at the time they enter school, but few people question why this is the case. Common sense suggests that there must be some biological phenomenon which slows learning down at about age 6. Uncommon sense suggests that we look at how the environment changes at this time and consider how it affects children's learning. The environment to which I am referring, of course, is school. Students are the *raison d'être* for establishing schools — yet few children would elect to go to school, given other options. They go because they are compelled.

Transition to School

Early on, children are excited about going to school. It seems to promise so much. Seeing their older brothers and sisters march off to the adult world, 4 and 5 year olds muse about wanting to go to school, about being included in this larger world. (The forbidden always looks so attractive!) As they play school with their older siblings and friends, these experienced school-goers subtly tutor them in what happens at school.

I observed Annie, a 12 year old, playing teacher with her 7 year old sister, and her friends (Cathy, Jackie, Jimmy, Paul, Tom and Susan). Annie designated herself as teacher and the others as students. She walked tall, surveying the seated, complacent group. In an authoritative voice she reminded Cathy, Susan and Tom, 'Raise your hand if you want to speak or if you want to leave the room.' When Cathy smiled at Jackie, Annie reprimanded her for not paying attention.

As the 'game' progressed, Cathy tested how far the rules could be pushed: she called out answers; she called out questions; she ridiculed Tom's responses; she asked to 'leave the room' three times. She tested the possibility that Annie would ridicule her, or eventually isolate her by sending her to the 'principal's office'. Annie continually reminded Cathy and the rest how to act. Students who called attention to themselves were labelled 'behavior problems'. (Receiving attention in schools is discouraged; students are rewarded for not needing attention, not needing help, not causing any attention to be drawn to themselves. They are rewarded for leaving the teacher alone and not making demands on her time.)

Although social behavior dominated the focus in these 'classes', Annie also dealt with academic issues. She announced assignments: 'study your spelling words; do your worksheets.' She distributed papers which she collected and graded. The papers of those with the top grades were displayed. Annie placed grades on work, but gave no assistance in interpreting her evaluation to guide future work. (See samples in Figure 2.1.)

Instruction was totally absent. Annie read *The Gingerbread Man* and then asked the group 'Who can tell me the story in your own words?' Following Tom's summary, she said, 'Draw your own pictures.' There was no apparent purpose for the retelling or the drawings. She sat at her desk grading papers as the students drew. When they were finished drawing, she graded these as well. Finally school was dismissed! Subtly, these youngsters were learning how to succeed in school as they 'played school' with a 12 year old. (Annie's perceptions were reflections of her own experiences 'going to school'.) Let us dig deeper into students' school experiences. We need to see school from students' perspectives, those who survived, those who were humiliated and those who flourished.

Reminiscences of Survivors

Elizabeth and Mary are typical students who survived.

Elizabeth

Elizabeth is a first year student at a suburban high school. Her academic schedule, which is typical of those given to most secondary students, is displayed in Figure 2.2.

'Having a schedule which changes every day, I get so confused. It's hard to keep track of where I'm supposed to go.' Elizabeth and her peers meet six different teachers each day, spending fifty minutes in each class. Some classes fly while others seem endless. She moves from one class to another, adjusting to different teachers' expectations and styles. Some of the teachers know her face, but few know her name without referring to the seating chart.

Figure 2.1: Anne's notes on student progress

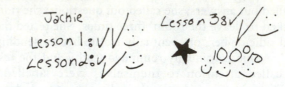

Nov. 24

Private Meetings:

Jachie - 100% works well lessons 1-3
Cathy - 80% works well needs improvement lessons 1-2
Jimmy - 95% works with a daze but is improving lessons 1-3
Paul - 75% needs special help is not paying attention
and not cooperating lessons 1-3
Tom - 85% works well but not clearly is improving L 1-3
Susan - 78% needs special help and is very consistently
complaining L 1-3

Figure 2.2: Elizabeth's academic schedule

Time	Monday	Tuesday	Wednesday	Thursday	Friday
8:15	— — — — — — — SCHOOL ARRIVAL — — — — — — —				
8:20 9:10	Spanish	Social Studies	Social Studies	Social Studies	Social Studies
9:10 9:21	— — — — — — SCHOOL NEWS BULLETINS — — — — — —				
9:27 10:17	Gym	Spanish	Spanish	FREE	Spanish
10:23 11:13	Math	Math	Gym	Math	Gym
11:13 12:03	— — — — — — — LUNCH — — — — — — —				
12:03 12:53	English	English	Math	English	English
12:59 1:49	Science	Science	Science	Science	Science
1:55 2:45	PACE*	Science Lab	PACE	PACE	PACE

* PACE stands for Performing Arts and Creative Experiences.

My Spanish teacher focuses on discipline: 'Why are you late?' 'Why didn't you go to the office to get a pass?' 'Don't talk to Hud now.' 'Don't go lying to me.' When he gives tests, he sarcastically tells us, '*Try* to spell them right!' He holds us after the bell to give homework assignments which he never checks, and makes us late for our next class. I've learned nothing this year in Spanish. My eighth grade teacher who I hated because she was so strict, had us do things like talk about *our* house for ten minutes in Spanish. It was really hard but my parents helped me. We do nothing like that this year — just asking him questions about *his* life — which we really don't care about.

Elizabeth describes her gym teacher as 'Chauvinistic'.

You're not a person with a name unless you're on varsity or a boy. He thinks girls can't play sports! . . . On rainy and cold days, we have to walk in our gym clothes through the school halls. Everyone stares and makes comments about us. Gym's just awful.

English is good if our teacher's in a good mood or bad if she's in a bad mood. When she's in a bad mood, she fills up the blackboard and says, 'You have to copy this down because it's going to be on the test.' Before we started to read *Romeo and Juliet* she read the entire summary. We were annoyed because we wanted a little suspense. We didn't want to know how it all worked out. On days when she's in a great mood, she lets us talk about things which are important to us, like whether Juliet's parents were right or wrong. She separates us into groups of four and we keep a good discussion going. The creative writing sessions aren't good. We never know what to do and there is so little time to really get started. A teacher can't be good at everything, I understand, but I have her again next year and so does the rest of the class. I'm real concerned about being able to write a good essay on my college application. I don't think she'll be able to help me.

Science [biology] is boring. He stands and talks and talks. We just sit and take notes on everything he tells us. I would rather be reading the textbook. It's really boring.

PACE [Performing Arts and Creative Experiences] is wonderful. My teacher says, 'Hi guys! What's wrong?' After we explain how bored we are, she says, 'So what do you want to do? . . . get into a shape that expresses how you feel now.' We go through basic definitions and variations and contrasts. In the beginning we didn't realize what we were doing. But as we go along, we get to connect verbal and non-verbal communication and we use our experiences to create powerful skits about life. We do a lot of brainstorming and experimenting. Then we revise our ideas and eventually we get it all together and even get it written up to share with others. It's really wonderful. I wish I had only PACE for the rest of high school.

Elizabeth bounces from a teacher who asks about *her* concerns to a teacher who doesn't even know her name, but lectures or ridicules, and then to one who encourages her exploration. Although this may seem schizophrenic, Elizabeth thinks it is the best that school can be. She appreciates having a few teachers whose classes she finds useful and exciting. She thinks expecting more would be greedy and certainly unrealistic.

Elizabeth's experiences are typical in that much time is devoted to moving from one room to another, and listening to the teacher discipline other students. Only occasionally does she feel intellectually challenged. Although she feels bored and demeaned in the main, she has learned to smile and endure it. She makes no waves, becoming anonymous, thereby insuring her survival. Her family looks on high school as essential for college entrance, a clear expectation. She has little choice but to endure schooling. There are many students like Elizabeth in our schools. School is not an intellectual resource for Elizabeth, nor is it for Mary, whose case follows, but it does provide an important social outlet for both.

Mary

Mary, a 12 year old, lives with her grandmother since her mother died of a drug overdose two years ago. Being very protective of her, Mary's grandmother allows her to go out only for school and church. Mary likes being in school because it is a place where she sees other children and is able to do things. She dresses neatly, but in clothes more typical of younger students. Mary explains that her grandmother selects all of her clothes while she is at school.

Her grandmother wants her to succeed in school. She monitors Mary's activities, allowing her to watch TV only on weekends. She checks Mary's homework nightly. When there is no written work for a subject, she writes to the teacher requesting written homework. Mary wants to please her grandmother and she wants to please her teachers, but she has difficulty mixing with her peers. Fearing her grandmother's displeasure if her clothes get dirty or ripped, she removes herself from all physical activity. Her grandmother restricts her activities at lunchtime as well, requiring that she remain within the school yard. She cannot arrange to meet others after school because her grandmother wants her at home. Thus, Mary's life is very confined. She understands why her grandmother wants to protect her, but this neither instills confidence nor strategies for protecting herself.

School is a bright light in Mary's life. Mary regrets when there is a week-end or a vacation. As she told her favorite teacher, 'I wish we didn't have vacation. Do they have to close school? Can I go home with you?' Summer vacation is the worst. She has to be home all alone with her grandmother. Although Mary does not find her classes at school exciting, they are more exciting than what she experiences at home, and they also allow her to do things independently, without close supervision. Mary feels good when she completes her assignments, especially when the teacher writes, 'Good' on her work.

It is a rare day when Mary actually participates in class discussions and then, only when the teacher specifically calls on her. As long as she turns in her assignments on time she is looked on as a good student, a label reserved for students who cause no trouble by being quiet and punctual. Intellectual advancement is not at issue here.

She does what she is told, copying from the board, reading, writing. She rarely volunteers to answer in class, being reluctant to speak, afraid that she will make a mistake and others will laugh at her. Mary looks forward to school every day because, in contrast to the rest of her life, she feels relatively free and unsupervised in school. Mary values the predictability and socialization available at school. She knows how to stay out of trouble and she learns while listening to others' conversations, even though she is rarely part of them.

Mary is a quiet student in class, happily accumulating average grades. She enjoys being part of the group and does not want to look different in any way. In high school as tests became more frequent, they were more difficult to pass. After speaking with her guidance counselor, she was placed in the non-college bound track where teachers give fewer tests.

Mary is oblivious to the future educational limitations resulting from this decision. This change in program removed a difficulty rather than helping her to conquer it. The 'protection' which her grandmother and now school provides, satisfies Mary's short-term needs, without any concomittant concern for the long-term consequences. Mary, being an unsophisticated adolescent, is unaware of the harmful neglect which she is experiencing. School, while serving as an important outlet from her home, is perpetuating the 'protective stance' without enabling her to accept increasing responsibility for her own life.

She is anonymous to herself and to her teachers. She never explores what she likes or what she values. She has no sense of herself as an individual, how to participate in society or to be responsible for her own survival. The school encourages her dependency, potentially limiting her life long possibilities. For Mary, although school is a refuge from the isolation at home, she is still imprisoned. She has no opportunity to confront problems and make independent decisions. School is continuing to imprison Mary, sheltering her from new challenges.

Reminiscences of the Humiliated

Some students rebel against the autocratic atmosphere in school. In the main, they are humiliated by the authorities, eventually leading to their premature departure from school. Yusef and Hector are examples.

Yusef

Teachers comment on what Yusef *couldn't* do, forgetting both that there were many things at which he was proficient, and perhaps even more importantly, that their role was to promote his learning — not to decry what they felt he was not able to do.

> He was a zilch, a mushroom. . . . He was totally overwhelmed by the other students. He didn't know how to go to school, how to study, how to do homework. He couldn't contend, didn't have the vocabulary. (Statement by, Yusef's former English teacher, after Yusef was arrested as a participant in a gang rape (Stone, 1989, p. 33).)

Teachers frequently told Yusef how dumb he was, humiliating him before his peers. The teacher's characterization removes any responsibility for Yusef's problems. He was denigrated for not knowing information that should be considered the responsibility of school. He was not helped to succeed in school. Yusef's experiences allow us to predict what will happen to Hector who starts out as a survivor, but, deprived of his social needs, quickly adopts a different stance.

Hector

Hector's family recently immigrated to Florida from Columbia. Hector rarely went to class or read on his own in Columbia, and never wrote unless told to. His parents wanted to get away from the crime in Columbia, a world which Hector found very exciting. One year on, his father was still looking for a job and his mother was working as an office cleaner at night. She was not learning English because the offices she went to were closed and there were few people with whom to talk. She wished she could help Hector, but felt inadequate for the task. She was very concerned that Hector stay in school and graduate.

Hector, a sophisticated 16 year old, was placed in eighth grade on the basis of his limited English proficiency. His brothers (aged 14 and 13) were in the seventh grade in the same school. Hector, taller than most of the students in his class, had a significant beard which he shaved daily. He 'made passes' at the girls in the class and all female visitors. He felt lonely and stupid because of his limited English proficiency which contrasted with the younger monolingual students in the class. The principal assured him that next year he would be placed in high school, but in the meantime he needed to learn English.

Hector had seven different teachers each day, all of whom spoke only in rapid English. Textbook readings intimidated him. He expected his ESL class for students learning English as a Second Language would help him to understand his books, but the teacher directed the ESL students to copy words onto their worksheets, and to pronounce lists of words. They focused a great deal on word endings such as: walk*ed*, house*s*; and min*e*. Although they became quite proficient at pronouncing these sounds with the teacher, they continued to speak in ways which reflected their first language proficiencies. Hector failed most of the tests he took. He wished he had more time to think before writing his answers. Also, spelling seemed to be of major importance. Hector chose to write only words he was confident of spelling, rather than attempt less familiar but more precise words, as errors jeopardize his grade.

When Hector came home from school each day, he had a predictable conversation with his mother, usually in Spanish.

Mother: How was school?
Hector : OK
Mother: What did you do?
Hector : Nothing
Mother: Do you have any homework?
Hector : I did it already.

Hector obviously wanted to avoid this interrogation. He had many explanations for this wish:

- She asks me the same question daily, but I know she doesn't understand how my classes work. I can't explain it all, so I'll just as soon move on to meeting with my friends at the corner.
- I'm not sure that anything *really* happened in school. I stayed out of trouble, so school was OK. I think she's really asking about my behavior.
- I have been pressured and told what to do by adults all day. By getting my homework done, I'm now free to decide what I want to do. Leave me alone!
- I have done my time — I stayed away from home for seven hours. Now I don't want to be bothered even thinking about what I did at school.
- School is so removed from my real concerns that additional discussion of an activity which has already occupied so many hours of the day is wasteful.
- There are so many things I do in school. I'm not sure what you might be interested in knowing. Are you concerned if I got in trouble? If I was honored? If I am confused? If I am excited? If I tried something new? If I discovered something? If I enjoyed something? If I did something I valued? If I spoke with interesting people? Until you give me a better sense of what you're interested in, I'm going to avoid saying anything else.
- You will not understand the denigration I've experienced. I need to forget what has happened.

These daily interchanges contributed to Hector's increasing anxiety. After enduring three months of this treatment, Hector was frustrated both in classes where he could not do the work and in classes where the work seemed babyish or unhelpful. He cut classes, hoping the teachers would ignore this. His teachers reported his absence to the attendance officer who visited Hector's home to emphasize the importance of regular school attendance.

Hector subsequently adopted a different strategy, having decided he needed to get out of school. Reflecting on his recent classroom experiences, he decided to copy the actions of students who were suspended from class and eventually removed from the school rolls. He knew that throwing paper and chewing gum annoyed the teachers. He replaced his princely behavior and astonished his teachers. When he then absented himself from class, they were delighted. Hector wandered around the building, finding other Spanish-speaking peers to talk with about the neighborhood and to share strategies to beat the system. Before the year was over, Hector dropped out of school, having found a job at McDonald's which respected his maturity and responsibility while allowing him to supplement the family income.

Hector's placement in eighth grade was insensitive to his emotional well-being, and the constant change from teacher to teacher made it increasingly difficult for Hector to become proficient at speaking English. Everyone was too busy with their other responsibilities to address Hector's needs. The teachers expected him to be docile, to listen and take notes. No one let him make any decisions. He was constantly told what to do. Being in a frustrating setting all day, Hector chose not to endure. So Hector slipped through the cracks and out into the streets — eventually into the world of the drug, crack.

One aspect which is particularly striking about these stories is that students lost the sense of confidence which they displayed prior to school. They were made to feel stupid and inept. The students who survived accepted this — and accepted virtual anonymity. No one really knew who they were. The ones who had problems getting through had called attention to themselves, trying to become noticed and implicitly valued by the people in school. Schools do not encourage such individuality, however. Successful students accept their anonymity as well as their boredom and frustration.

Those who have expectations of personal celebration and rewards are discouraged from holding on to these goals. Invisible students who get through the day succeed. There are few who ever get the top prize. Most accept their anonymity, and only want to be 'average', as Mike Rose (1989) vividly related from his own experiences in *Lives in the Boundary*. Others take one of two extremes: competing to be number one — and competing to be sanctioned the most and sent for disciplining. In both cases, the individuals are fighting for recognition — and fighting the system. Most in the system, however, are anonymous and rewarded for enduring such oblivion by being promoted and eventually receiving diplomas. Those who rebel find the system is stronger than they are, and it eventually wins — beating them into submission, or excluding them from academia. There is another group we need to consider, those who become stars, and flourish in school.

Reminiscences of Students Who Flourished

Noam and Angel's experiences contrast with those of Elizabeth, Hector, Yusef, and Mary.

Noam

It wasn't until I was in high school that I knew I was a good student. The question had never arisen. I was very surprised when I got into high school and discovered that I was getting all A's and that was supposed to be a big deal. That question had simply never arisen in my entire education. In fact, every student in the school I had previously attended was regarded as somehow being a very successful student. There was no sense of competition, no ranking of students. It was never anything even to think about. It just never came up that there was a question of how you were ranked relative to other students. Well, anyway, at this particular school, which was essentially a Deweyite school and I think a very good one, judging from my experience, there was a tremendous premium on individual creativity, not in the sense of slapping paints on paper, but doing the kind of work and thinking that you were interested in. Interests were encouraged and children were encouraged to pursue their interests. They worked jointly with others or by themselves. It was a lively atmosphere, and the sense was that everybody was doing something important.

It wasn't that they were a highly select group of students. In fact, it was the usual mixture in such a school, with some gifted students and some problem children who had dropped out of the public schools. But nevertheless, at least as a child, that was the sense that one had — that if, competing at all, you were competing with yourself. What can I do? But no sense of strain about it and certainly no sense of relative ranking. . . .

Well, then I got to high school, the academic high school in the public school system, which was supposed to be a very good high school, and it was a real shocker. For one thing as I said, there was the shock of discovering that I was a good student, which had never occurred to me before. And then there was the whole system of prestige and value that went along with that. And the intense competitiveness and the regimentation. In fact, I can remember a lot about elementary school, the work I did there, what I studied and so on. [High school's] almost an absolute blank in my memory apart from the emotional tone, which was quite negative (Chomsky, 1987, pp. 5–6).

Noam flourished when he was encouraged to pursue his personal interests. Competition and separation by ability were destructive to his intellectual initiative. He responded to being respected for his interests and accomplishments, a personal affirmation, much like Angel's response to Mr. Friedman's personal 'life raft'.

Angel

Angel vividly recalls his high school days. Feeling as though he was getting nothing out of school, Angel decided to cut class. He didn't think anyone cared if he was there or not, although he feared the consequences if his mother discovered his transgression. Absence triggered an immediate response from Mr. Friedman, Angel's guidance counselor. Remembering his own difficulties as a high school student, Mr. Friedman wanted to guard against other students falling through the cracks. He wanted to assure students that they were

Figure 2.3: *Student roles*

←— →

Privileged	Anonymous	Humiliated
Praised	Ignored	Ostracized
Flourished	Survived	Rejected
Noam	Elizabeth	Hector
Angel	Mary	Yusef

noticed — that *he* really cared that they attend school. When Mr. Friedman noticed Angel's absence for the 8:45 attendance check, he telephoned immediately. Amazed, Angel ran to school. Thereafter, every day, Mr. Friedman checked Angel's attendance . . . and Angel was there. Mr. Friedman introduced Angel to the baseball coach who invited him to join the team. Mr. Friedman continued to monitor his coursework as well as his progress on the playing field. Through the four years that Angel was in high school, the gym teachers and Mr. Friedman watched over him. They made sure he stayed out of trouble and that he graduated. Angel valued their concern.

Periodically he returns to visit these friends. Some fifteen years later Angel notes their attitudes have changed. They and the students are demoralized. They complain that the administration does not care either about students or teachers. They claim their colleagues are just putting in their time until they are eligible for retirement. In contrast to this disengagement, Angel realizes how fortunate he was to have been a student in the earlier years — when these teachers took an interest in individual students. Angel knows he would never have graduated without their support.

As inspiring as this story is, it is simultaneously depressing since much like Noam's high school years, Angel does not talk about having learned anything from his academic courses! Academic issues seem to have escaped attention, yet he still graduated. Angel entered the Coast Guard on graduation where they encouraged his continued education. He's currently pursuing a bachelor's degree on a part-time basis. He now knows he enjoys learning, but that's not what he typically experiences in his college courses which require considerable memorization of details and technical vocabulary.

Student/Learner Roles

We can place students' experiences along a continuum from Privileged to Humiliated with Anonymous Survivors being somewhere in the middle. (See Figure 2.3.)

The vast majority of students are anonymous, a status which virtually insures survival. Few become stars. Those who do, are applauded by adults for their achievements while being ridiculed as 'nerds' or 'eggheads' by their peers. Many more, and a constantly replenished supply, are ostracized, humiliated and eventually rejected. Boys tend to the two extreme groups, while girls tend toward the middle. In their interactional roles with adults at school, students are tacitly placed in one of three groups. These are neither equally accessible, nor are there equal numbers in each. While it is always possible to become a member of the Humiliated Group, it is much more difficult to gain access to the Privileged Group.

The Privileged Group receives most of the awards distributed in school — awards in terms of new materials, freshly painted classrooms, more frequent trips, more exciting teachers and high grades. For all of these rewards, they feel 'special'. Adults in school smile at them, and greet them by name. Adults expect these students will succeed and when they don't they investigate to find out why. Adults really care about these few students who are accorded admission into this élite circle. Angel worked his way into this group and Noam was there all along.

The group at the other end of the continuum is humiliated by schooling. In contrast to the Privileged Group, they are overtly ridiculed for their dress and their behavior. They are untrusted and therefore given few materials with the explanation: 'They'll never use them.' The few materials to which they do gain access, tend to be old, a phenomenon justified by 'They'll only lose them.' Instead of being called by their given names, they are frequently labelled 'pest' or 'big mouth'. These students who typically live in financially poor and educationally restricted homes, frequently play by different rules than the Privileged or the Anonymous, either intentionally or unintentionally; some know the rules and intentionally break them, while others never learned the rules and become victims of suspicion that they are intentionally challenging adult authority. Adults expect these students to fail. Angel was in this group briefly before being 'saved'. Yusef and Hector were in this group before finally leaving school.

The largest group of all is Anonymous. They are distinguished neither by praise nor humiliation, preferring instead to be average, to blend in, and thereby survive. This group engages in a great deal of avoidance behavior. Fearing failure, humiliation and ostracism they keep a low profile, accept a dependent, complacent stance having learned that helplessness is rewarded. They only do precisely what they are told, nothing more, and nothing less. Elizabeth, Mary, and most female students fit here.

Musical Chairs and School Success

The perspective that there are few winners is upsetting. It garners greater impact when we note that many school traditions (e.g., spelling bees and Musical Chairs), actually celebrate this phenomenon. Susan Holt observed her kindergarten students as they played Musical Chairs under the supervision of their music teacher, Mr. George.

OK Children, let's get ready to play Musical Chairs! First we have to count how many people we have. Please help me, Charles. [They count each student.] OK. We're twenty-seven. Now we need twenty-six chairs in the front of the room. If everyone brings up a chair, except for Charles, we will have the right number of chairs. [They bring their chairs forward.] Now we need to place them so they alternate directions: one faces the windows, the next faces the wall. How many people have played this game before? [Many hands are raised.] Great — then you'll be able to help the rest to learn to play it quickly.

Now I'm going to play some music and I want you to walk to the rhythm of the music. Let's try that first. [Mr. George plays some music and encourages students to walk as he demonstrates 'keeping pace with the music'.] Now the point is, you have to listen *very* carefully to the rhythm in the music because you are supposed to move with the music. After a while, I will stop the music, and then everyone is to go for a seat. But there are not enough seats, so one person will be out. We will continue to do this, until we have one winner. Everyone ready? Let's go. . . . Remember to listen carefully!'

Dana, who is a shy, quiet child, walked around, head down. Michael, being very cautious and determined to stay in the game, went for a chair while the music played. Jessica cried at the beginning of the game, unwilling to join. When she was eventually coerced, she just sat in the chair. But Andrew had a smiling face. He enjoyed the game, the only one in the group. Some had played previously and preferred to remove themselves rather than be excluded by others.[1]

As the game progressed, the first few students 'out' felt isolated. They were not sure what they did wrong, but they knew they were out. When more children joined the ranks of those who were 'out', this group became more comfortable. Those who remained in the game were increasingly aggressive; they knew that each time they went around, they were competing with fewer peers for one seat. The ones who remained developed aggressive, competitive strategies which were successful in sustaining their participation. Some held on from one chair to the next; others pushed peers once the music stopped.

Those who followed the teacher's explicit directions of 'following the rhythm' inevitably lost. The winners watched the teacher's arm movements when he started and stopped the tape recorder knowing he was controlling the presence or absence of the music — the crucial factor. Finally, Andrew was declared the winner. All were told to cheer his victory — when that victory was at the cost of everyone else's success — and when they all knew how he pushed them away from the chairs they wanted to sit on.

For Andrew, Musical Chairs was a wonderful experience. The 'game' of Musical Chairs provides a clear metaphor for the schooling experiences of many students. Children are schooled to accept the fact that few people will win — most will be anonymous. Most people recall a brief list of positive, mentally challenging experiences during the years of school. School experiences, painful in many respects, get relegated to the mind's recesses; we are happier to forget the humiliation endured. And yet the graduates are considered 'successes'. We can characterize the experiences of sucessful students: They get lost in the crowd and they accept being manipulated.

Lost and Manipulated

Students are grouped with twenty-five other students and separated from all the rest. They are treated as one mass, losing all identity and camouflaging their unique backgrounds. They are all expected to blend into one indistinguishable crowd. Individuality is lost in most school situations. Students are systematically turned off from asking questions. When they do not understand, they feel 'dumb', demoralized or frustrated, not realizing their peers have similar feelings. Emphasis is on conformity — not personal development or growth.

Students give up their identities and their self-esteem to fit into the school game, knowing the trump card is always held by the adults who decide who will graduate. Endurance is valued, not the unique challenges surmounted in each individual's work. After twelve or thirteen years of these displays, students expect to be rewarded with high school diplomas.

Schools from elementary to high school are similar. These commonalities provide a unifying effect for schooling whether placed in Arkansas, Alaska, or Australia. Schools focus much attention on behavior, particularly rewarding those who become invisible.

For increasing numbers of students, schools are more stable than their homes, providing settings which students can predict and grow to understand. Large numbers of children come together and students can get lost in the crowd of their classes. While this anonymity may become a sanctuary for children accustomed to physical or mental abuse, it neglects the need for nurturing each individual's intellectual development. Students are treated as objects, not individuals. For the most part, these individuals survive by their own initiative, but are not intellectually challenged or taught to become independent learners. Successful students do what they are told, making them dependent on others for directions. Such dependency makes school-time easy to manage, but the short-term benefits are outweighed by the long-term handicaps.

We repress our memories of boredom as we tell others of our school days. School frequently becomes idealized in our adult minds while children, if we listen, try to remind us how boring and demeaning it is. The teacher makes all the decisions and the work is the same for everyone in the class. Personal interests and experiences are not tapped. Why do students have to endure these experiences? The answer to this question will become clearer as we consider students' places in the total organization of schools.

Note

1   Susan Holt, paper presented at Fordham University, October, 1990.

'Wipe that smile off your face.'

Kindergarten teacher to class: 'Why can't everyone be as quiet as Janet?'

'This must be a really good school. You'd never know there were any kids here.'

Chapter 3

Managing to Survive in Classrooms

Pointing to a mark on the blackboard, the teacher inquired, 'What is it'? The kindergartners came up with fifty different ideas, including 'a squashed bug', 'an owl's eye', 'a cow's head'. The high school students unanimously agreed it was 'a dot on the blackboard' (vonOech, 1989, no. 30). To understand how this superficial response develops, we need to look at what happens in classrooms. To obtain this perspective I will sketch two representative experiences, drawing the more typical one from materials collected with my colleagues, John Mayher and Jo Bruno (Brause, Mayher and Bruno, 1982).

The Setting

The students quickly enter the classroom, going to the seats Marcia Perez, their teacher, assigned them. (See Figure 3.1.) Marcia arranged the movable furniture so that all students face the chalkboard. To maximize use of the limited space in the room, she has paired the desks so that there are two middle aisles, an aisle next to the windows, and an aisle next to the clothing closet. These decisions all carry implicit messages about the roles of teachers and students in the classroom and assumptions about how students learn. Let's consider three issues: the arrangement of the desks; the students' seating; and the atmosphere.

Marcia likes to walk around as she conducts her lessons, so the wide rows facilitate her movement. By placing her desk at the front of the room and the students' desks in rows, she easily monitors students at their individual desks.

Marcia is the center of attention. All students can see her. This organization indicates that the teacher is the center of all activity. Not only is she the source of all knowledge, but she supervises every student. Each student sits directly behind another, seeing many backs of heads, but rarely seeing another's face — or communicating in any way with anyone but the teacher. If a student violates any rule, Marcia can notice this quickly and put a stop to

Figure 3.1: *Marcia's second grade classroom*

			CHALKBOARD					
Marcia's desk							entrance	
W	X	X	X	X	X	X	C	
I	X	X	X	X	X	X	L	
N	X	X	X	X	X	X	O	
D	X	X	X	X	X	X	S	
O	X	X	X	X	X	X	E	
W	X	X	X	X	table		T	
S							S	

(X denotes a desk)

Figure 3.2: *Marcia's seating chart*

		Evanita	Kareem		Roberto	Sharon
Joan	George	Anna	Oswaldo		Janet	Julio
Robert	Teresa	Victor*	Rosa		Omar	Jose M.
Carlton	Maria	Ephraim	Nina*		Pharoah	Elyan
Sandra	Lawrence	Barbara	Mike		Mary	Obediah
Susan	Juan	Teodora	Steve		Carol	Jose B.
					Teacher's Desk	

* = absent

it. If students are not doing as she instructed, this too, becomes quickly visible, and she can comment on this behavior for the rest of the class to hear, subtly reinforcing her control. This room is organized to facilitate Marcia's day. It is an efficient way to seat thirty-four students, and it maximizes her control.

Marcia assigned seats using two criteria: height and sex. She was concerned that all students have a clear visual path to the front since she presents her lessons from this position and she regularly asks students to copy from the board. She placed shorter students closer to the front of the room, so students would not need to peer over the heads of taller classmates. (See Figure 3.2.)

She was equally concerned that students not talk during her lessons, so she devised an organization to discourage communication. She placed boys next to girls, hoping to separate students from their potential confidantes. The only students who were not seated using these criteria were Jose B. and Carol who said they had vision problems and needed to be close to the board. As the semester progresses, seat assignments remain relatively stable, with changes only occurring to handle discipline problems. When students are unsure about what to do, there are thirty-three other models around to surreptitiously emulate thereby conveying a physical display of with-it-ness. Thus, this seating gives students optimal opportunities for successfully following Marcia's directives.

The desk organization provides for constant monitoring, implying that students cannot be trusted. Students know Marcia is the sole individual who makes policy in the room. This is not a collaborative enterprise. Students are constantly under her surveillance. They are fearful of being ostracized for any transgression whether accidental or intentional. There is no sense of a community of learners which shares knowledge, interests or expertise, intentionally learning from each other. Students become anonymous to peers, seeing each others' backs, rarely seeing faces. Many compete for the limited turns-at-talk and for the teacher's recognition and approval. (Although Marcia accepted a more contemporary practice using her first name, her seating practices are reminiscent of Dickens' teachers.)

An Alternative Seating Arrangement

Not all classrooms are organized as Marcia has arranged hers. Some classrooms with the same dimensions have alternative arrangements as shown in Figure 3.3.

In Sallyanne's room there are several centers in the room, not one. Each table is a center of attention. When Sallyanne stands near the blackboard some students need to turn their heads or their chairs. But most activities are focused at the table. Students work individually and in small groups, most frequently, with Sallyanne moving around to the separate tables, talking with small groups of students while at other tables students talk with each other or work independently. This classroom seating establishes the possibility for frequent collaboration, allowing students to see others' faces, and to talk with each other. There is sufficient space for the teacher to sit with the individual groups, while being accessible to assist and monitor the others in the class. There is additional flexibility inherent in this design. More chairs can be drawn up to a table, to enlarge the group — or students can go off to a corner to work when this is preferred. This potential flexibility allows students to take control of some of their activities.

The students face each other and talk with each other. Students selected the table at which they would sit and thus who some of their tablemates would be. Inevitably, most of the tables were all boys or all girls at the beginning, but as the semester moves along, Sallyanne encourages some

Figure 3.3: *Sallyanne's second grade classroom*

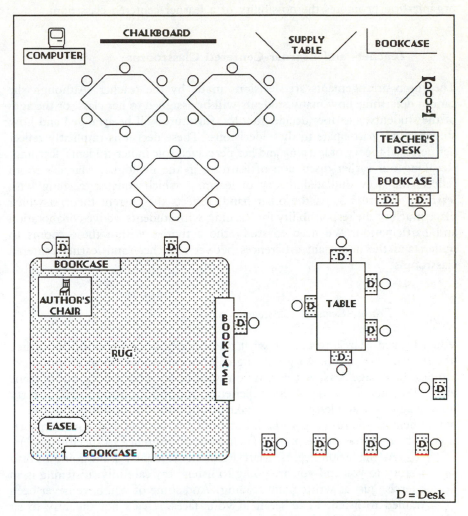

rearrangements, to draw on diverse talents represented in the larger group.

The seating arrangement in Figure 3.3 suggests that students do not need to be constantly monitored by the teacher. There is a sense of trust that students will act responsibly, both in their selection of tablemates and in their daily interactions. The cooperative spirit conveyed in the seating arrangement alone suggests a warm, happy, responsive and potentially lively class. The physical arrangement allowed for more independent and less formal activities during their six-and-one-half-hour days.

When rooms are arranged to encourage student collaboration, students learn to trust themselves and others. They also get a sense of responsibility to peers and to themselves, not only to the teacher. Each student's self-esteem and importance to the group is enhanced by this arrangement as well. This organization promotes the possibility of a learner-centered classroom.

Teacher- and Learner-Centered Classrooms

The room arrangements are decisions made by the teacher. Although she cannot determine how many students will be assigned to her class, or the ages of the students, she does decide how the furniture will be arranged and how students will participate in these decisions. These decisions implicitly reflect her personal theory of learning and her perceived role in her students' learning. Recalling our earlier discussion of learning in the Prologue, Marcia's room reflects the now outdated theory of learning which equates teaching with learning. Figure 3.3, on the other hand, reflects the current theories which place much of the responsibility for learning with students' active collaboration and participation. We need to study the activities within these rooms to understand the important differences between teacher- and learner-centered classrooms.

A Teacher-Centered Classroom

When I asked Marcia to tell me what the students were learning, she replied 'the regular curriculum. We go through all the curriculum areas: Math, Social Studies, Language Arts, Art, etc. If you want to see what we do, please come visit.' To convey a sense of this experience, we will focus on a typical forty minute language arts lesson. Try to take on the role of a second grade, 7 year-old-student as you read this verbatim account interspersed with some explanation. (The numbers in the margin facilitate later reference to specific lines.)

As the lesson begins, Marcia tells the students, 'I am going to read a story to you and you are going to listen very carefully. Listening is an exercise just as writing and reading. And some of you have never been trained to listen. I can see it in your faces. That's not the way to sit
5   when you listen. Sit up straight. The first thing is sit up straight. You have to pay attention. That's the first thing. Put your hands on the desk [so] that nothing distracts you. You don't play with anything that's around you. That's the second way to distract yourself and then, of course, you don't interrupt. All right? Other people who want to listen,
10   can listen. Everybody's with me on this?' Students nod agreement. 'Any questions?' Seeing no raised hands, Marcia proceeds. . . .

'Try not to interrupt the story until we are finished with it. All right? And then we'll go back and ask questions and we will discuss the vocabulary.' [She has conveyed her desire to avoid interruptions and to
15   get on with the story reading.] 'Now the story I'm going to read to you today is the story . . .' [Noting that Pharaoh's hands are in his desk, she

interrupts her own introduction] 'What are you doing darling? Where
are your hands supposed to be? You see how fast you forget and it
seems so easy.' Then, she spots Evanita raising her hand, 'Yes?'
20   [Evanita, thinking Marcia is looking for important questions, asks
about an ill student-friend who was escorted earlier to the nurse.] 'Where's
Nina?'
        [Marcia really wants to get on with the lesson. She does not under-
stand Evanita's question, and asks her to repeat it.] 'What?' Evanita
25 repeats her question, 'Where's Nina?'
        'Nina? I don't know. Do you know?'
        Evanita shakes her head negatively.
        Marcia, now getting increasingly agitated, responds, 'OK. Do you
30 think that's a pertinent question for now? Hm? Do you think that's
important — that's an emergency, that you should interrupt for that?
Think about it. No. Don't do it anymore. All right?' [At this point,
Evanita is confused. She has posed a question which she thinks is important, possibly an emergency. She is concerned about the well-being
35 of her friend. But this is not apparently a concern for Marcia who tells
her not to interrupt. Marcia, seeks to get on with the lesson.] She asks
impatiently, 'Anything else?' No other hands are raised.
        'OK. The story I'm going to read to you today . . . ' [Marcia,
notices Roberto's hand raised.] 'You have a question? Yes?'
40   'I didn't finish the writing [of the Agenda]'.
        'Don't worry about it. After lunch I'll give you a little more time
to finish. OK? Right now it's important that you learn to listen. Don't
think of anything else. Any other questions?' Finally, seeing no hands
raised, Marcia says, 'Beautiful. All right. I don't want you to fall asleep
45 either. I see somebody already falling asleep. Sit up straight. The story
I'm going to read to you, you probably heard. It is a well-known story.
Maybe you heard it, and maybe you didn't. I'm going to read it anyway
because it is one thing to have read a story and another thing to really
know everything about the story: characters and plot and sequence and
50 vocabulary. All right. I hope that you know the story, actually, because
when you know the story it's easier to grasp all of the details of it. OK?
The title of this story is *The Three Billy Goats Gruff.* OK? How many
of you have read it before?' Several hands go up.
        'That's very good. Excellent.' Encouraging them to keep their hands
55 raised so she can count, she repeats, 'How many? . . . Put your hands
down. How many of you never heard it before?' Several hands go up.
        'All right. So about half the class knows it. So the title is *The Three
Billy Goats Gruff.* Who would like to read that title for me?' Recognizing
Lawrence, Marcia says, 'OK.' Several students repeat, '*The Three Billy
60 Goats Gruff.*' 'Everybody knows what a goat is?' In chorus, the students
respond, 'Yes.' 'Now,' pointing to a picture of the troll, she asks, 'Is
this a goat?'

Some say, 'No.' Some say, 'That's a troll.' Others say, 'I heard this
story.' Marcia responds, 'Very good. All right. So we'll see what happens
65 in this story which is an old, old story. ONCE THERE WERE THREE
BILLY GOATS NAMED GRUFF. [Capitalized words represent text
material.] Now, you can imagine, because you are looking at the pictures
of what they would look like in real life.' She shows the illustrations.
'THEY WISHED TO GO UP ON THE HILLSIDE TO EAT
70 THE FRESH GREEN GRASS THAT GREW THERE. THEY WERE
VERY LEAN AND HUNGRY AND THE GRASS WAS ALL GONE
FROM THE SIDE OF THE MOUNTAIN. Did the goats have any
problems? . . . Yes', Marcia acknowledges Rosa who has raised her hand.
'They couldn't eat the grass.'
75   'They couldn't eat any grass. Do you know why?' Rosa answers,
'Because, the troll was under the bridge.'
'Oh, No. The troll was under the bridge? I haven't read anything
about any troll. I don't see any troll here on the first page that I showed
you — or on the second one that I just read. You are not listening.
80 You are remembering, but you are not listening to what I said. He
[pointing to Ephraim] was listening. Good boy. Marcia acknowledges
Ephraim's raised hand. 'Where were the goats going? Why were they
hungry?'
'Because the grass went away.' Marcia agrees, 'Yes. It went away.
85 It was all gone, right? It went some place . . . we don't know — maybe
it was eaten or whatever. Then, acknowledging Barbara, she says, 'Yes,
you want to say something else?'
'There was no more grass.'
'Because there was no more grass. We don't know the reason there
90 was no more grass on their side of the mountain.'
Carol speculates, 'Somebody took it.'
Marcia, not interested in brainstorming, asks rhetorically, 'Well,
who knows? Maybe it didn't rain enough. Maybe there were too many
animals and they ate it up. They don't tell us. We all know, though,
95 that the grass was gone, right? There was no grass and that was the
problem. . . . But you see, children, many of you know the story and
we did a practice exercise for listening and still when I asked you, you
couldn't answer. So, it's not that easy to listen. Right? Now you know
how to pay attention because when I ask you a question, I want more
100 people to answer, OK? So here we go.' [Marcia complains that they do
not know the answer to her question because they are not listening
carefully enough, despite the discussion about how to listen they had
earlier that morning. She asks for verbatim repetition and recounting of
the story. She rejects inferences students are making as they interpret
105 the story. Their understanding of listening differs from hers, yet this is
not evident to Marcia.] The students continued to raise hands believing
Marcia wanted them to say something. She acknowledges Lawrence's

raised hand. He, correctly inferring that Marcia wants only information which is specified in the text, states, 'It doesn't say.'

110 'It doesn't say. Right. All we know is that they didn't have enough grass. BUT THERE WAS A LITTLE STREAM OVER WHICH THEY MUST PASS TO REACH THE GREEN HILLSIDE. AND UNDER THE BRIDGE WHICH THEY MUST CROSS OVER, LIVED AN UGLY OLD TROLL.' As she shows the illustration, she

115 inquires, 'Is he ugly enough for you? . . . Do you see the troll? Where was the troll? Who wants to tell me? . . . Yes?'

'He was under the bridge.'

'Under the bridge. Very good. Was he handsome?'

Several students call out, 'Ug-ly.'

120 She repeats her question, 'How was he?' More students say, 'Ugly' but she is still not happy. 'Well I didn't hear everybody answer that. How was he?' And now most of the students reply, 'Ug-ly!'

Marcia repeats this response, 'Ugly. That's right. Was he young?' 'No', is the response.

125 Marcia repeats her question, seemingly unhappy with the first answer. 'Was he young?' Carol calls out, 'No!' Marcia clarifying that she wants a description of the troll asks, 'How was he?'

Several students shout, 'Old'. Marcia responds enthusiastically, 'Very good. More people are listening.' And then returning to the

130 book, she reads, '"I WILL GO FIRST", SAID THE LITTLE BILLY GOAT GRUFF AND HE STARTED ACROSS THE BRIDGE. TRIP. . . . TRAP. . . . TRIP. . . . TRAP WENT THE BRIDGE. "WHO GOES TRIPPING OVER MY BRIDGE ROARED THE TROLL?"'

135 As Marcia shows the illustration, she notices Roberto out of his seat. She asks, 'You can't see? Let me give you a closer look. Would you like to sit here [in Nina's seat] or would you rather sit here [Victor's seat, another absentee]?' Roberto takes Nina's seat. Marcia continues reading: '"IT'S I. I'M THE LITTLE BILLY GOAT GRUFF," SAID

140 THE BILLY GOAT. "I GO UP THE HILLSIDE TO EAT THE GREEN GRASS." "I THINK I'LL EAT YOU," SAID THE TROLL. How do you think the billy goat felt?' Marcia asked.

Lawrence called out, 'Terrible.' Rejecting his answer by not repeating she prompts for a different response, 'Probably very — what?' Now a

145 group of students calls out, 'Sad.'

Marcia, still not pleased, pushes further, 'How else?' Barbara suggests, 'Scared.' Marcia, delighted, repeats, 'Scared — a good word. He was probably frightened. He was probably scared. Right? OK.' Trying to clarify why the billy goat was probably frightened, she asks,

150 'What did the troll want to do to him?'

Rosa calls out, 'Eat him.' Marcia repeats, 'Eat him. More people are listening now. Very good. "OH DON'T DO THAT," SAID THE

BILLY GOAT. "MY BIGGER BROTHER IS COMING. YOU'D BETTER EAT HIM." '

155   Marcia, trying to engage more student involvement in the plot, solicits their reactions: 'What do you think of that? What do you think of that answer?' No responses are offered, so she suggests one, 'Smart?'
      Obediently, the students respond 'Yes!' in chorus. Lawrence and Carol explain, 'He doesn't want to get eaten.' 'He wants his brother to
160   get killed, not him.' Marcia repeats these and then asks the students if they think the little brother is being selfish. 'That's possible, right. Do you think he's being selfish that he wants his brother to get eaten up instead of himself?'
      The students, predicting Marcia's desire for a yes response, shout,
165   'Yes.' Marcia notices Kareem's raised hand. She inquires, 'What do you think he's thinking?' But Kareem is not ready with a response to her question. Rather, he asks, 'Can I sit up front?' [Speculation about the little billy goat gruff's strategy has been diverted.]
      Marcia responds, 'I don't know, darling. There are no more front
170   spaces. Where could you move? The only place you could move is right here [Victor's seat]. Want to sit there?' Kareem slowly nods affirmatively. Marcia, realizing this is not a happy solution, offers, 'OK. But I'll come to you so don't worry about it. I'll be coming to the back just as much as I am in the front. All right, anybody who hasn't seen the pictures,
175   raise your hand.' Marcia shows the pictures. 'You didn't see it? OK. What do you think the troll is going to do? Do you think he's going to eat the little billy goat . . . the little one . . . or is he going to wait for the brother?' Several students respond in chorus, 'He's going to wait.' Marcia, repeats their response, 'He's going to wait?' and adds, 'OK.'
180   [Now that we have a sense of the cadence of the lesson, we can focus on the dialogue which follows. Some readers may prefer to skip ahead to page 74 where this transcript ends. The total lesson is presented for two reasons: to enable readers to experience more closely what the children lived through, and to record the nature of these sessions where
185   access is restricted and published documentation is almost non-existent. T stands for teacher, and Ss for multiple students responding in chorus.]
      Ss: He's going to wait.
      T: He's going to wait? OK. We'll hear what he says. 'VERY WELL', SAID THE TROLL AND THE LITTLE GOAT CARRIED ON.
190   TRIP, TRAP, TRIP, TRAP, OVER THE BRIDGE AND UP THE HILLSIDE TO EAT THE GREEN GRASS. SOON AFTER, THE NEXT BILLY GOAT GRUFF CAME ALONG. TRIP, TRAP, TRIP, TRAP, WENT THE BRIDGE. 'WHO'S GOING TRIPPING OVER MY BRIDGE?' ROARED THE TROLL. Now
195   this goat is a little bigger than the first one. He's the bigger brother, the second. That's why the bridge went trip, trap a little louder. Well, now this one is going to have the same problem because the

troll still isn't going to let him pass, don't you think? How do you
think the second brother was?

200 Ss: Scared.

T: Scared? Do you think he was as scared as the little one?

Ss: No.

T: Not that much, right? Why is he not that scared? Because he's a
little bigger. He's stronger, so he knows he can defend himself a

205 little better? [noticing Omar rocking on two legs of a chair:] Don't
do that, you're going to fall. OK? (proceeding with the reading)
'OH DON'T EAT ME. MY BIG BROTHER'S COMING.
YOU'D BETTER EAT HIM.' 'WELL, BE OFF WITH YOU',
SAID THE TROLL. So he said the biggest brother's going to be

210 the best dish, right? So he'd better wait for the oldest one.

Roberto: He's going to be the worst dish.

T: Yes. Because you have an idea of what may happen, right? OK.
BUT JUST THEN, UP CAME THE BIG BILLY GOAT GRUFF.
TRIP, TRAP, TRIP, TRAP WENT THE BRIDGE. 'WHO GOES

215 TRIPPING OVER MY BRIDGE?' ROARED THE TROLL. See,
he's big now [showing illustration] He has big horns, right? You
see him? . . . Bigger than the troll, OK? 'IT'S I. I'M THE BIG
BILLY GOAT GRUFF. I GO UP ON THE HILLSIDE TO EAT
THE GREEN GRASS.' 'NOW I'M COMING UP TO EAT

220 YOU', ROARED THE TROLL. [shows illustration]

Lawrence: He's not scared!

T: Do you think he's scared?

Ss: No.

T: He doesn't look scared to me.

225 Ss: He looks mad. He's real tough.

T: 'COME ON, THEN', SAID THE BILLY GOAT GRUFF, WHO
HAD A GREAT HOARSE VOICE OF HIS OWN. HE
LOWERED HIS HORNS AND WHEN THE TROLL CLIMBED
UP ON THE BRIDGE, HE STRUCK HIM. [shows illustration]

230 Barbara: I knew it.

T: You knew it?

Ss: Let me see.

T: It's upside down already, can you see it? OK. THE OLD TROLL
WAS KNOCKED DOWN INTO THE WATER WHERE HE

235 CHANGED INTO A GREAT STONE. IF YOU GO OVER
THE BRIDGE, YOU MAY SEE IT THERE TO THIS DAY. So
what do you think the billy goats are going to do?

Mike: Eat him up.

T: They can't eat him because he became a stone. You weren't

240 listening. What do you think the billy goats will be able to do
now?

Ephraim: Eat the grass.

T: Very good. You are a good student. You listen the best. Yes,
     they're going to eat the grass. I'll read the page to you. AND THE
245 BILLY GOAT GRUFF WENT TRIP, TRAP, TRIP, TRAP,
     OVER THE BRIDGE AND UP THE HILLSIDE TO EAT THE
     GREEN GRASS. [shows illustration] You liked it?
Ss: [clapping]
T: OK, very good. Now, listen. We only have about ten minutes or
250 so, so what I'm going to do is give you some coloring paper. I'm
     going to give you some words that you should remember about
     the story. You're going to write them down. You can color a
     picture of the part you liked best and I'm going to lend you the
     book so that you can look at it and pass it to your friends, OK?
255 Everybody's going to see it for a minute. I'll give you paper. You're
     not going to use your notebooks. [Marcia starts to distribute paper.]
Carol: I don't have any crayons.
T: Don't worry. We'll share. I have some crayons. All right. This is
     what I want you to do. Listen. That word 'listen' is very important,
260 you know.
Oswaldo: I don't want to draw.
T: Excuse me. What did you say?
Oswaldo: I don't want to draw.
T: You don't tell me that. Will you please apologize.
265 Oswaldo: Sorry.
T: OK. That's better. [Marcia holds a sheet of paper — see Figure 3.4.]
     What I want you to do is this. I'll give you a sheet of paper. You're
     going to write the title of the story on the top of the page. I will
     write it on the board for you so that you know how it's spelled.
270 Then you're going to write some of the words that you should
     remember about the story. I will write them on the board for you.
     Then, on the second part of the paper, big, as big as you want to,
     you can draw your picture of the part that you liked best. You can
     begin as soon as . . . You can write your name very close to the
275 top. Don't write a big name. That's going to take half the page.

Figure 3.4: Arrangement of information on paper

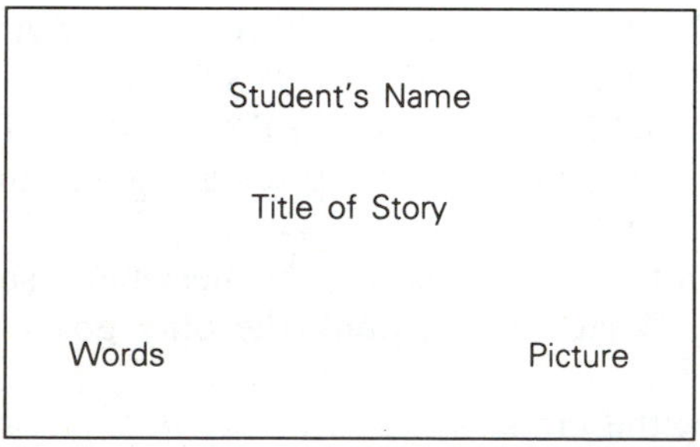

Student's Name

Title of Story

Words   Picture

Mary: Write with pencil?

T: You write it with pencil, yes. Take out your pencil and crayons, those of you that have them. If you don't have them, we'll help. Can you let her share your crayons?

280 Carlton: If she's careful.

T: What?

Carlton: If she's careful.

T: She's going to be careful, right? She'll let you share. Do you have crayons? You're going to share yours, right?

285 Obediah: Should I hold my paper this way?

T: What?

Obediah: Should I hold my paper this way [vertically]?

T: It's better this way [horizontally]. You have better space, all right? That's good. Anybody who doesn't have paper, raise your hand.

290   So this is the title of the story. [She writes *The Three*.]

Omar: [interrupting her writing] Are you going to pass the book around?

T: What?

Omar: Are you going to pass the book around?

295 T: Yes, I will. I will pass it that way. You'll get it. You wanted something else? You wanted the book? OK. It'll get to you. . . . Don't keep it too long. Pass it along. When he passes it to you, you look at it fast and you pass it to him, OK? And this way . . . Now on the top of your page, let me see. Carol already

300   wrote her name. This is very nice, but I don't want you to write the title of the story under your name. I want you to write the title of the story bigger, in the middle of the page, on the top. [Marcia demonstrates.] See, over here. I'll write it for you on the board. Some people are not paying attention. I don't know how you're

305   going to do it. I'll write it here [completes title on board]. Everybody, look up. That's the title of the story over there. Everybody can see it?

Ss: Yes. Three Billy Goats Gruff.

Joan: Can we start?

310 T: Yes. Also, I'm going to give you the words you should have — just a few words, OK? Copy them on this side of the page [shows on paper] as straight as you can, on this side. Everybody's listening?

Ss: Yes.

T: On this side, you make a list of the words. I don't want the words

315   flying around the paper. A list of the words on this side, so you have space for your picture. [writes: GOAT, GOATS, BRIDGE, TROLL, GRASS, UGLY, OLD, HUNGRY, MOUNTAIN] I'm going to open the door because it's getting extremely hot and we can be quiet and work. [to Lawrence] If I were you, I would get

320   to work. [to class] Now it's a little cooler. We're getting some

breeze. Are you going to be talking to her all the time? You are talking too much. . . . Thank you.

Janet: Are we supposed to write the words?

T: That's right. You have to copy the words.

325 Rosa: Are you going to go over the words?

T: What did you say?

Rosa: Are you going to go over the words?

T: The words. . . . I'm going to review them. [to Oswaldo] Sit down. [to class] Please look up for a second. Let's review the words

330 together. Say 'The Three Billy Goats Gruff.' Say it.

Ss: The Three Billy Goats Gruff.

T: [pointing to list on board] Goat

Ss: Goat

T: Goats

335 Ss: Goats

T: All right. What's the difference between those two words [goat and goats]? [T. acknowledges student raising hand.] Yes

Ephraim: One means a lot and one means one.

T: Which one means a lot and which one means one?

340 Ephraim: The one with the . . .

T: You read it. You tell me. Which one means one?

Ephraim: Goat

T: Very good, and the other one means more than one. [T. acknowledges student raising hands.] Yes

345 S: One has the *s* and the other one doesn't.

T: One has the *s* and the other one doesn't. Very good. So I'm going to teach you something today. When it's only one we say that is singular. Say it.

Ss: Singular

350 T: Yes darling. How are you doing? [Student whistles.] I don't like that whistling. Who did it? [Lawrence shakes his head 'no'.] I know it wasn't you. Who did it? [T. whispers to Carlton, then addresses class.] Remember, children, when you have one thing, one person, one animal, we say it's singular. Say it.

355 Ss: Singular.

T: All right. When you have more than one, when you put the *s* to mean more than one, like in this case, goat — goats, we say that is plural. Say it, plural.

Ss: Plural.

360 T: All right. We'll go back to it. It's just so that you'll hear the words. Let's look at the third word now. Bridge.

Ss: Bridge

T: Say it.

Ss: Bridge

365 T: Do you think you know how to read it, everybody?

	Ss:	Bridge
	T:	Yes, but do you know how to spell it?
	Ss:	B-R-I-D-G-E
	T:	Very good. You are good spellers. Very good.
370	Carol:	B-R-I-D-G-E
	T:	OK — pretty good — This is not easy to spell for many people; all right. Those of you who know how to spell it, that's great. Let's say this one, Troll.
	Ss:	Troll
375	T:	Troll
	Ss:	Troll
	T:	OK you know what it is. It's the ugly, mean man that was under the bridge. . . . Grass
	Ss:	Grass
380	T:	Grass
	Ss:	Grass
	T:	And what is this . . . what is this grass?
	Kareem:	It's on the ground
	T:	What color is it?
385	Ss:	Green
	T:	Green, that's right. And who eats it?
	Ss:	The goat
	T:	Not only the goat, but many animals. Right? . . . Anna, when we're reading words, darling, we don't get up to color. We pay attention
390		for a few minutes. . . . Ugly
	Ss:	Ugly
	T:	Give me the opposite of this word. [Acknowledging Anna's raised hand] Yes?
	Anna:	Pretty
395	T:	Pretty, very good, or beautiful. . . . Old, read it, Old.
	Ss:	Old
	T:	What is the opposite of this word?
	Ss:	Young
	T:	Young, very good. . . . Hungry
400	Ss:	Hungry
	T:	Hungry . . . when do you feel hungry?
	Ss:	Now.
	T:	When do you feel hungry? Raise your hand.
	Ss:	Now
405	T:	Now is one time. Because it's before lunch. But when do you usually feel hungry? . . . Somebody? Carlton? [who is turning around, avoiding a turn-at-talk]
	[Carlton does not respond.]	
	T:	When do you feel hungry? [T. acknowledges Steve with raised
410		hand.] Yes?

Steve: In the morning
T: OK — But when in general?
Lawrence: When you're eating.
T: No, I don't mean at what time. I mean, when do you feel hungry
415   in general?
Jose B: After school.
T: OK. But when, in general, do you feel hungry, even if you don't
go to school or even if it's not evening?
Carlton: I know when
420 T: When?
Carlton: The whole day.
T: Not really. Do you feel hungry after you've eaten?
Barbara: Lunchtime?
T: I'm not sure you understand. You're giving me specific times,
425   but I want in general. . . . When do we feel hungry? Think about
it.
Teresa: When you're on the train?
T: I don't always feel hungry on the train. What if I just had lunch?
When would you feel hungry? Think about it. When do you feel
430   hungry? You're not thinking.
Kareem: When you have dinner?
T: When you have dinner? All right. Listen. No other ideas? Listen
then. Yes?
Oswaldo: When you come back from school?
435 T: Well you're giving me specific times. What happens when you
don't go to school? You don't get hungry when you don't go to
school? So when do you get hungry? . . . In general.
Juan: In general?
T: Yes. It means no matter what, wherever you are or whatever you're
440   doing. When do you get hungry? I'll tell you. Listen. You get
hungry when you haven't eaten in a long time. No matter where
you are and no matter what you do, and no matter where you go.
If you haven't eaten in a long time, you get hungry. So when is it
that you are not hungry? When you just ate! It doesn't matter
445   whether you are in school or whether it's morning or evening.
You are not hungry when you just ate. Right, Ephraim?
Ephraim: Right.
T: And you get hungry when you haven't eaten in a long time,
therefore, why are you hungry now?
450 Susan: Because . . .
T: Because you haven't eaten in a long time. That's right. OK. Not
because it's lunchtime. Because if you had a snack of milk and
cookies, maybe if it were lunchtime you wouldn't be hungry, right?
It has to do with your stomach. Not with the time of day or whether
455   you go to school or not. Do you [addressing Carlton] understand

that? I don't think you're listening. If I were to ask you when do we get hungry, would you know how to answer? Go ahead.

Carlton: Sometimes when I'm at home.

T: Listen. I want to hear what he says. When do we get hungry?

460 Carlton: [repeating] Sometimes when I'm at home.

T: You see. He wasn't listening. He said sometimes when he's at home. No. . . . I told you the answer but you weren't listening. Put your hands close to your desk. You're not going to borrow any more crayons. Put your hands on your desk. Push your chair
465   in. [acknowledging Teodora's raised hand] Yes?

Teodora: When you haven't eaten in a long time .

T: Very good. She was listening. Say it loud.

Teodora: When you haven't eaten in a long time.

T: When you haven't eaten in a long time. Very good. [to Carlton]
470   Use these crayons and you mind your business. I don't want you to turn around anymore. What are you standing for, George? You didn't raise your hand. Mountain, Say it.

Ss: Mountain

T: Mountain, say it.

475 Ss: Mountain.

T: All right. What's a mountain? [T. acknowledges Mary's raised hand.]

Mary: Something that we climb.

T: That's right. Something that you climb. Although not only that,
480   you could climb a staircase or tree and that's not a mountain. [Acknowledging Anna's raised hand] Yes?

Anna: It's like a hill

T: It's like a hill. Very good. It's like a large hill. All right. It's a bigger hill. That's what it is. [Acknowledging Lawrence's raised
485   hand] Yes?

Lawrence: And it's tall

T: OK. Listen. We are going to go to gym to dance and then I'll bring you to lunch after gym. So if you please, let everything be the way it is — and we'll come back to it after lunch, and finish it. Row
490   one, stand up. Row one, you're not listening. Row two, stand up. Stand by your chair. OK. Let's line up this way. Row one line up outside. Row four stand up. Five. Let's go darling . . .

Let's reflect on this lesson from Marcia's perspective and from the students' perspectives.

The Teacher's Perspective

The students were learning what I taught: how to listen, the story of the Three Billy Goats Gruff, the spelling and vocabulary, and incidentally generalizing about conditions such as hunger, and distinguishing between singular and plural. I know they learned because they were listening. I had most of the students' attention most of the time. They in the main, followed all that I told them to do. When there were some minor transgressions [ll. 16–19, 205–6, for example] I stopped these quickly.

I posed questions to determine what students knew and then instructed based on these responses. I get answers — from one student and assume: (1) if one student knows the answer, the rest probably do as well, and (2) those who did not know the answer when I posed the question, know it now, because they heard a peer's answer and my repetition of it. I repeat answers to make sure students have heard the correct response. This also reinforces those answers. I assume students learn by absorbing what they are told. I present information. I transmit my understanding to the students — explaining *when* people are hungry [ll. 438–45]. I confirm by asking the students to repeat my words. I attribute students' limited participation and erroneous answers either to their *not* listening (ll. 79–80, 96–8, 239–40, 460–1) or to 'laziness'. I modelled my reading strategies, identifying issues, interpreting, predicting and comparing (ll. 67–8, 142, 150, 157, 201). But Carlton is unable to explain my understanding of hunger (ll. 401), although he heard my statements. I have mentioned and exposed students to many important topics.

The students seemed to follow the story, and they seemed to like it because they did as I asked. Many students participated verbally in the lesson [twenty-three of the thirty-two attending].

The Students' Perspectives

We are in school to learn from the teacher. We must be quiet and follow what she tells us. We learn by repeating. We absorb the teacher's statements, thereby learning. Our repetitions of her utterances are evidence of our learning. We get all of our information from the teacher. She tells us where to write our names, how to hold our paper, and when we can talk. When we listen to her, we do not get in trouble. I do not want to get in trouble.

I am very bored and confused in this class. I follow what the teacher tells me to do. I stay out of trouble by not talking. But I don't understand why I am doing all these things. Each day I hear new stories and get new words to study. I hope I get good grades on my report card because that will make my parents happy. Learning is a simple process of hearing and repeating information. The more often the teacher tells me my answer is 'good' the better I feel about myself as a learner and the more I must be learning.

My Critique

Marcia had good intentions with this lesson. She sought initially to establish control and discipline. Once she had that discipline, though, she never got the students involved in learning as defined in the Prologue. There was the illusion of learning. The implicit consequences of Marcia's decisions alienate, bore and control students (the ABCs of school) and they trivialize and impede consequential learning. In this teacher-centered classroom, pseudo-learning replaces real learning. Although Marcia believes she has 'taught' a literary classic, along with spelling, vocabulary, and how-to-listen, there is no evidence that these activities increased their understanding of the world, — or their proficiencies at participating in society.

There is no dialogue, no discussion of different interpretations or understandings, no exploration of what students understand. Most students are not making any connections with the story or the other aspects of the lesson. Marcia states, 'We all know that the grass was gone' (ll. 94–5, for example). Yet there is no evidence of that general knowledge. The students connect neither the story or any of the other topics to their personal experiences, nor do they explain their understanding. When they try to draw on their previous experiences with the story, in fact, they are reprimanded.

This is a teacher-centered activity. Students are asked to read 'for me' (l. 58) and 'tell me' (l. 116). They heed her desire, 'I want more people to answer [in chorus]' (ll. 99–100, 129, 151–2). She gives permission where students may sit (ll. 136–8, 167–71). She paces their work, confusing matters by assigning two different activities then blaming the students: 'When we're reading words . . . we don't get up to color' (ll. 388–9). Marcia tells them what to do and all must follow. Oswaldo says he doesn't want to draw. She responds, advising him that he does what she wants him to do (ll. 261–5). She tells them what writing instruments to use (pencil and crayon), how to hold the paper, and what to write (ll. 272–7, 285–8). There are no decisions made by the students. They learn to follow what they are told, without getting opportunities to consider decisions for themselves or collaborate with the teacher. Marcia makes the decisions and the students follow her directives. They depend on her for decisions and thus are not learning how to consider alternatives on their own.

She rewards mind-matchers — those who respond in the way she wants: 'You're good students', 'Very good', 'Good' (ll. 54, 129, 243, 249, 343). She tries to read their minds, assuming she understands their meaning. She does not ask Roberto to explain why he believes the oldest will 'be the worst dish' (l. 211).

Marcia constantly interrupts during the lesson, despite her explicit admonition (l. 12). These contradictory messages leave the students unsure of what is acceptable. Most students, not being clear about what is acceptable, adopt a 'low profile' and only participate when explicitly told to do so, rather than risk negative comments from Marcia.

Two students had as many as six turns, most had less than two, with an average production of 4.1 words per turn-at-talk. The average student in the forty minute class, then, spoke twice independently, uttering a total of eight words! The verbal contributions among all thirty-two students account for

Table 3.1: Turn allocations

Turns-at-Talk	Average Number of Words	Range	Total Number of Words	Total Turns Allocated
Teacher	25.3	1–129	3,088	122
Individual Student	4.1	0–9	269	65
Chorus of Students	1.6	1–6	72	46
Total Student Words			341	
Total Teacher Words			3,429	

approximately 10 per cent of the total talk. Marcia talks 90 per cent of the time (see Table 3.1). Her turns are considerably more extended than the students' contributions.

She views learning as a simple outcome from her direct instruction. For her, the learner absorbs, memorizes, and repeats information. There is only one right answer — particularly to the questions she poses. The implicit model in the lesson is that listening and reading are verbatim recall tasks. She even notes to Carlton (ll. 455–62) that the reason he does not know the answer is because he was not listening, never questioning her assumption that hearing is equivalent to understanding. When students' answers do not meet her expectation, she dismisses the responses, seeking others who will meet her expectations (ll. 142–8). She expects them to display their listening by repeating her words (ll. 77–9).

They have confidence that being quiet will protect them from Marcia's criticism. They take few opportunities to check their understanding by way of questioning or responding. The rare questions they pose most frequently address procedural issues: Will you read the words? Where should I put the words? Their successful survival in this setting denies them opportunities to clarify or extend their understanding. This is confirmed by Marcia's 'Beautiful' (l. 44) when there are no questions.

Although the word 'thinking' appears several times, we are hard pressed to find any evidence that the students are thinking. Marcia asks 'What do you think he's thinking?' (ll. 165–6) 'What do you think of that?' (l. 156), but she leaves no time for students to contemplate. She answers her own questions — 'Do you think he's being selfish?' (ll.161–4) 'Smart?' (l. 157). When Evanita asks where Nina is, Marcia asks, 'Do you think that's important . . . that you should interrupt? Think about it.' But immediately she negates her own suggestion, 'No. Don't do it anymore.' (l. 32). Implicitly, only Marcia is allowed to think. Marcia presents a few options, but these are not explored or explained (ll. 85–6, 148, 176–9). She limits discussion, 'because "they" don't tell us.' (l. 94)

When students suggest the second goat was scared, she rejects their response, saying the second goat was less fearful than the first, clearly a related, but different issue. She leads them to reverse their response without engaging in any discussion of the students' perspectives. Ultimately, she imposes her interpretation on students without explanation, 'He doesn't look scared to me' (l. 224).

Marcia is concerned that they will fall asleep (ll. 44–5). She recognizes this is a real possibility, without thinking it might reflect boredom on the students' part — a consequence of her lesson plans. She seems to have forgotten that she said they would talk about characters, plot, sequence, and details, and particularly that those familiar with the story would know 'everything' about the story (ll. 48–50).

The students never got to talk about many significant issues:

What's the story about?
How does the story connect to the words and the drawings?
Why is there no grass?
Why did the troll bully the billy goats?
What motivated the younger billy goats to tell the troll to wait for their oldest brother?
Why did the troll turn to stone?
What moral decisions did the three goats make?
What moral decisions did the troll make?
What would you do in that situation? . . . in comparable situations?

Marcia's assumptions about listening and learning — or teaching and learning need to be challenged on four counts;

1 Hearing does not guarantee understanding. Understanding requires us to make connections between new information and our existing knowledge and personal experiences. If our minds are not actively involved, we do not learn. Learning is an active process, as explained in the Prologue.
2 Students may understand, without being able to explain their understanding. There might be other more valid ways to check their understanding. If the concept of hunger were placed in a meaningful context, perhaps students could provide evidence of their understanding of "when" they are hungry.
3 If the information is important for them to learn, the teacher is responsible for finding ways to get students interested, so they will learn. She needs to figure out why students are so uninvolved in the story.
4 Learning is not analogous to stringing beads. Students need to build on their experiences and knowledge. Reading a 'classic' does not insure student understanding of the themes implicit in the story. They need to be helped to develop these concepts and interpretation strategies. The listing of plot elements is not the crucial learning point, rather students should be learning about life as they read literature, something which seems alien to the activities in this class. This class session,

however, might be lauded E.D. Hirsch (1987) and his focus on 'cultural literacy' where an emphasis is placed on knowing names, not concepts. Hirsch believes students' primary learning should focus on the 'facts' from a relatively restricted range of literary texts. The consideration of characters' values, goals or strategies is secondary to the repetition of 'facts'. In his view, students need to first learn the facts in a story, much as Marcia directs attention in her so-called discussion of *The Three Billy Goats Gruff*. By focusing on isolated facts, students rarely consider conceptual issues. Nor do they discuss and become more proficient at interpreting texts. These practices fly in the face of Hirsch's acknowledgment of the complexities inherent in understanding text and the importance of promoting learning with the collaboration of more proficient guides such as teachers.

In Marcia's lesson there is no opportunity to explore ideas, to speculate, to consider alternative perspectives. The teacher transmits her knowledge with the expectation that students literally absorb what she has said, and thus have learned. There is no connection between the students' experiences and what is happening in the classroom. Those who were familiar with the story were not encouraged to rethink their understandings of characters' motives, for example. They have no sense of why they listened to the story or why the story is considered a classic. They blindly follow what Marcia tells them to do, and get rewarded for doing so.

They moved through the lesson, following Marcia's instructions: listening (not talking), responding in chorus, copying, and occasionally getting a turn-at-talk. They epitomized vonOech's (1989) characterization in which he identified, 'Much of our educational system as an elaborate game of "guess what the teacher is thinking". Thus, many of us have been taught to think that the best ideas are in someone else's head' (no. 47). These second graders have learned to read their teacher's mind fairly well, as have the high school students who describe the mark on the blackboard as a dot.

A Student-Centered Classroom

Now let's visit Sallyanne's classroom whose physical organization we presented in Figure 3.3. Sallyanne's class of second graders was planning a new project with a kindergarten class, a group they had collaborated with on several projects during the semester. This time, Sallyanne decided to share one of her favorite stories, *Alexander and the Terrible, Horrible, No Good, Very Bad Day* by Judith Viorst (1972). The students are seated in the rug area as she reads. This activity encompassed forty minutes, but most of that time was small-group work. The resulting transcript then, is much shorter than Marcia's.

Sallyanne's class discussion of the book follows:

600 'I've brought one of my most favorite books to share with you today — and then for us to share with our friends in the kindergarten. First of all, I'd like you all to get very comfortable, so we can enjoy the story. [She motions to the students to move onto the rug area.] Is everyone comfortable? [She looks around and all seem content; no hands are raised.]

605 OK. [She opens the book, resting the edge in her lap with the pictures and words facing the assembled students. And she reads the entire text page by page, uninterrupted.]

On closing the cover, Brian says, 'I feel just like Alexander! My brothers are always picking on me.'

610 Mark adds, 'Yeah! Mine too!'

'Is there anything we can do about these experiences?' Sallyanne asks. 'Does anyone have ideas for Alexander — and for Brian?'

Suddenly there's much grumbling, and then many 'I do' with raised hands.

615 'OK, let's brainstorm some of these and get back together.' [The students still sitting in the rug area, turned to neighbors, shared experiences of 'favoritism', and then tried to deal with alternatives. During this time, Sallyanne moved around to help the students get their stories started — and to direct their focus from their stories to their

620 solutions for others' problems.]

[In one group Terri talked about how her sister always changes whatever TV program she has selected, and Terri never gets a chance to see what *she* wants. Nadine understood what Terri was talking about, and complained about her brother who always makes fun of her when

625 she tries to play softball. They then tried to help each other solve their problems: Nadine suggested that Terri talk with her mother and get her mother's approval for what program she can watch — so her sister can't fight with her over the TV. Terri connects her own soccer experiences with Nadine's softball ones, and offers that maybe Nadine could get her

630 brother on a softball team, just like she's on — and get him out of her way! They are quite engrossed in these stories and solutions. After fourteen minutes of this interaction, Sallyanne called the group back together.]

'Well, how did you do? I know that Bruce and Darryl have been

635 dealing with some very difficult issues. Who would like to share a story with us?'

Terri retells her story, explaining Nadine's suggestion for what to do next time. Sallyanne then tells them that she has more copies of the book — enough for each to share with their kindergarten friends.

640 'Can we go down there now and read this story to them?' Michael asks.

'Sure! Does anyone have any ideas of how we might work with our kindergarten friends with these books?'

'I do! We could read to them — and then we could talk with them

645 — and help them if they have older brothers and sisters who try to take
advantage of them.'
      'That sounds like a good idea. Maybe you'd like to read the story
over to yourself before we go down there. Practice might help a little.
I'll give you ten minutes to get ready and then we'll go down. The
650 books are over on the bookshelf — so take a copy and look it over.'
[Sallyanne walks around, suggesting some students consider dramatic
readings, while helping others pronounce 'Australia' and other unfamiliar
words.]
      After ten minutes elapsed, the class lined up and went down to the
655 basement where the kindergarten class was meeting. They sat on the
floor behind the kindergartners, and listened as the kindergarten teacher
welcomed them and then asked what they had planned for today.
      Brian offered, 'We'd like to read a great story together.'
      'What's it about?' asked Xavier.
660 'It's about a kid, just like us — and his family. . . .'
      This activity continued for another thirty minutes with students
sharing the books and their experiences. They moved in and out of
small groups, ending with a suggestion to create their own books connected to Alexander's experiences to share in about one week's time.

The Teacher's Perspective

We are a community of learners. I share my experiences with my students,
and I encourage them to share theirs. These experiences provide the opportunity
for us to reflect on our understandings and to learn from our experiences. I
really love the *Alexander* story, so I was interested to see if they could identify
with Alexander's problems and maybe come up with some strategies for
getting more control over their lives. I also wanted them to realize that they
can be more responsible for what happens to them, and be more successful in
planning their encounters with others. By arranging for them to work with
the kindergartners, I was hoping they could take on a 'big brother' or 'big
sister' role, and help others from their own experiences.
      All of these activities were enjoyable for the students. They were com-
fortable listening to the story and they were mesmerized as I read. Then they
were happy to share their experiences (although a couple needed to be prodded
a little). They felt quite confident when they arrived at the kindergarten
classroom, since they knew the story and had opportunities to go over questions and strategies for dealing with problems from previous about the story
experiences sharing.
      The students were each learning more about story structure, and the
importance of understanding themes in stories in promoting their ability to
deal with life situations. They were each talking considerably more than they
would in a teacher-centered activity, allowing them to gain proficiency in

expressing their ideas in an elaborated and extended discussion to responsive listeners. They were gaining more confidence in their own abilities as well as learning that they can learn from their peers as well. It's this type of activity I really enjoy with my students. I'm so happy to have a colleague in the kindergarten who is willing to collaborate with me on this project. I also learn from and with her as we collaborate and reflect on these sessions.

Walking from group to group, I get a sense of which students are more relaxed and confident, and which would benefit from additional encouragement. I also see which ones are sensitive to word choices, and which focus on the story line. From these observations I'm able to plan additional activities which respond to the specific needs of each student.

The Students' Perspectives

I can't believe it's acceptable to have so much fun in school. I enjoy hearing these stories and talking with my friends about my problems. I also like to see the kindergarten kids — because then I can remember how much I've changed since I was in kindergarten. I enjoy sharing my experiences with those kids and they are so happy when we bring them our books; it makes me feel real important. I also like to tell my parents about the stories I've read in school and sometimes my mom lets me buy some of them for my own library. Other times I take the book from the school library or the public library. Sometimes kids goof off — and try to avoid doing work — but we all get back to work eventually. In contrast to my first grade class where the teacher gave us so many workbook sheets and boring stories, I'm really enjoying second grade — and I think I'm learning a lot, too.

My Critique

Sallyane has orchestrated a long-term project with several short-term products which sustain student interest. The students are heavily involved in the activity — reading, writing, interpreting, creating alternative strategies. They are thinking about issues which are important to them while becoming more proficient at communicating their ideas and understanding others' perspectives.

By arranging the students in small groups, she is encouraging the students to accept some responsibility to the group while carrying individual responsibility for the success of their interactions with the kindergartners. Students, then, are controlling many of the decisions which are being made — in contrast to Marcia who tells the students what to do and how to do it. Sallyanne's students are gaining con-fidence in their ability to consider options, to select strategies with a view to-wards subsequent reflection on those decisions. Ultimately, they each become more self-confident and proficient at decision-making.

Table 3.2: *Teacher-centered and learner-centered classrooms*

	Teacher-Centered	Learner-Centered
Teacher roles	Tells, monitors, evaluates, decides unilaterally	Guides, provokes, supports, collaborates
Student roles	Follows, repeats, completes	Shares, explores, decides
Outcomes	Alienation Accumulation of isolated facts Dependency on leader/teacher Unquestioned obedience Boredom Pseudo-learning	Growing proficiencies using diverse resources and strategies Increasing personal knowledge and self-confidence Increasing proficiency at responsible and independent decision-making Thirsting for knowledge Authentic learning

Students learn to be resourceful learners. They do not restrict their resources to the teacher's knowledge, but call on their own experiences and knowledge as well as that of their peers. Students become increasingly independent and responsible for their activities, particularly their learning activities. They build on their knowledge store and they explore issues of interest to themselves.

Learning occurs in the process of students participating with the teacher in this project. As they go about all their activities, they increase their understanding and their strategies for accessing resources. They work independently and collaboratively, planning, speculating (ll. 644–6), and exploring (ll. 628–31). They understand that there are many ways to view an issue, not just one. All perspectives are potentially valid. Each person gets opportunities to present personal experiences and viewpoints. In addition, they draw on historical, social, and geographical resources as they brainstorm. They regroup, categorize, get new understandings (l. 660). The teacher serves as a guide, supporting their inquiries, provoking their interest, challenging their ideas. She is a *Learning Specialist*, not a deliverer of information. The students are enthusiastic and involved. They feel responsible for the project, which they can see progressing over a period of time. They develop increasing confidence in their own abilities to learn.

The teacher moves from group to group where students collaboratively brainstorm, search for resources, and allocate assignments. They share their knowledge and experiences, and ultimately hold each other accountable for producing a proportionate share of each project. The teacher serves as a catalyst, a supporter, a tutor, a collaborator. The students become increasingly responsible for completing their projects, and increasingly proficient at identifying choices and making decisions as they engage in these activities. They all form a learning community, working together to accomplish important tasks. This is a learner-centered classroom.

There are major differences between the activities within these two classrooms. Distinctions characterizing the teacher-centered classroom and the learner-centered classroom are listed in Table 3.2. While most classrooms function like Marcia's, Sallyanne's is more unusual, but certainly not unique. (See for example, Gamberg *et al.*, 1988; Moffett, 1973; Wells, 1990; Atwell, 1987.)

As we consider the differences between these two classrooms, the experience of describing the dot on the blackboard becomes more understandable. A clear outcome of the teacher-centered classrooms is the conformity of response. Students' thinking is uniform. Their creativity is squashed. They conform to the teacher's directions and thus are well-disciplined to follow others' rules. They are reluctant to be different; they are prepared to flourish as a herd of sheep.

Is this the outcome we seek from twelve years of schooling? Teacher-centered lessons remove the responsibility for learning from students. Students depend on others to tell them what to do and how to do it. These dependencies, while effective in teacher-centered classrooms, are counter-productive for surviving in the world outside of school. Learner-centered classrooms like Sallyanne's support students' developing responsibility and independence in their learning and in their decision-making. Surviving in teacher-centered classrooms requires accepting a dependent stance, the antithesis of our educational goals. We must consider why so many of our classrooms are teacher-centered, the focus of the next chapter.

'Teachers insisted I use my right hand for writing, but paid no attention to which hand I used when drawing!'

[Reflection of a 66-year-old left-handed artist]

Chapter 4

Teachers

Teachers typically have two distinct perceptions of their roles: visionaries who have created models in their minds of how classes might be, and followers who expect others to tell them what to do and how to do it. These contrasting perspectives influence much of what happens in classrooms. Let's consider the experiences of the visionaries first.

Visionary Teachers

Teachers who are visionaries devote considerable time to contemplating the activities they plan for students. They think about their own experiences, read about and explore others' memories, and investigate professional education resources, all in the continual process of creating a setting which will be conducive to their particular students' learning. Frequently, many of these reflections are initiated in a teacher-preparation program designed for inexperienced teachers. Let's consider Maureen's case.

On her application for admission to a teacher education program Maureen explains her intentions.

In the short space that follows, I must try to write with clarity why I sincerely want to give up a lucrative career in international finance to attend a graduate program that will prepare me for a career in teaching.

It was a personal triumph for me earlier in the year when I finally realized that I could pursue my long-held aspirations in the field of education. I felt like a burden had been lifted off my shoulders when I was finally able to admit that I do not derive satisfaction from selling financial products to banks. Somehow at the end of the day, I am left wondering just exactly what I had done to help make the world a better place.

Over the last few years I have often let my mind wander to the question of what I would do if I had the freedom (which of course I do) to pursue any field I wanted. The answer has always been to teach . . . because the ability to learn is so important in today's society. If I could help others obtain such a critical skill, then at the end of the day I would certainly know that I was doing my part to make the world a better place.

My interest in teaching has deep roots. Both of my parents were teachers and they instilled in me a keen appreciation for the value of education. My first job after graduation from university was teaching English in Japan. I truly enjoyed the challenge of planning and carrying out classes that would build on my students' previous achievements to improve their English language abilities. My seemingly unlimited patience which can be a hindrance in the world of finance, proved invaluable to me as a language teacher.

When I returned from Japan in 1983, many large financial institutions were extremely eager to hire people with Japanese language skills. I had never considered going into business, but I was intrigued by the opportunity offered me to become an international banking officer. I was ultimately lured by the so-called 'upward mobility' such a career would offer. I didn't realize at the time how keen my interest in education really was.

The experience and extensive training I received during my career in the business world have enhanced my analytical and communication skills. However, I miss the considerable personal satisfaction I found when I was teaching. I am therefore, now seeking to return to that field. . . .

Maureen's statement is both compelling and classic. Her perspective is typical, as noted in a Metropolitan Life Survey (1990):

New teachers (who graduate from education schools) come to their schools full of optimism and idealism. They are virtually unanimous in believing that all children can learn and that they can really make a difference in the lives of their students (p. 1).

Like most new teachers who have completed cohesive teacher preparation programs, Maureen hopes to make a major impact on learners and thereby on society, and she has visions of how she might do that, even prior to her enrollment in a professional education program.

Maureen joined twenty-five others in a program designed to prepare new teachers. A capstone of that program involves a university-supervised internship, sometimes called student teaching. Education students are placed in classrooms for extended time periods, collaborating with experienced teachers and teacher educators. One of Maureen's classmates, Pat, ruminates on her concerns in her journal:

> Will I be able to realize my goals? How can I handle the conflict between my idealism and the realities I am confronting in the classroom?
>
> I want to teach them the world, but I feel I know nothing of it. Will they be able to understand me as I zip along in my garbled speech? Or, will they even bother to stop me and ask 'Why?' I have great expectations, but will they collapse to the ground because I have built them out of fragile stuff? And how does one master a cackle (required in the Macbeth STANDARD LESSON PLANS distributed by the department chair)? How to cram so much into their heads (they made me say it) or pull it out?
>
> . . . I'm ready to take twenty kids, cart them off to the back woods in West Virginia, and REALLY teach them something. So the question is, How do you do what you are REALLY supposed to do within the limits of the SYSTEM? For starters, get rid of those horrendous value questions. Enough is enough. What we have done in two weeks could have been done in two or three days. Ironically, it's not the kids who are slowing the process; the culprit is the Standard Unit Lesson Plan (the devil's tool). . . .
>
> If the SYSTEM wants them to examine their values, why not have students see how their values hold up under the strain of a controversial issue? That's a challenge; that's interesting; and I'll bet they'd rise to meet the occasion. Why not talk about South Africa and apartheid (all but one are minorities in my class) especially in light of the recent release of Nelson Mandela! The kids would learn something about current events and think about an important issue and write about their opinion of it. No, instead they write about, 'I am the type of person who . . .' Broaden their horizons! . . .
>
> Ah, such are the problems of student teaching. You're probably saying, 'Why not implement these ideas in your classroom?' Yes, but you forget about the creature called COOPERATING TEACHER. I am a student teacher, and ultimately I must answer to my cooperating teacher. She is teaching me a particular style of teaching and I don't always have the final say in matters. Next year, I keep thinking. Then it will be MY class, not someone else's.

Teachers like Maureen and Pat start with high levels of enthusiasm and creativity, but quickly become frustrated and disillusioned about the possibility of really making a difference. What happens to beginning teachers? Let's consider Jennifer's situation.

Jennifer's Tale

Jennifer is a recent graduate of a twenty-four credit teacher education program, which supplemented her Art History major and Sociology minor. As part of the teacher education program, she completed a six-month internship with Lena, an experienced and enthusiastic teacher. She interviewed with a local school board in the spring, receiving encouragement, but no commitment from the district until September 1, when she received a contract indicating she was assigned to third grade at PS 8. She is very enthusiastic about starting to teach, but she is equally intimidated. Her fears result from two factors: she had only one week's notice to prepare for the beginning of classes and she will be responsible for organizing activities for thirty third grade students every day — for every subject (reading, language arts, social studies, mathematics, science and art).

Although she completed her student teaching internship successfully, she now will be totally responsible for thirty students and isolated all day, with rare opportunities to confer or collaborate with more experienced colleagues. The certification she received from the state to allow her to accept such responsibility is necessary but insufficient for Jennifer. She is mindful of her limited experience and the magnitude of her responsibilities to each of these students. To prepare for the awesome task, Jennifer decides to visit PS 8 the next morning — to plan her travel route as well as to get as prepared as possible at the school.

After a twenty minute drive through three different communities, Jennifer arrived at the school. Just seeing the building's exterior was comforting, having graduated from a similarly designed one. Once inside, she was easily able to find her way, but only custodial and clerical workers seemed to be around. She introduced herself to Sheila, a secretary who told her what room she was assigned to, and gave her the keys to go up and look around. Although she was happy to know a program had been set for her, she wondered how they made these decisions and who made them. She found five sets of textbooks — *History of America; Mathematics — Grade 3; Reading About the City; Science and You;* and *Correct Grammar and Usage — Grade 3.* Books were already selected and in place. While this was reassuring (there would be materials for the students) it was simultaneously disconcerting; Jennifer had been denied any say in these decisions. With the short time available, however, Jennifer felt relieved at the sight of these books. Tables and desks were pushed against the windows facilitating the semi-annual floor washing. She moved the tables around to create a large rectangle (see Figure 4.1). Seeing empty bookshelves under the windows, she made a mental note to bring in some books from her personal library. She moved the large desk and chair to a corner.

As she looked around the room, she was still dissatisfied, although happier than her first glance into the room. She wanted the room to look inviting and exciting. She made another note to get some plants, some fish, glossy paper and posters.

Figure 4.1: *Jennifer's original seating arrangement*

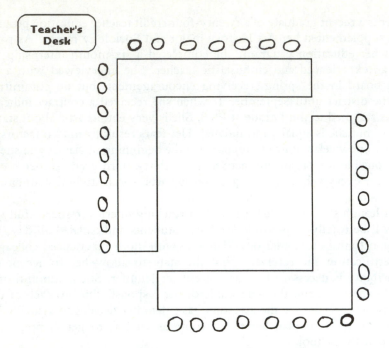

Taking one copy of each textbook and the teacher's manuals, she returned to Sheila in the main office hoping to find some way to learn about her students. There were a few other faculty members socializing, but all taught upper grades and said they didn't know her students. Sheila offered her the filebox which contained her students' records. After glancing at a few comments, she stopped, realizing only negative remarks were recorded. She decided to use the cards only to create a list to practice pronouncing names for Tuesday when she would meet the children. This completed, she returned the records and the keys for 'her room' and went to shop in a local stationery store. While there, two youngsters were looking at school supplies; increased her anticipation of meeting her own students.

Jennifer returned Friday, after reviewing some of the stories in the reader and glancing at the table of contents in the history book. She was getting increasingly anxious about how to organize her first day of school and sought the assistance of Annie, an experienced teacher at PS 8 whose classroom adjoined hers. Although Annie was currently teaching fourth graders, she had taught third grade many years ago.

Annie tried to pacify Jennifer by showing her the schedule: Monday 9:00–9:45 — Reading; 9:45–10:30 — Social Studies. Annie explained that Jennifer needed to plan short activities in each area for each day. To help in her planning, she gave Jennifer curriculum guides and told her to look them over, especially in the back where there were 'real lessons'. She also told her to stick by the teacher's manuals for the books, because they were pretty good. Above all, Annie told her, 'Have loads of work for them to do so they are busy. You don't want them to get out of their seats and get in trouble.' She also advised that she rearrange the furniture in the room so that all the desks faced front and place her desk at the center of the front of the room. After this conversation, Jennifer had mixed feelings.

Her relief came from the time schedule Annie offered her. By dividing the day into small blocks, Jennifer felt confident at structuring these times, using the textbooks in the classroom to center students' curricular learnings. She appreciated advice on how the day is organized, since in student teaching, her students worked on projects for extended time periods — integrating reading, social studies and music. Last year, Jennifer's cooperating teacher seemed to have so many materials which she had collected over the years, as well as the support of the school librarian who collaborated with her, gathering supplementary materials. The PS 8 budget did not include a staff librarian, and Jennifer's resources were restricted mainly to the class textbooks.

Jennifer was a little uncomfortable with Annie's advice about the desks, especially since she had really enjoyed working with students last year in collaborative groups, but she figured that Annie knew best — particularly about what was acceptable in the school, and what these kids would expect. And so she changed the seating design to conform to Annie's suggestion (see Figure 4.2).

Jennifer had never seen this school functioning; she had no idea how students or staff were organized. She had no idea what was acceptable or unacceptable. She worried about these matters as she rearranged the furniture and wrote some welcoming comments on the board. Later in the morning there was a faculty meeting. The staff gathered in the auditorium. The principal, Mr. Norris, stood on the stage and called to the teachers, 'Move to the front, please.' Slowly, most accommodated his request. The assistant principal, Ms. Romero, was standing at the side of the auditorium checking the attendance.

Mr. Norris distributed several mimeographed pages. It was easy now to figure out who the old timers were from the new people. Annie had seen this document many times before. Traditionally, at the first meeting the teachers received a list of the holidays for the year, the school organization chart, the fire drill procedures, the dismissal procedures, and the schedule for report cards. Annie knew this information would be important to refer to in the future. Jennifer read everything, trying to store the information for ready reference. After a few minutes Mr. Norris started to read the documents to the entire group, admonishing them that he did not want to hear at a later date that they were 'never told'. He welcomed them back, announced the names of the new teachers, and wished them well. As far as he was concerned, the school year had been launched. Two major issues become clear: (1) This year starts just like last year — and all the years before it; and (2) The teachers

Figure 4.2: Jennifer's revised seating arrangement

are excluded from the policy-making, even how and when they will report to parents and students on academic progress. There was no reflection or evaluation of the effects of practices such as grading.

The teachers who left exhausted in June had not collaboratively reflected on their experiences — to celebrate their successes, to discuss uncertainties, and to consider alternatives to current practices. Acknowledging the limited time available at the start of the new year, they viewed this as an expedient approach to take. When Jennifer thought about 'starting', her mind was filled with images of freshness and newness, but the only new elements were the students' names. The practices were repeated with no time for reflection. And so, each year looks quite similar to the past.

Mr. Norris neglected to inquire about what each of the teachers wanted to do — or how he might support their work. In this short time, however, he subtly established important principles which will influence much of what will and will not happen during the year. Teachers will be isolated and history will repeat itself. There will be no collaborative establishment of goals or discussions of strategies for achieving objectives. Tradition will prevail, more as an expedient than anything else. With only three days to get ready, there was no time for these serious discussions. Jennifer moved along with the other teachers, feeling pressured to prepare for her students.

Ms. Romero approached Jennifer, introducing herself and confirming that Jennifer has seen her room and gotten her books. She told Jennifer that if she needed help, she should not hesitate to come to her office, room 312. She reassured her that she will 'do fine. After all, they are only third graders!'

'Yes', Jennifer thought, 'but there are thirty of them and I really don't know what I'm supposed to do with them in reading or science and I have them *all* day, *every* day! I have only witnessed first days of school as a student. As a student-teaching intern, I came into a pre-existing classroom. How am *I* to start this year? But nobody seems to care how I feel. They all expect me to carry on. They must have forgotten what it's like to be a beginning teacher.'

Over the holiday weekend, Jennifer copied plans from several different manuals. Remembering Annie's advice she created one work sheet for each period of the day. She wrote the kind of plans her cooperating teacher loved but she was wary of them because Jennifer remembered that Lena's best lessons took more than forty-five minutes. She visualized different scenarios, how she will greet her students, and how she will organize the first day.

After a sleepless night of anticipation, opening day arrived. Her students seemed as nervous as she was when they all came together in the school yard. They wanted to make such a good impression on each other, somehow knowing the importance of first meetings! Taking her cues from Annie, Jennifer paced activities during the day showing she was 'in charge'. When students said they were not ready to move on, she raised her voice, told them to hurry, gathered their materials and moved them to the next activity. She ended the first day reading from *Charlotte's Web* by E.B. White (1952), and then led her students to the yard for dismissal. Relieved, she returned to the office where she observed the experienced faculty returning keys and checking out. Although it was noisy, the conversations resonated with remarks about school being in full swing already — but Jennifer felt she had only just begun.

Jennifer went back to her room to clear her desk of the papers she accumulated and to organize for tomorrow. She hoped her lessons would continue to work as well as they did today. The students were so attentive and cooperative, but they were not very spontaneous, nor was she. It all seemed so artificial and mechanical. 'Maybe that's how a beginning is supposed to be', she thought.

She was thrilled, exhausted, tense . . . so many feelings at once. She wished she had time to talk with Annie and her group at lunch; they seemed so confident. She missed lunch because she wanted to clear her desk from the morning materials and get ready for the afternoon session. She really liked her students. Kaisha and Edward seemed so interested, so lively, so cooperative. She just hoped that what she was doing was right. Mr. Norris passed by her door, but did not come in. She sensed that he liked to check up on things but she was not sure what he was looking for. She would need to find out somehow.

As the days passed, Jennifer occasionally saw Ms. Romero and Mr. Norris in the hall. She also passed many other teachers. They smiled as they passed, occasionally asking, 'How's it going?' but moving on without talking about how it *really* was going. Everyone seemed to be so busy, they had no time to hear how she was doing or to offer any advice. There was seemingly no time to converse or for Jennifer to learn from her more experienced colleagues. There was a tacit agreement that the experienced teachers would not 'interfere' with Jennifer's experiences (trial by fire, some called it). In return, Jennifer would not seek their assistance. It was every man or woman for himself or herself. Each teacher had such a great burden that taking on additional responsibilities (such as helping new colleagues) was considered foolhardy by some, and somewhat arrogant by others. ('She thinks she's so great', jealous colleagues would comment in private.) So beginning teachers like Jennifer are totally isolated and left to survive on their own resources.

As the weeks went by, she continued working her way through each of the books and the students usually did as she told them. Although her students were not as lively as she would have liked them to be, Annie told her to be happy that they were doing as she told them. She was constantly responding to requests from the office about long range plans, attendance reports, book counts, lunch passes, bus passes, emergency cards, health cards . . . the list seemed endless. She never had a moment to talk about or think about how or what her students were individually learning. She really wanted ideas about how to make things more lively in her room. She was getting bored with the lessons in the teachers' manuals. What kept her going was her feeling that her students liked her; several asked permission to stay after school to help her. During that time she engaged them in conversations about their lives as well as listened to their stories. Getting to know each of them was very important to her. They asked her to start a drama club where they could act out plays after school. It was during this activity that Jennifer was convinced that her decision to become a teacher was the right one.

As the semester moved along, she noticed her frequent state of exhaustion, never having energy to see her college friends or do anything but prepare for her students. A poster announcing a conference sponsored by the local teachers' association caught her attention. Jennifer decided to go to the Saturday meeting which included demonstration lessons. There she participated in discussions about good teaching and learning. When she returned to school on Monday she wanted to tell Annie about her experiences, but Annie did not have any time to listen. Jennifer gave her copies of some of the handouts she received and asked Annie to join her in trying some of the ideas she heard others talking about, but Annie said she had no time to try them. Anyway, she was quite happy with her own activities, thank you.

By December, Jennifer had completed all of the exercises and activities in her assigned books. Pleased with this accomplishment, she went to Ms. Romero to select new, more exciting materials. Ms. Romero looked at her strangely asking, 'How could you possibly finish all that work? I can't believe that students have learned it all. Why don't you go back and teach it now!' Jennifer was upset. Was Ms. Romero suggesting that what she had been doing up to this time was not teaching? She knew she had carefully gone through the books, and the students had been very conscientious about doing all the worksheets. Most of them passed the tests on the material, with some getting 90s and 100s. She was not sure what was going on, so she went to Annie for advice, first telling her what happened.

'How could you?' asked Annie incredulously. 'I don't believe you actually went to Romero and said that to her. Do you know what she's likely to do? She'll come to your class now and ask your kids about the topics in those books and you'd better hope they can answer her. Before she comes around, though, you might get your kids involved in acting out one of the stories you read with them or something like that to impress her. She really likes dramatic activities.'

Shortly after this conversation, Ms. Romero entered Jennifer's room and casually walked to the back of the room, motioning to Jennifer to keep on with what she was doing. At this time, the students were writing stories and Jennifer was helping individuals. Ms. Romero sat next to Jeremy and read his work. Noting many spelling and punctuation errors, she told him to be sure to check over his work carefully. Then she read several other students' work. As she left, she asked Jennifer to stop by her office.

In the conference which followed, Ms. Romero criticized the students for superficiality in their story plots and urged Jennifer to be more demanding. Jennifer, now on the defensive, suggested that if Ms. Romero looked at the individual folders, she might see the progress they made since September when they only wrote three or four sentences. Disturbed by this conference, Jennifer tried to make sense of the situation.

Her students were not complaining. They were doing OK. Parents were not complaining, and neither was the administration. Up until then they all seemed to trust her to succeed, but suddenly she felt that trust was replaced by suspicion, just the reverse of what she expected to happen. When she started out, she had little faith in herself, but everyone left her alone, implicitly trusting her. With time, she thought she was proving that she could do it, thereby confirming their original trust. However, by doing something different (asking for additional books) suspicions were aroused. Only now was there an interest in what students were actually doing. Even that interest was not focused on individual progress in communicating ideas, but only on superficial conventions of spelling and punctuation. From Ms. Romero's criticism, Jennifer realized the initial trust was changing rapidly to mistrust.

Having no one to turn to at PS 8, Jennifer decided to contact her college supervisor from last year for some advice. Frank McDonald invited her for coffee the next day after school. For two and a half hours they talked. They talked about how Jennifer felt about her students (really good), how confident she was they had learned what she had taught (not sure), how pleased she was with what she was teaching (not sure), and how happy she was with the professional spirit in the school (not at all). After much sharing of anecdotes from Jennifer's class and Frank's early teaching experiences, Jennifer asked Frank what he would do in her situation. He suggested she consider taking a graduate education course where she would be able to talk regularly about important, professional issues, much like she experienced at the conference but for lengthier and more regular time periods.

She followed his advice and enrolled in a 'Seminar for Reflective Teachers'.

She met other new teachers and some with considerable experience who shared their concerns and probed issues of how students learn. She looked forward to these weekly sessions and the readings and projects she worked on in preparation for class. In the process she realized she was recapturing the idealism which somehow had gotten buried since September. Debbie, another graduate student, mentioned there were two positions becoming available in her school and encouraged Jennifer to apply for one. From all that Debbie said, Jennifer believed the school might be more receptive to her concerns, and she was enthusiastic about the possibility of talking with Debbie on a daily basis. Maybe they could even work together on some activities. Optimistically, Jennifer arranged to talk with the principal. After an intensive hour's conversation about children, learning and Jennifer's successes and wishes, Jennifer was elated. Mr. Foreman seemed earnestly concerned about students and her desire to become a better teacher. His priorities were similar to her own. She was overjoyed when he asked her to join the staff.

As she drove home, she reflected on her experiences at PS 8. Mr. Norris and the other administrative staff were totally removed from the day-to-day school activities. She never had the opportunity to engage in professional discourse with the administrative or instructional staff, and she felt so overwhelmed. Jennifer and all new teachers are given the same responsibilities as Annie who had fifteen years of teaching experience. They gave her the same size class, while providing no special support in recognition of her limited experience. They did not seem to remember themselves as new teachers and all that they had to learn, much as they removed themselves from the complexities of student learning. They also believed that they had earned the right to easier assignments, since they had survived their early years with no assistance. Jennifer's comparison of PS8 and Mr. Foreman's school helped her understand her conflicted situation. Her initial, vague visions were becoming clearer.

Sheila, Karen and Other Visionaries

Sheila Rosenberg recalls an episode during her first year of teaching. She attended a meeting convened for the purpose of familiarizing the staff with the newly prescribed science curriculum. Unlike most of her colleagues, Sheila made time to read through the materials prior to the meeting. She was intrigued by the topics to be studied and sought to understand the content of the curriculum.

As Sheila read, she became aware that the 'compass lessons' emphasized that the needle always pointed north — a fact she was both unaware of, and unclear as to why that is the case. Since the phenomenon was not discussed in the materials, she asked how she might answer a child who might make a similar inquiry. The principal asked, 'Did a child ever ask you why a chicken lays eggs?' When the laughter from her colleagues subsided, an experienced teacher volunteered, 'If I had a kid ask a question like that, I'd tell him to go home and write a ten page report. He'd never do that again.'

Sheila was appalled at the principal's perception of the teacher's role as well as her colleagues' desire to squelch student interest by imposing additional homework. While Sheila believed the session (and school itself) was a place to learn and grow, she found herself holding a minority viewpoint. From the administration's perspective, school was a place where students (and teachers) accepted without any further thought whatever the teacher (and the principal) told them. They were not encouraged to think or question. Sheila quickly realized her educational values conflicted with the established bureaucracy and that she would need to conform to established policies or leave.

Teachers quickly change from idealists who want students to enjoy learning, to discipline demons who bully students into obedience. Before Karen reported for her first day as an intern at Martin Luther King, Jr. High School, she spoke with me about her dreams for teaching. She wanted to 'fire up the kids, to bring life into the classroom'.

A mere two weeks after that, having been in a classroom for a total of thirty hours, she was concerned about maintaining order, having forgotten totally about student interests and learning. She rattled off several rules without a moment's hesitation: 'If they are late they have to get a late pass. If they are out more than four times, they fail for the semester. If they don't do their homework they fail.' All of these are negatives — if they do *not* do — and the adversarial relationship implicit in the They–I dichotomy is noteworthy as well.

When asked to consider the contrast between her original goals and her newly acquired ones, Karen was initially dogmatic, just as her cooperating teacher had been when informing her of the rules. Then, recognizing the contradictions, Karen was appalled at herself. She realized how quickly she had adopted these autocratic rules without considering students' perceptions about why they cut class or failed to bring homework assignments. Karen and her cooperating teacher were responding to the realities of the time-pressured system, and neglecting their students' feelings and needs in the process, much like the teachers had been treated as they were issued administrative dictates.

Teachers like Jennifer, Karen and Sheila are isolated. They have few opportunities to confer with colleagues on professional issues, and when they tell of their experiences in the teacher's room, they are admonished to keep their war stories to themselves. Teachers themselves avoid talking about teaching or learning, knowing most teachers trivialize teaching, or are so appalled at their compromises that they choose not to consciously deal with the complexities of teaching and learning. Those who do admit to having problems are frequently considered to be inadequate to the task.

Most people who complete professional preparation programs prior to initial teaching, have high ideals about teaching as a transformative activity. While many feel called to teaching to right the wrongs they experienced as students, the bureaucratic system subtly socializes its neophytes so quickly and powerfully that they are not initially even aware that they lost sight of their original goals. They become members of the establishment, thereby contributing to the reproduction of the status quo. There is no time for taking teaching seriously, something new teachers like Jennifer, Karen and Sheila surely do. Teachers are deskilled (Apple and Jungck, 1990; Giroux, 1991). From the initial intent of getting students excited about learning and enhancing their self-concepts as learners, they are moved to focusing on discipline, control, and behavior. The goal of engaging minds is forgotten as is the opportunity for discovering how to promote each student's inquiry. Both the teachers' own growth and that of their students is denied in this context.

Teachers are expected to be experts from the beginning — experts at getting students to display the same 'learning' behaviors that ideally the experienced faculty obtain from their most proficient students. These expectations camouflage any real inquiry into which classrooms are most effective in promoting student learning — and perhaps even more basically, what knowledge is of most worth and what processes are most effective in promoting that learning? Those who remain, frequently give up their original ideals and become followers.

Followers

In contrast to teachers who have visions of how to promote student learning, many individuals enter teaching expecting to be told what to do and how to do it. Such individuals do not have a professional perspective on teaching and frequently enter teaching with no professional preparation. They therefore are unschooled in theories about learning, for example. These individuals are very different in important ways from the visionaries. Let's see how Kim's beginnings are different from Jennifer's.

Kim

Kim, a native of Madison, Wisconsin, graduated from Stanford University in California. She participated in an eight-week program at UCLA during the summer, in preparation for her teaching position in New York. She had always wanted to live in New York and sees joining 'Teach for America' as a way to get to New York with a job in hand. She was not sure what she wanted to do for the rest of her life, and was considering law school or business school, but had not really decided. In the interim, she intended to teach, earn some money and then figure out what she wants to do 'when she grows up' as she put it.

Teach for America is a richly funded program seeking to attract Ivy League graduates to teach for two years. It is organized to attract 'intelligent, dedicated college graduates' to take a 'crash teacher training course and spend two years teaching as a form of public service' (Yarrow, 1991, p. 35). The name of this group connotes a concern for developing citizens who will sustain the American ideals of freedom and democracy by teaching. Teach for America's strategy is to 'recruit only from colleges known for high SAT scores . . . [and] promises those recruits a minimum of pedagogy during the training prior to actual teaching' (Steffensen, 1991, p. 40). One of its participants explained, 'I saw Teach for America as very idealistic, a way to give something back to society' (Yarrow, 1991, p. 33). Implicit in the organization of the program is the denial of the value of studying pedagogy, a significant distinction from Jennifer's experiences.

Kim arrived in New York in time for an intensive, three day workshop with others from the Teach for America program. The topics they considered included: negotiating the streets safely; keeping attendance records; filing for health benefits; an explanation of many of the abbreviations used in 'the system' (ESL, G&T, MIS-1) and other aspects of 'the system' which they were likely to hear during their intended brief stay. She and her compatriots were told how to plan lessons, how to set up their classrooms and how to keep students in line. They took copious notes on the procedures, realizing a heavy emphasis on discipline.

As for curriculum and learning issues, they focused on how to read the teacher' manual, how often to give tests, and how to enter grades in the marking book. The major element of the orientation program is to induct new teachers into the established traditions of the system. They are treated as technicians who are responsible for following orders. So these new teachers were told explicitly and implicitly to continue the prevailing practices without considering their effects on student learning. They were particularly guided to use the published curriculum guides and teachers' manuals accompanying the textbooks. They were schooled in delivering a prepackaged curriculum and in maintaining discipline. These materials were frequently called 'teacher proof' by publishers promoting the view that these materials not only were effective without any teacher contribution, but they were impervious to individual idiosyncracies. (This practice denies the potential value of professional judgment and the complexities inherent in promoting individual learning as noted in the Prologue).

Armed with this orientation, Kim arrived at her assigned school, with a clear message as to what the system wanted her to do to organize her room. The rows of desks and chairs need to be well spaced so students do not talk to each other or hit each other. She counted the textbooks to verify there were adequate numbers for each student to have one. She recalled her own school days and tried to remember how her teachers maintained silence and discipline. She has been filled with information from her courses at UCLA, and now from this orientation program. Much of this somewhat contradictory information transmitted in a brief time period, with no opportunity to test out the effects of any of the suggested strategies or to consider personal goals for students' achievement. There was no time for such serious contemplation. . . . the students would arrive in two days. It was up to her to make a go of it.

Kim had conflicting thoughts: she wanted to see New York but she also wanted to be prepared for her students. Accepting the impending arrival of her students, she asked her supervisor, Mr. Kasper, where she could find paper supplies, bulletin board charts, and other instructional materials. He informed her that these were all on order, and would arrive soon. In the meantime, she should make do as best she can. He handed her a sheaf of paper, 'Here are some lesson plans that should get you through the first three weeks!' One of these is presented in Figure 4.3.

Figure 4.3: Sample commonsense lesson plan

Objective: Students will comprehend the passage on the disease AIDS by relating it to their previous knowledge of the disease.

Aim: What do you know about AIDS?

Procedures/Activities:
- Motivation:
    What do you think you know about the disease AIDS?
    What else would you like to know about it?
- Transition:
    In history, were there any other diseases as fatal as AIDS? (Discuss)
- Distribute copies of the article, 'Will AIDS Make the Black Death Look Pale?' Have the students read the article carefully and then answer the following questions which you write on the board:
    (1) Make a list of any words you don't understand.
    (2) List anything you learned about AIDS you didn't know before.
    (3) What do you think is the main idea of this article?
    (4) Underline the section of the article which best expresses this main idea.
- Go over the answers to the questions. Elicit meanings for unfamiliar words and answers to the other two questions.
- Distribute the comprehension check using the standardized style for comprehension questions (see below). Elicit answers.

    _____ 1.   The tone of this article is (a) passionate (b) fearful (c) objective (d) persuasive.
    _____ 2.   The author supports his statements by (a) citing facts and expert opinions (b) giving examples (c) providing detailed descriptions (d) supplying many details.
    _____ 3.   The author most probably feels (a) the Black Death was not that terrible a disease (b) Otis Bowen gave a realistic appraisal of AIDS (c) TB is still a danger to health in the US (d) Rosenkrantz's historical perspective helps us understand the AIDS phenomenon.
    _____ 4.   We can most safely conclude from this passage that in the US (a) many cases of AIDS go unreported (b) AIDS will kill a million people in the next ten years (c) heart disease is a more serious illness than AIDS (d) AIDS is transmitted in the same manner as tuberculosis.
    _____ 5.   According to the article, the widespread fear of AIDS in the US results from the (a) shock it has given our egos (b) fatal nature of the disease (c) way it attacks people in the prime of their youth (d) similarity it has to tuberculosis.
    _____ 6.   It is clear that AIDS is not similar to tuberculosis regarding the (a) number of people it affects (b) age group it attacks (c) hidden nature it sometimes has (d) the social status of its victims.

Assignment: Select any common disease or illness. Write a 150–200 word essay on how people feel about it and respond to it. Be objective.

Understandably, Kim was nervous about the first day of school. She had little confidence in herself as a teacher, mainly because she had so little professional background. As a result, Kim copied the established, enduring procedures. She organized her class just like most of the experienced teachers in the building and she planned her lessons, relying heavily on the teachers' manuals and ditto sheets which seemed to be omnipresent. Kim's acceptance of the *status quo* helped her to fit in easily with her colleagues and her supervisors. They knew she would follow the manuals and guides they provided. Here is a clear example of how schools perpetuate the *status quo*, by employing individuals to follow what they are told rather than to accept professional responsibility for promoting each student's learning.

Kim was connected with a support group of other teachers from Teach for America, all of whom went through the same preliminaries. They met monthly to talk about their experiences and share strategies for surviving. Some were pleased with their interactions with their students and wanted to find ways to help them. Many were just trying to survive to the next day of planning lessons, grading papers, calling homes, and supervising lunchroom activities. For her part, Kim was appalled at her school' s facilities, something her demoralized students take for granted. She secretly wondered if she could transfer to one of the newer schools where some of her college friends were teaching. She realized that the clock on her two year commitment was ticking, and she had fewer days remaining. She was sure she would be able to hang in there, and if she could not, she did not envision any repercussions. Kim's commitment to her students was quite limited, and is thus similar to her colleague, Beverly.

Beverly

Beverly was a recent college graduate who finished her undergraduate courses but still was unsure of what she wanted to do. Her parents refused to continue to support her, so she needed a job. Teaching seemed a reasonable alternative, at least until she had some clearer ideas. She thought: 'How difficult can teaching English be? I speak it quite well and have received high grades in high school and college.' With this self-assessment and the knowledge that there were many openings at a junior high school in a depressed part of town, she visited the school. The office assistant, after briefly chatting with the principal, ushered Beverly into his office. After confirming that she had her bachelor's degree, he arranged for her to get a temporary waiver from state certification since his school had 'difficulty' getting staff. Thus Beverly met Kim in the brief orientation program — both being introduced to the district's teaching policies in preparation for their first teaching assignment.

Beverly, however, did not have the exposure to the eight weeks of 'training' that Kim had, so the information she received was less contradictory for her. For both, however, the instructions and advice are desperately sought.

They were guided to follow prepared recipes for instruction as though they and their students were cake ingredients — not individuals with unique personalities, experiences, and interests. Beverly's initial bravado gave way to a recognition that working with thirty or more students in a room can be a challenging experience. From the beginning, both Kim and Beverly were concerned about maintaining discipline — and getting through the day and the year. Their preparation was different and their goals were different from those with a professional background like Jennifer. Most directed, new teachers will make it through that first year . . . that is, they will not give up the position before the end of the term. Many of them will stay on, particularly because they evaluate themselves as becoming more proficient at following procedures establishing discipline and following the curriculum guides. Since their perceptions of their responsibilities differ so much from Jennifer and other visionaries, their reflective evaluations are different as well.

Some Reflections

Beverly and Kim represent a very large group of teachers. Some have a short-term perspective on teaching — something to do for a brief period of time. Others consider teaching as an innate ability which is impervious to education — people are 'born' teachers. Some believe that their experiences as students are sufficient for their preparation to teach.

Surviving Year One

The Visionary Teachers and the Followers survived in very different ways. Jennifer was frustrated. She wanted to find a place where she had the opportunity to discuss professional issues with colleagues. Kim had mixed feelings. She was expected to complete the two-year term, but she inadvertently realized that there was more to teaching than she originally believed — and was attracted to the dramatic impact a teacher may have in a student's life. She is now taking her teaching quite seriously, and is considering enrolling in a graduate program at night.

Beverly, on the other hand, decided that teaching was easy. She could teach the lessons and distribute the worksheets. The salary was OK — at least for the time being — and she did not have to give her teaching much attention. Her evenings and weekends were free. Her supervisors were pleased that she showed up on a regular basis, that she kept the students in line, and that she turned in her reports on time. She decided to stay on, and pretty much follow the same strategies she used the first year. She knew that she must complete four courses in education before starting her third year of teaching — but that seems far off. Maybe she will find a quick weekend program to fulfill that requirement. Thus we see from these three different 'beginning teachers' that all beginning teachers are not the same. Those who become long-term teachers

frequently expect to be told what to do, while many of those who start with
personal visions are disillusioned and leave, dismayed. Thus, schools become
havens for those who do not take teaching, or learning for that matter, as a
serious, professional concern. They see teaching as a 9 to 3 job which frees
them up for summer vacation and most evenings. When the numbers of these
people who trivialize learning and perpetuate ineffective practices exceed those
with high ideals, the latter group becomes discouraged and leaves. As depressing as this reality is, there is more disturbing news.

Those who remain infer an important strategy for surviving: *be invisible*.
The advice to teachers (and students) is to have a low profile, to make no
waves, to go along with the status quo, thereby becoming invisible. Principals
like schools to be quiet. They like students to be in their seats within the
classroom and abide by the adage, 'Children should be seen but not heard.'
Silence (both in terms of not questioning policies or issues and in not calling
attention to one's actions) buys freedom from harrassment. By filing reports
on time and avoiding confrontations, individuals become invisible, blending
into the building. As long as no attention is called to the teacher's actions or
those of her students, she fits in with the school community. Such cooperative
souls are rewarded by being ignored. Not much attention will be paid to the
quality of learning occurring in the classrooms where people play by the
accepted rules. Those who violate this rule (as Jennifer and Sheila did) find
their every move being monitored.

Another dimension of this silencing is concerned with the content of
instruction. Teachers are issued curriculum guides and textbooks much like
soldiers in an educational army. These tomes list topics and provide sample
lessons and activities. When these materials are supplied, teachers infer that
they need to organize their instruction around them. One justification for this
practice is that uniform examinations are perceived as easier to write when
common materials are used. Use of these guides and texts implies an imposed
curriculum, not one which is determined by the professional educator in the
classroom working with specific students. Teachers, particularly those with
limited or no professional preparation, frequently consider themselves un-
qualified to decide 'the curriculum', believing there is some higher authority
which should decide. Administrators frequently seek to make courses 'teacher
proof' as evidence of their limited faith in teachers' knowledge. Publishers
accommodate these fears by producing costly, if unreadable textbooks to sell
to schools with limited budgets.

Administrators hold contradictory views about teacher qualifications.
There is an implicit assumption that teachers need to be all-knowing. They
should be able to answer all students' questions and they should be spoon-
feeding information to the class. This perspective on teaching flies in the face
of current knowledge that:

1 there are many facts, but few which are uncontroversial; and
2 knowing facts is not the same as being knowledgeable.

We do not know how we think, or how to prevent war, for example, yet these issues are of basic concern for our survival and development. Expecting recent college graduates to be experts is unrealistic. Although they are specialists, they are clearly not experts. (See Stewart, 1989, on English majors, for example.) Their specialist knowledge can be used in two ways: sharing their enthusiasm for a particular subject, and sharing the learning strategies they acquired in their process of becoming specialists. Expecting them to be all-knowing intimidates anyone but the arrogant, but especially the novice teacher is threatened by such expectations.

Teachers who are viewed as all-knowing experts are placed in an untenable position. It is particularly unrealistic to expect teachers to be experts or even specialists in all subjects, such as math, science, social studies, language arts, and art, for example. Yet these are 'subjects' which are included in the elementary curriculum. The knowledge base from which experts need to draw is so far-ranging it is acquired only by the most erudite individuals, usually well advanced in years and experience as well. Fearful that their less-than-expert knowledge will be discovered, many adhere closely to the 'curriculum' and other texts distributed by the administration.

The teachers who 'follow the curriculum' are rewarded by being left alone; their curriculum is not scrutinized. By following established practices, teachers avoid negative comments and questions from supervisors and colleagues. Only those who seek to modify the traditions find their administrators and colleagues questioning what they are doing and the effects on student learning. Change and difference are viewed with suspicion. Much like the teachers and students who seek to be invisible, the principal seeks to keep the school activities invisible. By sustaining the *status quo*, that invisibility is assured.

In a setting where this rule of invisibility prevails, people are docile. There are no intellectual discussions. They become automatons, controlled by the bureaucracy. Contemporary issues such as the demise of communism in Eastern Europe, the elimination of apartheid in South Africa, homelessness and other inequities in our society are not explored. 'Facts' are learned and repeated, but as McNeil (1986) shows, even the facts they are told (that Columbus discovered America, for example) are fictions. These 'facts' are then made meaningless by becoming lists to be memorized, like those devised by E.D. Hirsch (1987) in his call for 'cultural literacy'. School is perceived as a place to accumulate details and follow established tradition, not a place in which to become an active inquirer. This silencing serves to deny teachers important control over their professional lives (Fine, 1989). It also serves to limit students' intellectual involvement, frequently resulting in their dropping out of school (Fine, 1991; Brause and Hodge, 1987; Lanzone and Brause, 1990).

There are major staff problems in schools. Not only do students endure schools, but teachers are expected to endure them as well. The initial excitement for most students and teachers quickly turns to boredom, drudgery and degradation. There is little support for new teachers in most settings. (The first item removed from the education budget in the 1991 New York State fiscal crisis was the mentoring program to help new teachers. Cynics explain education is a low priority, since students cannot vote.) If visionary teachers survive the first year through resourcefulness and intense commitment, they frequently find their idealism replaced with cynicism. They feel overpowered by the strangling system. Either they conform to the system, or the system will seek to discredit them. This phenomenon is as true in journalism (Chomsky, 1989) as in education.

Carnegie Foundation studies (1988a,b) report teachers feel disrespected and undervalued and become disheartened, an inevitable result of being excluded from deciding how the school should be organized, how teachers and students be should instructed and evaluated, and who the new administrators and teachers should be. The work-conditions are considered 'intolerable' in 30 per cent of the schools. One-third of teachers are characterized as 'coping', struggling to do the best they can under the circumstances. Another third have high absentee rates and low morale, while only one third have high morale and a sense of accomplishment (Corcoran, Walker and White, 1988).

> Good teachers' morale is low. . . . They are frustrated by large classes,
> frequent interruptions, scarce supplies and administrators with no time
> for instructional concerns. . . . This list begins to suggest how working
> conditions must change if schools are to retain and support their most
> able and committed staff (Johnson, 1990b, p. 1).

The challenge is clear. Society needs to find ways to sustain the idealism and commitment of visionary professionals.

Ironically, current practices implicitly assume that when a person is appointed, she is supposed to be as knowledgeable and proficient as experienced teachers despite the subsequent need to meet permanent certification requirements, or more importantly, to remain a lifelong learner. Beginning teachers do not gradually accept increasingly complex and more demanding responsibilities. The initial appointment becomes total submersion. Other professions organize an extended sequence of experiences during which time the experienced physicians, lawyers and financiers, work with the neophytes. In the process, these newcomers grow to understand how the experienced members of their profession go about making decisions. In contrast, new teachers work in isolation from colleagues yet assigned the same or heavier responsibilities as the most experienced teachers. Rare are the opportunities to profit from others' experiences or engage in professional discussions.

The complexity of the evolution of a teacher is denied in employment practices. With a constant supply of idealists, and those desperate for a salary, schools readily replace the now demoralized, cynical and burned out former visionaries, creating a revolving door scenario for the teaching profession and for students' education. New teachers are perceived as relatively easy to mold into the system. Those who are not, are rapidly replaced. This process sustains the status quo. The demoralized teachers implicitly convey their low self-esteem to their students and keep students hostage to the system's rules.

Beginning teachers become experienced teachers, or they leave. There are few actual dismissals of teachers for incompetence. [For example, in New York City, between April of 1979 and September of 1988, of 60,000 teachers, thirty-one were dismissed for professional incompetence (Freedman, 1990).] Approximately 40 per cent of teachers leave before completing their second year. This bare fact is testimony to the major hardships and problems in this transitional period alone (Darling-Hammond, Gendler & Wise, 1990). From these stories, we can only assume that many of the visionary and best teachers leave. The system perpetuates the status quo and schools endure. Expedience replaces excellence once again.

Personal Reflections

Like Jennifer, when I started teaching, I had great hopes of transforming the system so that students had exciting and productive educational experiences. I quickly found such goals are not supported in most settings, however. Schools are not places where knowledge and traditions are shared and questioned, people think about important issues and leaders for future generations are launched. I assumed that I would be participating in mind-expanding experiences with my junior high students. I believed I was entering a community of learners. Significantly, my idealism was not reflected in my own experiences. In fact, I was denying all my experiences as a student and student-teacher.

I did not question the system early in my career, being too immersed in the day-to-day stress to obtain a clear perspective on the larger issues of what was happening. This pressurized setting was ideal for socializing me into the system. I responded to requests for reports, reducing time available to think about the effects of my plans, or what my students really needed. By keeping busy with trivial reports, I was systematically removed from considering the big issues:

- Why do we have to give uniform exams?
- Why are scores on reading tests used to restrict the range of grades we can give on report cards?
- Why are students with first language proficiencies in Spanish and French denied access to those and other courses based on their English reading scores?
- Why are we so inundated with clerical work?
- How do the administrators help us to help our students learn?
- Why don't teachers have time to engage in professional conversations with colleagues?

- When is there time to consider how we can share and speculate about improving our educational practices individually and collectively?

We were putting out the proverbial fires instead of feeding students' burning questions. Ms. Parker, the assistant principal whose office was directly opposite my room, emphasized the primacy of quiet. Periodically, she would open the door to the classroom; her presence caused all noise to cease. I looked totally inept — implicitly being reprimanded by my supervisor for not keeping the students quiet. Without any focus on *what* I was teaching, she emphasized that discipline had to come first. Her constant monitoring intensified my concern for discipline.

The monthly, forty-five minute meetings of the English department centered on distributing books and tests, and creating uniform mid-year and end-year exams. We were given our programs, informed which books were ordered, and told when exam grades were due. The few times when we 'discussed' procedures for evaluation we never established policies based on any consistent theory nor was there evidence of concern for our effectiveness in promoting student learning. Our programs scheduled us to meet new groups of thirty-five students every forty-five minutes, totalling 175 students per day. There was no time for us to engage in these discussions — just as there was no time for students to really get immersed in a project — or for us to get to know very much about the individual students in our room.

There was a conflict between the school's goals and my own. The school, as represented by Ms. Parker, was concerned with silence and control. I was concerned with involving students in exciting activities. These seemed at odds with each other and the external pressure jeopardized my untenured position. While constantly striving to get better control of the class, to pacify Ms. Parker, I dreamed up many new strategies. Monday's lessons frequently included comments like, 'I've come up with a new plan' or 'I've had a new idea!' I was constantly trying to start over — to turn over a new leaf — to turn the tide so I looked like the person in charge of the class while stimulating student involvement. With Ms. Parker's comments, I felt as if the students were 'taking advantage of me', speaking out without permission, and talking among themselves. I never questioned why I or Ms. Parker wanted them to be quiet. This was a common sense expectation. I never thought, 'maybe what I'm teaching is irrelevant'. That did not seem to be the issue. It was the students' responsibility to listen to the teacher. And it was my responsibility to tell them what they had to learn. The rebelliousness, particularly in teenagers, was inevitable.

I vowed that my second year would be different. I would let them know who was boss and much of my summer was devoted to designing strategies to present that persona. Much to my amazement and chagrin, I was able to accomplish this, obtaining accolades from my administrators. The system had driven me to this extreme. I had been subtly socialized into the school community's expectations and traditions despite my desire to be different. Luckily,

I recognized quickly the conflict between my ideals and my practice and was able, gradually, to establish a balance between the administration's desire for quiet with my desire for students to enjoy learning.

Realizing the gap between initial idealism and the reality of a teacher's life, many colleagues leave teaching. Susan Moore Johnson (1990a) reported 37 per cent of 'good' public school teachers who were considered to be making positive contributions to their schools, either were considering leaving teaching or had already decided to leave. Some experienced teachers forego their idealism for 'reality'. Many good teachers inevitably drop out of teaching.

Teachers become dismayed at their inability to implement their initial idealism in these settings. They become demoralized, being deprived of any professional respect. People leave teaching in droves. It is not a lifelong career for most who enter the profession. Major reasons teachers cite for leaving the profession are: feeling powerless and demoralized; inordinate stress; and insufficient support. Comments from former British teachers, published in *The* (British) *English Magazine*, 1989 provide representative concerns:

> I left mainly because teaching . . . left little time or energy for anything else. . . . I'm amazed at how hard English teachers work and I wonder if I could ever go back to working under such pressure (p. 21).

> Pupil disaffection was far too prevalent. On top of all this a continuous stream of 'initiatives' was being imposed by bureaucrats on an already overstretched teaching force . . . the levels of stress we experienced as teachers [also contributed to my decision] (pp. 21–22).

> The cut-backs . . . produced intolerable working conditions and have made teaching . . . draining and distressing. Ideals I believed in such as mixed-ability teaching and collaborative learning were impossible to carry out. . . . The main difference between my job now and teaching is that I have time to think out ideas (p. 22).

Perhaps the problem for these new professional educators is that their professional background was inadequate. According to the Metropolitan Life Survey (1990), 'Most new teachers (by 58 per cent . . .) would have liked to have had more practical training before beginning to work on their own in the classroom' (p. 6). Two other interpretations need to be considered: (1) professional education made them incompatible with the established system. Individuals without an informed professional perspective (those with no professional preparation) might be happier teaching in the current schools; and (2) beginning teachers need programs which gradually demand increasing professional expertise. It is unconscionable to give the same or heavier responsibilities to neophytes. The experienced educational staff (including administrators) must accept some responsibilities for educating both the students and the new staff.

We must consider the processes by which individuals are given teaching responsibilities. There are a variety of routes to achieving teaching positions, with professional education programs being only one option. Most states identify 'alternative routes' which make participation in professional education programs unnecessary, superfluous, or merely perfunctory.

Visionary educators are the lifeblood of the profession. Graduates of visionary professional education programs have important understandings which include:

- teaching and learning are highly complex activities;
- effective teaching is a lifelong quest;
- study at an Ivy League institution does not guarantee effective teaching;
- teachers are introspective and responsible pro-fessional educators. In fact, education might very well be the most demanding responsibility in our society.

Jennifer and other visionary educators proudly discuss their constant development as teachers — reflecting on early days with nostalgia, but prouder of more recently developed abilities to nurture student growth. Teachers who follow others' directives, on the other hand, perpetuate the *status quo*, and their students become professionals at acting like students, without becoming more proficient at accepting new challenges. Ultimately, the students make the inference that nobody really cares about them! Our current staffing practices display little respect for the profession of teaching or for students. Such practices make it possible for schools to endure, but we lose our best students and teachers in the process. We must find ways to change.

Mrs. Thomson did not keep her teaching job at our school, but I was one of the lucky ones to have her . . . and my life is different because of her. She befriended me, talked *with* me, not *to* me, and made me feel like a very special person. She treated me (and all the others in the class) with total respect.

Jean Winter

Chapter 5

School Staffs

Jennifer and Annie teach in separate, but adjoining rooms in the same school. Their school day, however, has been virtually organized for them prior to their arrival in September and is fairly predictable from previous years' schedules. They are told how many students they will teach. They are told which books are available for their use and they are told to adopt new initiatives from the district.

For example, in September, Mr. Norris informed the teachers of a new district policy: 'The district superintendent wants to see the aim for each lesson placed on the blackboard. He's going to come around to verify that we're doing this. He believes the aim should come from the students and within the first five minutes of each lesson. In this way, students will know what they're doing, and they have a say in what they're doing. They are to copy that aim into their notebooks.'

Annie interrupted, 'What form should it be — a question — or a "to do" something?'

'Whichever you're comfortable with,' Mr. Norris responded.

Bruce said, 'It's much easier to get the aim of the lesson from the students at the end of the lesson — when they see where the lesson has gone.'

'But the point of the aim is to know where you're going. The aim *must* be up on the board within the first five minutes.'

Mr. Norris did not consider that Bruce's suggestion might indicate a misunderstanding of the policy's intent. Nor did he question the wisdom of predetermining one specific purpose, particularly the teacher's purpose. To question this would necessitate questioning whether writing lesson plans one week in advance of their projected use really responds to students' needs, either. But he did not engage in a discussion. He was adamant that the policy be implemented 'across the board'. As the semester went along, teachers contrived many ways to fulfill this charge. A classic example from Annie's room follows:

Annie: Who remembers what we did yesterday? Timmy?
Timmy: We were discussing the first chapter of *The Pearl*.

Annie:	Good. Now, what do you think we'll be doing today? Julia?
Annie:	We're going to discuss the next chapter.
Julia:	OK, Now who can phrase that as our aim? Lawrence?
Lawrence:	To discuss Chapter Two of *The Pearl*.
Annie:	Very good. I'm going to write it on the board. I want each of you to copy it into your notebooks.

Although the superintendent believed the policy would promote a student-centered learning environment, nothing in this dialogue suggests the students are at the center of what is happening. They are playing a role in a repeated scenario, telling Annie what she wants to hear, so the lesson can move on. They are perfunctorily responding to Annie's questions. They know what she is looking for, and being obsequious students, they feed the lines that move the lesson along. The statement gives no clue about the content of the discussion, only the text materials which will serve to launch the discussion. Ultimately, this statement has only moved along the lesson routine, not student understanding.

Much time elapsed before some teachers began to realize the implicit intentions of the policy. The superintendent did not advocate that students become mind readers. Rather, he wanted the teachers to *listen* to what the students' concerns were, and to use those concerns to create classroom activities.

But Mr. Norris never pushed that added dimension, and the superintendent never came into the classrooms or heard the teachers complain about the emptiness of what they were doing. So the disparity between his intent and their practice was never attended to. The teachers were accustomed to having such seemingly arbitrary 'innovations' imposed on them. Old timers would cynically identify these new policies as trivial and forecast their rapid replacement with a new idea. Newcomers were in a quandry about the purpose of the policy — but the policy itself never was discussed. Why does this happen?

Let's consider how schools function. Sarah, Tanya and Mike teach at the Longwood Elementary School along with fifty other classroom teachers, five assistant teachers, a special education teacher, a librarian, a guidance counselor and a remedial reading teacher. They all work in the same building from September to June, attend the same monthly 'staff' meetings, and over the course of several years meet the same 1,200 students. Collectively, they comprise the faculty of the school, with each teacher having specific, independent responsibilities. 'I do my job,' experienced teachers will say, 'I "respect" my colleagues' professionalism by allowing each to "do their own thing".' In some large measure, teachers become isolated in the guise of professionalism.

We have glimpsed into individual classrooms, but we need to consider the relationship between the separate rooms to understand more fully why school practices endure. While each school is organized somewhat differently, the strict hierarchical structure is fairly commonplace. Teachers perceive

Figure 5.1:   The Commonsense school design

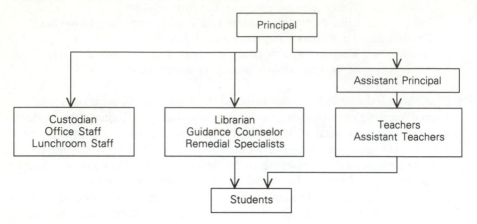

themselves as being 'monkey in the middle' between the students and the administration while students consider themselves the underdog, as realized in Figure 5.1. When the school structure is viewed from this perspective, it appears that the principal dominates the situation, and is autonomous. Teachers frequently comment, 'We have no say in what happens here. We just do what we are told to do.' Students echo the same sentiment.

School Bureaucracy

Principals are appointed to schools and usually do not select their staff. Teachers usually do not pick their principals — or their colleagues. These personnel decisions are usually made at the district office.

Many other decisions are made either at the district or the school and typically prior to the start of each school year. These decisions include: funds available for staffing and accessing educational resources; the specific number of classes to be scheduled; the assignment of each student to a specific classroom; teacher assignment to specific responsibilities; instructional materials to be made available; and staff appointments. These decisions are made by the administrators who are in charge of the school building. Administrators may exclude teachers from the decision process 'because there's not enough time' or 'because they're not around', 'or because teachers don't understand these concerns.'

Administrators who note that teachers do not really understand the issues, while probably accurate, do little to change this situation. Administrators may be given budget information in the middle of August when teachers are on vacation. During the academic year, the teacher's time is completely scheduled to work with students, reducing the opportunity for participation in these decisions. Administrators decide to be efficient in their use of time by consulting with few individuals. Efficiency, a key concern, has the effect of denying staff expertise, or opportunities to realize the visions of the professional staff. 'Efficient' use of time displaces the opportunity for excellence.

Delivering Education in Classrooms

One teacher, appointed to a junior or senior high school, may 'teach' as many as 150 different students each day. With thirty students in each class for forty-five minutes, there is little chance to know more about the students than their names (and some teachers never even learn that). Teachers tend to be so involved with moving each class along every forty-five minutes that the clock gets more attention than learning does. A teacher might try to create neat packages which have a beginning (motivation), a middle (medial summary), and an end (follow-up or homework assignment). Secondary students systematically move through the day, attending seven such classes where they are delivered pre-packaged, overstuffed lessons, and their teachers efficiently move with them through these classes and thus through the school day and school year. They act as if students are learning, denying the reality that they are not.

Experienced teachers become expert at planning forty-five minute lessons, much like newscasters fill the scheduled TV time. Teachers are happy when they get through their planned lessons, and students are jubilant when they get through the lesson and the day. At the end of the day the students and teachers are drained from the constant time pressures. Students and teachers go from day to day — and month to month — surviving in part, by anticipating the next holiday from school. Their perspectives on the effectiveness of these practices — or on alternative organizations, are not sought. The school program seems to be fixed in cement.

The major differences between elementary and secondary schools are found, not so much in the time schedule, but in the number of teachers each student works with daily (or to put it another way, the number of students each teacher gets to know). Elementary students and teachers remain together for extended times during the day. To accommodate the diversity of federally mandated and locally designed special programs such as 'gifted', 'remedial', and 'special education' as well as to meet union contractual agreements (for example, forty-five minutes daily to 'prepare'), elementary schools establish schedules which look much like those in secondary schools. Although students move in and out of the classroom at different times, a large portion of the class remains fairly stable for long periods, accommodating the possibility for engaging in projects which take more than forty-five minutes to complete. Also, since the elementary teacher meets considerably fewer students each day, she is more likely to get to know her students better, making her more able to design activities which capitalize on her specific students' interests and needs.

While there is much in this elementary organization which is laudable, particularly in contrast to the organization of the secondary school, there are many organizational decisions which might be subjected to professional reconsideration with teachers, specifically: Why don't principals teach? Why do we group all 8 year olds in one room? Why do we change teachers every year? Why do we place all those with similar standardized test scores in one group? What would happen if we grouped students by interest, placing those with similar interests in one group, despite age or score on a test?

Teachers rarely meet with other professional colleagues to explore these or other professional issues. Teachers mainly work directly and continually with 'their children'. They infrequently confer with colleagues who are assigned similar subjects or grades, or with the teachers these students had in previous years to share understandings about how to be particularly effective in promoting each student's learning. Although teachers work in adjoining rooms and inhabit the same building for 180 days, they rarely engage in extended dialogue beyond the perfunctory 'crazy weather we're having' or 'when are the attendance reports due?' The assigned schedules designate responsibilities (supervise lunchroom, teach thirty students language arts) for every minute from 8:15 to 3:00. Collaborating with colleagues is not included as part of our responsibilities. Jane Tompkins (1990), a college English teacher, decries the avoidance of talk about teaching, much like the avoidance of talk about sex. Teachers' schedules do not encourage these interactions, and their supervisors expedite matters, making major educational decisions in isolation.

When teachers are so excluded they are denied roles which other professionals are normally accorded. Physicians, lawyers, and architects establish policies about the best way to handle specific situations and they implement their plans in concert with their professional colleagues. Their professional preparation and continued education provide them with the knowledge essential for such decision-making; their continued professional growth is dependent upon their collaborative reflection on the impact of their decisions. So it is with teachers who, as professional educators charged with enhancing learning for all, acquire a core of knowledge which needs to be constantly increased by subjecting it to personal and collaborative review, reflection and revision. Thus, by denying teachers' these decisions, teachers are denied their professional rights and responsibilities. Such traditions, while expedient, have far reaching, negative consequences. Specifically, teachers are silenced and thus disempowered (Giroux, 1988; McLaren, 1986; Maeroff, 1991). They also accept little responsibility for student learning; focusing on instruction, they implicitly equate teaching with learning. There is no time in their schedule to question this assumption.

Autonomy?

Within the classroom, the teacher is responsible for students' instruction and student behavior. The teacher decides what the focus of the lessons will be, guides students through lessons, and evaluates their performances. Teachers frequently comment, 'What goes on in my room is my business.' They say this to emphasize their professional autonomy in deciding what is best for students. By isolating themselves they are responding to two different, but related phenomena. They are exercising their professional expertise in the privacy of their own rooms, but they are not concurrently growing as much professionally as they would if they discussed their teaching with their colleagues. When teachers isolate themselves in their classrooms, they insulate themselves from their professional colleagues' comments. While this isolation gives them a sense of autonomy, it also deprives them of learning from and with their professional colleagues. Their students, therefore, are deprived of teachers who are becoming increasingly proficient as professionals.

Teachers who seek to innovate are told they are free to do so in their own classrooms (for example, to establish 'whole language' programs or thematically organized activities). Their freedom, however, is restricted from several quarters, some real, some imagined. The forty-five minute periods deprive students of the opportunity for intensive involvement in projects and deprive students and teachers of the opportunity to really get to know each other. Teachers fear that next year's teacher will complain that students 'didn't learn anything last year'; parents are concerned that their child is being deprived of what everyone else is doing; and students complain if new expectations are imposed on them. Some colleagues who are threatened or jealous gossip about unusual activities. All of this serves to perpetuate established practices which continue unquestioned despite increasing criticism of school effects on student learning.

As professionals, teachers need time to engage in professional discourse, and time to reflect on the effects of our practices, to learn from experiences, and improve the settings for students' learning. Such time allocations are missing from most teachers' schedules. The bureaucratic organization which is intended to expedite the process of getting school moving and to respond to external demands, eventually becomes dogmatic. In place of improving educational practice by engaging all the available expertise, few people take responsibility for most decisions and generally perpetuate enduring traditions. The concern for excellence is displaced by the demand for immediate action and efficiency.

Principal's Responsibilities

Lest we get the sense that principals are autonomous, we need to look at the school organization more holistically. While principals might seem to be all powerful in their buildings, they are not really independent either. Principals inherit a highly tenured staff — or a totally new but pre-selected staff; and they get many directives from their boss, the district superintendent. The staff hold different and frequently contradictory educational philosophies and have no time to become conscious of these differences and their influence on daily practice. Thus, multiple and frequently conflicting philosophies are practiced within one school program. Tenured staff have little responsibility for continued professional education. Since administrators frequently have shorter tenures than the teaching staff, most teachers establish their autonomy from the administration saying, 'I was here before he came and I'll be here when he's gone. I can't be bothered trying to please each new principal who comes through this building.' Thus, administrators frequently feel as if they are between a rock and a hard place.

These realities reduce the principal's influence on those who are assigned to his building and thus on the programs offered at the school. In the case of the highly tenured staff, the principal feels constrained since these experienced staffs are guaranteed positions unless found guilty of some egregious deeds. With highly transient faculties, principals are happy to have sufficient teachers to cover the assigned slots. Expectations for academic excellence in these settings are rare (and we know expectations greatly influence outcomes from the classic study by Rosenthal and Jacobson, 1968). The administration puts out fires, expedient for the moment, with no attention to the long-term effects on student learning. Principals are not happy with these decisions, but rationalize that they are pragmatic, and this is the best they can do under the circumstances.

Again, they feel isolated and pressured to get things moving, and so they establish practices which give the appearance of education-in-progress. For example, principals have little opportunity to confer with other principals, or their professional staffs, to consider alternative strategies for organizing the school. Typical administrators act more like managers than the visionaries, head teachers or the strong leaders which effective educational institutions need, according to Lieberman and Miller (1990).

Principal's Cabinet

Principals establish 'cabinets' comprised of the administrative staff which meet regularly. The cabinet is created to support the principal's initiatives which come from two main sources: the superintendent and the principal. The superintendent's initiatives take priority over the principal's, strictly for bureaucratic survival of the principal. A typical cabinet meeting with principal Charles N. Blaine covered many topics, namely:

1　A hall duty schedule;
2　Substitutes — can we get more? What do they do when they come to class? Are there any we should eliminate?
3　Test preparation materials distributed by the district office — in anticipation of the State reading tests. When should we distribute? What information should we give?

4   Schedules for testing and teacher coverage — what assignments should be given to the specialists and to the new teachers?
5   Bus company's complaints about student fighting;
6   Neighborhood merchants' complaints about stealing of gum and candy;
7   Union grievances about assigning colleagues to substitute for absent teachers.

The agenda for this meeting filled the whole morning. There was no time to talk about individual teachers or students, particularly how the two new teachers were doing, and how the newly enrolled students from Columbia were settling in. Nor was there time to consider the educational program from a cohesive or philosophical perspective. They are reacting to the school's immediate needs, implicitly deferring for some undetermined time the consideration of broader issues about providing for educational excellence. To understand more of the issues which contribute to this problem, let's consider a profile of a specific, but typical principal.

Charles N. Blaine

Charles N. Blaine is the principal of John Glenn Elementary School. He has been at this post for five years, having served as a physical education teacher in the local junior high school for the previous eight years. Blaine has been promoted in recognition of his acquiring an administrative credential from the state and his reputed success with children. He is mostly noted for keeping them in line! Teachers comment that when Mr. Blaine was a teacher they sent him their discipline problems, and he 'took care of them'. Students, on the other hand, looked forward to their gym class, when they could move around the basketball court developing proficiencies shooting baskets, a welcome change from sitting at their desks filling in boring worksheets.

Mr. Blaine runs what he calls a 'tight ship'. He tells the teachers exactly how he wants the halls (empty) and their rooms (organized in rows with decorated walls). He brings students he encounters in the hall to their rooms, inquiring if it was 'necessary' for the student to be out of the room. He visits rooms to check that his directives are being followed. Teachers value his brief handwritten notes of commendation. He subtly coerces others, inquiring when their room decorations and bulletin board displays will be ready, because he wants to bring some visitors to the room.

Mr. Blaine arrives early and tends to correspondence. He is proud of his practice of ending each day with a clean desk, assigning unfinished matters to be completed by his underlings. He believes by getting to his desk early, he gets ahead of the increasing number of reports on attendance, test scores and demographic data requested from the district office and governmental agencies. He gets no assistance nor commendation for tending to the implicit task of school principals: nurturing student achievement.

When his secretary arrives, she duplicates and places documents in designated teachers' letter boxes including a reminder of the 'staff' meeting scheduled for the following Monday afternoon. Despite the fact that these are called staff meetings, Charles sees these as *his* meetings, times when he tells the faculty how to act in *his* school. The monthly meeting is a misnomer. While it does occur on a monthly basis, it really is a session where Mr. B. presents monologues stating policies, for example, placing the aim of the lesson on the board, or dealing with students with AIDs and those with repeated discipline problems.

Mr. Blaine frequently attends conferences within the district as well as in the state. He takes the opportunity at the monthly staff meetings to criticize the staff, 'Why don't we have a school newspaper like Middletown Elementary?' He prides himself on showing the staff their insufficiencies, never letting them feel pleased with their achievements. Announcements about procedures for completing report cards and attendance usually close the meeting. What annoys most staff about these meetings, is that because the topics are repeated each year, they get nothing new from attending the meetings, yet they are contractually mandated to be present. Most attend in body only.

In the past five years there have been eight new staff members. Two of these were tenured teachers transferring from other schools within the district. Two other positions have been filled by a series of teachers with none achieving tenure. Mr. Blaine has a reputation for rarely renewing contracts of the few untenured faculty in the building, believing the need to keep a fresh perspective is addressed by constantly bringing in new staff.

The teachers call their principal 'Mr. Blaine' to his face, but when his back is turned, they refer to him as 'Napoleon' (expanding on his middle initial, 'N') or 'Mr. B'. Mr. B. goes much beyond the basic responsibility of principals, who, according to Bradley (1990) typically are responsible for 'conducting drills; keeping records; following due process; displaying the American flag; and supervising student savings plans' (p. 5). Mr. Blaine makes unannounced visits to classrooms to keep teachers on their toes. Heather confides that Napoleon made fun of her pronunciation of 'tomato', testimony to the many years she lived in Boston. Mr. Blaine loves it when these stories get around, hoping this will cause them to do a better job. Teachers and students clear a wide path for him, fearful he will find fault with something they do. Parents are greeted curtly outside his office.

Charles N. Blaine places a heavy emphasis on efficiency, monitoring and controlling. He bullies some teachers, intimidating most of the school with his actions. Although he says he is concerned with the quality of the educational experience the students are having, he is never seen talking with students as they engage in their classwork. He does not solicit any dialogue about what students are learning or why so many get good grades but hate school. Nor is there time for discussing with the professional staff such issues as the goals of the school, and how these are implemented during the many years the students attend or realized in some demonstrable way as they graduate.

Charles frequently telephones the district superintendent, asking Dr. Harris' advice. He makes no secret of his desire to be promoted to a post in Dr. Harris' office, so he solicits his approval and brags about what is happening at John Glenn despite his complaints to the staff at their monthly meetings. Parents, while pleased with the discipline in the school, wish there were more student-oriented activities at the school for their children. Many students seem to have anxiety-induced stomach aches, but parents are reluctant to question, fearing the potential repercussions on their child for their inquiries. At the beginning of the year, many attended the parents' meeting and volunteered to assist on committees (report card, social, fund-raising, and health). Only the fund-raising group met; the others never found a convenient time. As the year progressed, fewer parents came to the monthly meetings. While the parents individually are somewhat distressed by these events, they have such busy lives they never meet collectively, so they do not realize the pervasive unhappiness within the school community.

The hierarchical mind-set inherent in the school organization is exemplified in the distribution of furniture as well. New furniture is placed first in Mr. Blaine's office. If there is a surplus, it is sent to a favored assistant. The top-down distribution continues with the assistant principal sending her discards to some preferred classroom teacher, who accepts the 'new' larger sized chair, sending her old chair to another colleague whose chair is in disrepair. New teachers feel lucky to have any chairs at all.

Another example of the hierarchical mind-set is evident in the talk about Mr. B. moving *up* from teaching to administration, and from building principal to the district office staff. Some teachers have commented to peers about a national trend of shifting authority *down* to the school site from the district office to encourage 'shared decision-making'. The hierarchical organization is pervasive, however. The local principal may consider himself subservient to the district office while he is told he is autonomous. He is allocated funds with specific formulas for spending; he is assigned students and teachers and he believes he is responsible for sustaining the *status quo*. This hierarchically organized school is not concerned with reflecting on and improving its improving its effectiveness with specific students.

In previous years (when Mrs. Shutman was there), parents and children designed and built the school playground. Parents also assisted in the auditorium productions, and the read-aloud program. In general they felt comfortable and welcome in the building during the regular school day. With the arrival of Mr. Blaine, however, the atmosphere seemed to change and parents felt superfluous. They are optimistic about Mr. Blaine's promises that their children will be eligible for gifted programs in the middle school based on the rigor and discipline he is instilling. Many parents wonder if their children have to suffer so during their education. Some are banking on Mr. Blaine's prediction that their children 'will blossom' once they get to middle school. Others suggest, 'Of course they will blossom when they get out from under the rigid structure of this experience.'

Teachers speak fondly of their former principal, Mrs. Shutman who, while monitoring, encouraged each teacher to explore new ideas. They reminisce about how she gave them examination copies of books she received, and asked their advice in ordering materials, telling them the budgeted allocations and seeking counsel on how to spend that money. She encouraged their conversations on teaching and supported their attendance at conferences and visits to neighboring schools. She knew many of the children's names, making a practice of greeting them as they arrived in the morning, engaging them in discussions about their school projects. They now reflect with amazement at how they took for granted their professional relationship with Mrs. Shutman. Some teachers are now counting the days till they are eligible for retirement.

Principals are overburdened, responsible to the students, their parents, the teachers in the school and the district superintendent. Presumably, all have a common goal, namely establishing and implementing an effective setting for learning, but rare is the day when they ever get to talk about these issues; rarer still for all levels of the hierarchy to come together on such concerns.

There is an adversarial relationship between the principal and the teachers. Because their power is unequal, and there is no real communication, all are suspicious of each other. There is little time to arrive at any consensus on an educational philosophy or long-term educational goals. Principled decision-making, therefore, is absent, replaced with lists of rules, many of which exemplify the tensions for power and control: students are not to wear hats or chew gum; teachers are to assign a minimum of thirty minutes of homework each weekday night. A chart of the typical school bureaucracy reflects this one-way flow of power. (See Figure 5.2.)

Significantly, there is no arrow connecting students to the others in the organization. The authoritarian organization implicitly conveys that one person decides the total educational program for all. Although the organization has many individuals with professional titles, the strict hierarchical organization excludes collaboration among all these professionals in deciding educational policies. The students who participate in this system are similarly deprived of the collected expertise which could shape more effective schools. In such a hierarchical organization, efficiency and expediency replace a concern for excellence.

Figure 5.2 captures the essence of the typical school bureaucracy. The school board, which may be elected or appointed, selects a superintendent who is charged with the responsibility for educating all children in a district. Since it is impossible for the superintendent to know what quality of education is being experienced by 20,000 to 1,000,000 children, he designates others to supervise, monitor and implement those tasks. Assistant superintendents appoint others to design curricula, select tests, establish promotion and graduation policies, order materials, and analyze test and attendance data.

Ultimately all are responsible to the superintendent, but everything is not wonderful in the superintendent's office either. There are major pressures here, too, with the expectation that they deal with

Figure 5.2: School district organization

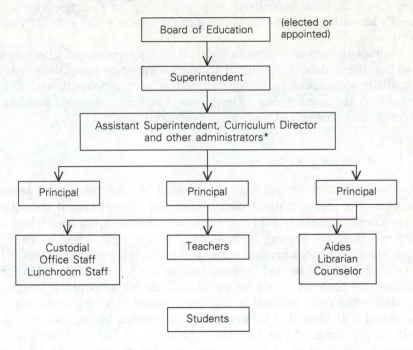

* In large school districts, 'other administrators' may mean 25–500 people.

Source: Fernandez, 1985, p. 30

reading scores, disenchanted teachers . . . crumbling buildings, squabbling politicians, declining tax revenue, and intractable problems associated with poverty . . . collective bargaining, special interest groups, AIDS, and drugs, . . . they have to be regular 'Renaissance men'. . . . The average tenure in the job has dropped to about 2.5 years (Daley, 1990, p. Al).[1]

The responsibilites are onerous and far reaching. Major changes are needed to establish more effective educational units.

The superintendent 'negotiates' with the local politicians for budget allocations, and is fiscally responsible for the expenditure of funds. The assumption implicit in these negotiations is that the funds are adequate for the task. The superintendent must defend as beneficial to the students the educational practices engaged in by his staff. When we view schools from a larger perspective we can understand why many practices endure. Teachers are only accountable to principals, and principals to the district superintendent, who in turn is appointed by the board of education. Students and parents are totally excluded. The same people who appoint and fund hear about problems. This Catch-22 situation impacts most negatively on students who are frequently blamed for not learning, instead of the system which may deny success to students.

School districts are notorious for their gossip — principally because there is so little 'hard' data. This paucity of clear inform-ation leaves each individual potentially vulnerable. In the district and in each individual school, being invisible is the safest policy. Thus, what has been, remains, avoiding the attention that change and innovation potentially bring.

A Personal Reflection

I became frustrated in just such a system. I blamed those who made the decisions (the administration), and complained to professional colleagues in other schools, but rarely did I dare confront the issue in my own school. Not only was there no meeting time allocated in our tight schedules to discuss these issues, but more pragmatically, I liked working with students. I liked what teaching could be, and I wanted to keep my job so that I could continue teaching. If I objected — or even questioned our traditions, I felt I might lose my job (before I was tenured) or that 'they' would make it uncomfortable for me once I was tenured. I believed it was expedient for me not to rock the boat. My colleagues had become cynical about our students and their responsiblities to them. I found it demoralizing to work with 'colleagues' who did not have the same professional commitment I had. But their perspective made it possible to appear daily, albeit without any professional responsibility, without any vision or investment in improving schooling. Instead of adopting their perspective, I and like-minded colleagues left teaching in the secondary school. The system needs to nurture professionals. We need to make it possible for professional educators to establish educational programs within institutions which promote excellence. Endurance should not be the criterion — excellence should be. But how do we get there?

Taking an Alternative Perspective

Thomas Sobol (1990), New York State's Commissioner of Education, reflected on these problems:

> . . . You can't regulate excellence into [the system] because excellence is the product of the energies of the people who are most intimately engaged, the kids themselves. It's a product of the hearts and minds of the people who are actually doing the work. And the only way you can engender excellence in the system therefore is to energize those hearts and minds and create a context of direction and support wherein their energies can be used to the best effect.

> . . . We've been trying to run it from the top down in a system that emphasizes compliance with procedural prescription. . . . The implicit assumption has been that if the regulations are followed, and if the norms of good practice are pursued, the kids will learn. Well, some do, but not well enough and not in sufficient numbers.
>
> Top-down efforts have not worked. . . . We need a new kind of partnership, a new compact for learning to create such a partnership without being overly prescriptive or overly *laissez-faire*. . . . One of the things that we need to do is to give every person at every level of the system genuine ownership of it; a feeling that he or she has some control of it, can make those changes that make sense to them in their own schools. . . . We also need sanctions, if things don't go well in a school . . .

Bureaucratic organizations establish rules and monitor their observance. While this organization may be efficient, it is counterproductive in establishing effective learning settings. The organization of responsibilities needs to be reconceptualized to tap the wealth of expertise available. The hierarchy needs to be flattened out, so that the decisions reflect shared understandings of all members of the educational community. By sharing the expertise available in the larger educational community, many benefits will be realized:

- teachers will get respect for their professional expertise;
- students' ideas and experiences will considered;
- administrators will have access to the expertise and experiences of their professional colleagues;
- the tensions which separate the levels will dissipate, increasing collaboration on crucial professional issues; and
- ultimately, the students will participate in much more wholesome and more effective educational programs.

To accomplish these idealistic goals, we need to acknowledge the importance of three related phenomena, namely: time, innovation, and beginnings.

Time is needed to do anything well, particularly something as complex as establishing an educational program appropriate for students from age 5 to 18. The programs which are currently in operation are in need of reconceptualization. We need to establish time for all members of the educational community to participate in this reconceptualization. The new organization needs to incorporate time for collaboration as an integral part of the on-going program. The summer months, which have traditionally been 'vacation', could be allocated for long-range planning, devoting extensive time to reflecting, evaluating and designing new programs. Time is also needed for this during the academic year.

When educators are able to devote extensive time to redesigning educational programs and school structures, then the 'beginning' of the school year might really become a new beginning, rather than a repetition of the ones which have preceded it. As educators discuss how schools need to change, innovation needs to be encouraged. Defensiveness for perpetuating established traditions jeopardizes the possibility of creating more effective settings. In the next chapter we consider the still broader contexts which affect schooling practices.

Note

1 Members of the board of education are known to appoint individuals to administrative posts as rewards for supporting candidates for local and national election (Barron, 1990). The number of administrative posts tend to increase despite declining enrollments (Hechinger, 1990). Educational expertise and vision may not currently be the crucial criteria used in selecting individuals who are charged with providing educational programs for the community's youth. When well-qualified individuals are selected for these posts, there is still no guarantee of educational excellence, considering the traditional hierarchical structure which pervades many of these settings.

Duke removed his winter coat and threw it on his desk. He was shirtless, dressed in overalls. He slumped down in his chair, munching on a sandwich.

At Teacher's College they told us to lay down the rules on the very first day and stick to them.

'There's no eating in the room, so put away the sandwich.'

Duke shut his eyes, nodded his head knowingly, and said softly (but not so softly that I couldn't hear), 'It figures.'

But he didn't leave it at that. 'I ain't had breakfast, so I'm just fillin' up early on my lunch.' He studied my reaction with cool disdain.

I looked at him angrily. He went on eating.

'What do you mean?' I asked, uneasily, annoyed that he'd triggered off such a strong reaction in me. What was really bothering me was that I didn't know if he was putting me on or not. Maybe he *was* being sincere.

'Just gimme two seconds,' he promised, his mouth crammed with salami. 'There . . . only one bite left,' he mumbled, chewing hungrily. Then he smiled: 'All gone! Now what was so bad about that?'

I closed my eyes, shook my head indicating that I wasn't to be questioned further. There was an uneasy silence.

'Listen,' I said, putting an end to the awkward moment. 'It's all right.'

He looked at me, then nodded impertinently. 'Thanks, man. You can relax now, right?'

McLaren, 1989, p. 41

Chapter 6

Communities for Learning

In this chapter we will consider the physical design of the school community as it affects student learning.

Main Street School

Driving into a new community, we easily identify Main Street School, a low, free-standing unit with an American flag prominently displayed. Although there is constant bustle in front of the city hall and the library, we see people at the school only at predictable entrance and dismissal times. The physical setting suggests the school is important, but this setting also creates barriers which separate the school from the rest of the community. We notice that fences, shrubs and vacant land mark off the school. The school building seems to be an ornament rather than an integral part of the community.

The geographic placement of the school systematically isolates learners from stores, zoos, museums, offices, laboratories, hospitals and factories. By isolating the school building, student learning is isolated, making school remote from the rest of life's activities. By removing students from other worldly activities, students' opportunities for seeing and working with others actively engaged in community-oriented projects are reduced. Separating students from these activities changes their experiences to a series of simulations as preparation and rehearsal for active engagement in authentic projects. The physical isolation handicaps learning, as discussed in the Prologue.

Building Exteriors

Despite the geographic setting and the grandeur of the exterior, the interior is cold and remains virtually unchanged from the day the building opened. School buildings, especially those in older urban areas, are not maintained. It is not unusual for twenty years to elapse between paint jobs. The walls are covered with posters and pictures which serve two purposes: to conceal the chipped and peeling paint and to conceal the 'institutional color' walls. Splintered desks and broken seats are avoided, when possible, to preserve clothing. The flooring is uneven as floor tiles are missing. Holes in the floor are covered with large pieces of wood. Strategically placed waste baskets catch the rain water. Some teachers are able to camouflage much of the disrepair to outsiders, but students and teachers are not deceived. They feel unimportant, uncared for, and abandoned by the rest of the community once they have entered the 'twilight zone' of the decaying school building.

According to Prud'homme (1989), at least half of New York City's 1,100 schools are over fifty years old, and two-thirds need major work. Some buildings use coal for heating, increasing air pollution. The quantity of electric outlets has not kept pace with the current demands for computer access and other technological resources. Air conditioning is rarely found in schools. Telephone access, taken for granted in most settings, is difficult to obtain in schools today. Even toilet facilities are limited. (Teachers talk about 'running' while students do busy work. Telecommunications are virtually non-existent. The facilities are functional — but convey none of the grandeur or importance suggested by the exterior of the building. Students and teachers deal with dehumanizing facilities. Why does this happen in buildings costing millions of dollars?

An Overview of the Interior Design

Architects have been employed by school board members to design the Main Street school to accommodate 800 students ranging in age from 5 to 12. In addition to accommodating these students, there is provision for a limited number of administrative offices. The common-sense design of the first floor is presented in Figure 6.1. The architect allocated more space to administrative offices than for student learning. The principal's office and the main office take up as much space as that allocated to a hundred students. The quantity of space devoted to non-educational tasks is troubling, particularly because of the implicit message that students are less important than those who administer those programs.

When administrative offices are in a prominent location in the building, they highlight the bureaucratic organization which predominates in most schools. This design flies in the face of the belief that schools are established for *students'* learning. The simple act of placing administrative offices more centrally in the building than student resources, subtly (or perhaps not so subtly) focuses the priorities of those responsible for approving the school design.

The library, a premier learning resource is isolated on an upper floor, accessible to small groups of students at prearranged times. All students of one

Figure 6.1: Main floor plan

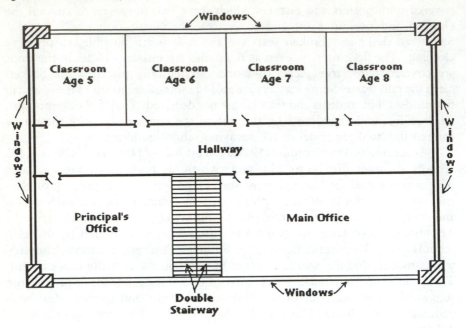

age are grouped together. This organization is predicated on two assumptions about learning, neither of which is valid: (1) All students of the same age have the same experiences and knowledge base; and (2) It is easiest for students to learn when everyone has the same knowledge base. These assumptions are invalid, as revealed in recent research (Barnes, Britton and Torbe, 1986; Donaldson, 1978; Wells, 1986, and Wells, Chang and Maher, 1990 for example). Despite the fact that these designs are inappropriate considering our current knowledge, the use of the space has not been modified.

An alternative design, consistent with our current knowledge about learning, displayed in Figure 6.2, gives prominence to adjustable space and centrally located resources. While we cannot guarantee that the activities occurring in Figure 6.2 will necessarily be more productive, there is a greater likelihood that students will learn when they have access to resources when there is flexibility, and when they feel important.

The design needs to cater to the real purposes to be served by the building, namely student learning. Administration needs to be viewed as an adjunct to that learning, and appropriately located out of the mainstream. In addition, the library needs prominent and more extended space for the simultaneous access of larger numbers of students to rich data bases. When student learning is clearly at the heart of the school, the design provides clear evidence of that priority.

Figure 6.2: *An alternative design*

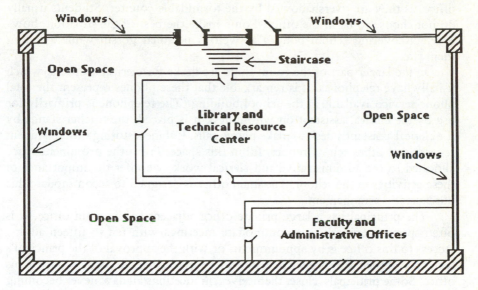

Typical Building Organizations

The building space is divided into three main categories: Offices, Hallways, and Classrooms.

Offices

There are administrative offices and professional offices. The main office is the center of all administrative concerns. It also is the communications center for the school, additional evidence of the centrality of administration to the school functioning. There is a formidable counter in the main office which divides the area into two discrete, unequal sections. In the smaller section we find the teachers' 'mailboxes' and bulletin boards announcing professional opportunities. Mailboxes are two-inch vertical slots mounted against the wall. Personal mail is sorted daily and placed in these boxes along with occasional telephone messages. Official announcements pertaining to student activities and staff responsibilities are duplicated and placed in these boxes as well. Teachers pass through this area to 'check their boxes'. Keys to classrooms are stored overnight in a locked, coded box near the mailslots. (Key storage facilitates access on the few days when teachers are absent. But the teacher constantly feels like a transient soul, never entrusted to hold keys to her room.)

Students sent to the main office for some rule infraction (absence from school, unsigned report card, fighting in the yard, etc.) are dealt with individually, and in isolation. Smaller students are frequently unnoticed in the office, as they are overshadowed by the formidable counter. Students usually do not choose to be in the office. Some make the best of the situation, however, discovering school politics as well as personal gossip while awaiting their fate.

In the larger part of the room there are desks for clerical workers, which usually have telephones. It is remarkable that these phones represent the total phone service available in the school building. The telephone is primarily for use by the clerical assistant on whose desk it is placed; the teacher stands by the clerical assistant's desk to make phone calls. Cabinets storing official student records and other school reports fill in this space. From the prominent space allocated to the administrative and clerical work, we infer the importance of these activities in the school. The main office is designed to accommodate this bureaucratic arrangement.

The principal has a large private office adjacent to the main office. It is often spacious enough to accommodate meetings with ten to fifteen adults. Access to this office is by appointment, or with the approval of the principal's secretary. When the principal wants to be accessible, he comes out of his office. Some principals 'closet themselves' in meetings all day, never becoming involved in the activities or interests of students and teachers during the school day.

Additional office space is assigned to the assistant principal, nurse and guidance counselor. These rooms are considerably smaller than the principal's, and distanced from the main office. They may have a telephone, but more frequently have an intercom which connects to the main office.

Professional offices (in contrast to administrative offices) are almost unheard of. Faculty rarely have offices to meet with colleagues, parents or students in private, to work quietly, referring to professional journals, to make telephone calls to parents, professional colleagues, publishers, or other educational resources or to store professional materials. They have no place to work at a desk away from their students.

The infrequent times when parents visit school to discuss their child's progress they converse in public areas such as the hall, the large main office, or the teachers' room, a common room for the entire staff's eating, lounging, and writing. When teachers want to review work with students and/or parents, they are restricted not only by the lack of physical privacy, but also the limited time available to them. Parents are discouraged from consulting with teachers, since there is no real space or time to meet. The only comfortable space in the building seems to be in the principal's office.

Halls

Wide halls accommodate large numbers of people moving simultaneously. The halls contain water fountains which are frequently inoperative, and bulletin boards which when covered, display student work, commercially prepared materials and public announcements. Often they are outdated or defaced.

Although largely ignored by students and teachers, they seem to concern administrators who delight in showing these to visitors.

There are doorways which lead into staircases, classrooms, offices, closets, and toilets. Some of the doors indicate a special area, such as Library, Assistant Principal's Office or Teacher's Room. Other doors have class designations such as Class 5-401. (The number before the dash indicates the grade level of students assigned to that room; the numbers following the dash indicate the room number. In this case, we know a fifth grade class meets in the first room on one end of the fourth floor corridor.) Frequently the window pane in the door is 'decorated', obscuring visibility into the room from the hall. The doors are usually closed, and frequently locked with access either by knocking or by using a master key.

Students and teachers move through the halls on their way to and from classes, with traffic volume reminiscent of a mid-town street at rush hour! This particular 'rush hour', however, occurs up to ten times per day, with each passing taking approximately six minutes. So, for one hour of each day the halls are crowded. (The rest of the time, they are intentionally deserted.) These passings are timed events, causing considerable hustling, particularly for those students and teachers whose assignments require getting from one end of the building to another. A visitor in the hall at the beginning of such a passage is in very real danger of being stampeded! Every forty-five minutes the school community rushes like lemmings to their next destination, without a spare moment to reflect or chat with others about what they are feeling, doing, thinking or learning, and they spend one hour of the day in these 'passes'.

Administrators monitor the halls, verifying that students are in their assigned classrooms. Teachers also monitor student activity as they carry messages and gather materials during their 'preparation periods'. As people walk through the halls, they look into the few undecorated classroom windows, much as one looks from the street into store windows. In this process, passersby nod to friends while making assumptions about what is happening in the classroom. The halls are unlike streets, however, in that conversations are discouraged for they may disrupt classes in progress, and the passersby are discouraged from exploring what is actually happening in the classrooms.

Classrooms

Schools are intended to be places for students and teachers to work together. To accommodate this goal there are a number of large rooms with approximately thirty small desks (one for each student) and one large desk (the teacher's). Desks are important in schools. They come in different sizes, denoting different status. The larger and newer ones have higher status, going to older, more senior students and more senior faculty. The classroom may be organized in a variety of ways, but are most frequently formatted in lines of student desks in rows facing the teacher's desk and the chalkboard (as in Figure 6.3).

Figure 6.3: The common-sense classroom

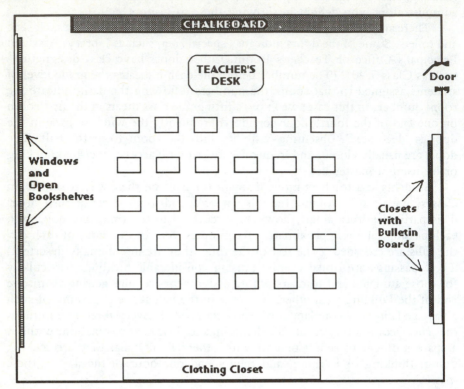

The common-sense belief that the teacher transmits her knowledge to the students is conveyed in a setting such as Figure 6.3. Students are responsible for listening carefully and absorbing the teacher's words of wisdom as shown by Marcia's teaching technique in Chapter 3. John Mayher (1990) presents a critical analysis of these settings, and emphasizes the importance for adopting an *uncommonsense* stance. He defines uncommon sense as 'a capacity to question received wisdom — to ask why and not be satisfied with a conventional answer' (p. 3). In contrast to such a setting, common-sense classrooms emphasize the teacher's dominance in the situation: the teacher stands and the students face her, seeing only the backs of their peers' heads. This classroom configuration is not conducive to creating a collaborative, inquiring, learning community.

In some rooms, movable desks are arranged in clusters of six (as in Figure 6.4). Even though the configurations in Figures 6.3 and 6.4 are vastly different, the teaching-learning philosophy implemented is frequently identical. Students may be restricted from talking with each other about their work, considering such interaction 'cheating'. Students are usually expected to work independently and competitively. The teachers in most classrooms unilaterally determine the process and products of all activities. Students work in

Figure 6.4: *An alternative classroom*

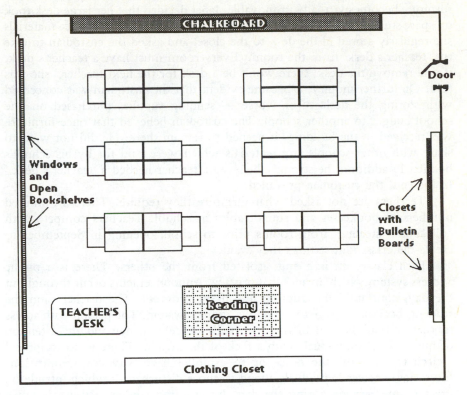

isolation, competing with classmates to achieve the limited number of external rewards.

The windows which open onto the street are large, providing an enormous quantity of light in the room. Spectacularly clean at the start of the school year, they become increasingly cloudy as the year progresses. Few people realize this, since the windows are generally off-limits. Students are warned to get away from the windows — both to ensure that they will not fall out, and to discourage their interest in what is happening on the street.

Broken glass and errant softballs on the floor testify to activities during non-school hours. The windows may not be replaced for many months, leaving everyone inside vulnerable to the cold, rain and wind. Some schools are designed as windowless to save the cost of replacing broken windows; others cite conservation on fuel costs in winter and summer as reasons for architects eliminating windows in the original design. The result is identical: students are totally walled inside. Windows to the outside world become barriers. These windows do *not* serve to open students' minds, contrasting with Vining's (1952) concern in *Windows for the Crown Prince*, for opening windows through education.

Most classrooms have identical furniture. Janet's story is typical of how furniture becomes virtually immovable. Janet decided that her large desk took up space students needed for group work. She moved the attendance materials she regularly stored in the desk to the closet and asked the custodian to take the 'teacher's desk' from the room. 'Every room must have a teacher's desk; if you remove the desk, there won't be a desk for the next teacher,' she was told. On further inquiry, it became evident that the custodian was concerned with storing the desk — or worse — sending supplies purchased on one school budget to another school. The custodian believed that once furniture was received in the building, it needed to remain there. He did not want to share with other schools any materials which were paid for by his school's budget. In addition, he strongly believed a teacher needed a 'teacher's desk.' In the end, the custodian prevailed.

Teachers are not asked what furniture they require. There are limited numbers of bookcases and round tables in school. Teachers compete with colleagues, 'stealing' from rooms prior to school opening in September to create the classroom settings they want.

Each classroom is a unit, isolated from the others. There is a public address system which invades that privacy. Announcements occur throughout the day, constantly interrupting lessons in progress. The teachers and the students become hostage to the public address system. The person with access to that system (housed in the principal's office) can demand the attention of hundreds of individuals with a flick of the switch. There is no reciprocal switch to turn off the noise or to establish two-way communication. Increasingly fewer individuals attend to those disturbances which intrude on greater time periods during the day. Interrupting student activity is taken lightly, with priority given to administrative concerns.

Classrooms are mislabelled as centers for learning despite recent studies documenting the restricted activities engaged in at school and the dismal record of student achievement (Educational Testing Service, 1990). (See the Prologue for an expanded discussion on these issues.) Classrooms are designed to be expedient and efficient without concern for what is best for student learning.

Constant Shuffling

It seems that the objective is to move everyone through the school day, eventually moving them out of the school. Keep them moving; keep them busy. Little concern is evident in the design of the school building for learning, thinking, or growth. That students move from room to room taking different subjects only contributes to the illusion of learning. Instead, there is constant turmoil with no place to call 'home' despite student assignment to a 'home-room'. Students and teachers constantly move around, never feeling 'at home'.

Despite the fact that hundreds, and sometimes thousands inhabit the buildings, each person is isolated. Students and teachers work individually —

deprived of the experiences and insights of their peers. They are treated like robots in a factory, moving systematically from place to place, emphasizing efficiency in place of excellence.

Problems with School Designs

Architects, collaborate with construction budget directors and school administrators in designing schools. They do not question how existing school buildings are functioning. They do not inquire as to whether there may be a need to reconceptualize the existing practices to accommodate current needs (Schön, 1983). The highest priority in designing schools is cost effectiveness, not educational effectiveness.

School buildings are designed for large numbers of students. The school capacity is determined by the number of desks and seats which can be accommodated in each room. For example, a school planning to increase by 600 students, designs twenty new classrooms to house thirty students in each room (Lyons, 1989). There is no concern for additional library space or computer access for the additional enrollees. Schools are designed to accommodate each student at one desk for hours on end. Instead of accessing to resources as the need arises, students are restricted to desk assignments through most of the day.

In more congested urban schools, however, chairs never get an opportunity to cool down. When one class goes to the library, another group comes in to use their space. Students are restricted to prearranged forty-five minute time slots (with one class of thirty having access to the library weekly for forty-five minutes, for example, thereby excluding all others from the library for that time). Students in these types of schools have a nomadic education. They never engage in longterm projects because there is no space for storing works-in-process. Worse still, they perceive learning as isolated, short-term, superficial and imposed; they are told what to do and not expected or encouraged to initiate or take increasing responsibility for their own learning. They inappropriately infer that learning occurs instantaneously as the teacher transmits information.

But this is not the case in all schools. Students in some schools read in comfortable, quiet spaces, while others paint at tables, confer, or work at computer. Students may leave work in progress, and return to it the next day.

School designs need to change in important ways. We need to address specific issues: How can schools be designed to promote educational excellence? What designs would place learning at the heart of the school? What designs are both educationally effective and cost effective? How can schools become integral to the community as a whole? How many people are ideally grouped in a learning community? How are they grouped? What type of physical facility is most conducive to learning? I invite you to consider some of these issues, drawing on your own experiences:

Who would be included in your learning community?

How many people would you have in this learning community?

What criteria would you use in grouping them?

Draw a floor plan for a physical structure to house your learning community.

An Alternative Learning Community

Some 200 students and their teachers who comprise an alternative school. They were visibly happy to see each other and to start their day together. This alternative school had clearly stated goals and a specific focus: Each student was to become fluent in two languages — their home language (English, French or Spanish) and a second language (chosen from the same group). The parents elected to enroll their children in this program because their values were similar to the professionals who had established it. Importantly, this was a small program, with 200 students who worked together on many projects. Having participated in the establishment of the goals, the parents and teachers invested in the program's success — and each student's success. Such collaboration was initially time-consuming, but over the course of several years, served to create a cohesive and clearly focused staff and school community with student learning as the priority.

Several years later, returning to the same alternative program, which was deemed 'successful' by external observers (in large part based on the high test scores and increased enrollment) I had a different reaction. Despite the principal's valiant efforts, it was impossible for her to know all 1,200 students in the same ways she had known the 200. Each teacher focused on the students assigned to her room, changing the sense of community previously established. This evolution was predictable in two ways: success would lead to an increased demand for opportunities to enroll in the school, and increased enrollment would lead to anonymity and an emphasis on efficiency. Bureaucratic rules disabled this previously inspired community. In contrast to my earlier observations of excited students, I now saw students much like those in most other schools: invisible. Eventually the principal initiated a program to divide the school into four sub-schools to regain the earlier community and enthusiasm. (We will look at this program more closely in the last chapter.) Why, we might ask, are students and teachers so dejected when they enter conventional schools? What distinguishes the excited group at the alternative school from more passive ones? Let's consider some issues.

The Excited Group vs the More Passive One

When there are relatively small numbers there is greater possibility for each person to become known individually for his or her artistic rhythm, verbal facility or physical dexterity. The interests and proficiencies of each individual can be nurtured in such a setting, in contrast to larger settings where only the aberrations are attended to, 'the squeaky-wheel-gets-the-grease phenomenon'. When there are large numbers, total obedience and conformity are considered to be an ideal, but these are antithetical to what education is all about. In larger settings, the focus is on keeping control *before* engaging in learning activities. In smaller settings, control is kept *while* they are actively engaged in learning; learners get more attention and assistance in advancing their knowledge and students become increasingly responsible for controlling their own behavior. These settings provide important models for promoting excellence in learning.

Individual Responsibility

In most schools, the numbers of people coming together range from 200 to 4,000. These numbers are particularly daunting when one person is perceived as 'in charge'. By designating the principal as 'in charge', we create a bureaucratic organization which, with a short-term perspective, quickly establishes policies to make the flow of the day possible. These efficient procedures frequently result in denigrating the individuals who are subjected to these rules. They feel unimportant in this setting; not only have they lost their identity, but they have lost their ability to influence what happens to them. Instead of feeling autonomous, they feel imprisoned.

People in schools are socialized to participate almost as if they are anonymous members of a crowd. Individual identities are lost to the collective group. In settings where so many people share the same facilities, schedules become essential — but they are also problematic. Many practices deny individuals' autonomy. For example, times are scheduled for guidance, lunch, and 'recess'. Programming our bodily functions and our personal problems to fit a prepared program is efficient but insensitive to human needs. There are large numbers of people whose lives are so scheduled. If the group were divided, the need for such rigid scheduling could be reduced, and individuals could negotiate these opportunities more humanely.

How do schedules enhance students' opportunities for learning? Schedules need to meet students' needs. Because people do not know each other, and there is no time provision in these settings for such familiarity to occur, the principal establishes schedules for all to follow. This efficient, objective practice removes any sense of trust about the judgments of the students and teachers in this setting. To save time, the rules are established, but concurrent with the administrator's efficient use of time, the others feel excluded from any responsibility or power over what happens to them. Ulti-mately, they felt untrusted and unrespected, unresponsible and unaccountable.

A seemingly infinite number of rules are announced as laws in schools. Many of them promote the hierarchical organization while restricting student academic and social learning. For example, schools establish rules to keep students in their assigned classroom, denying access to toilets until 10:00 am. The inflexibility of the rules to accommodate unusual circumstances is particularly objectionable. These rules are presented as non-negotiable; all must adhere to them, or be ostracized. These rules restrict behavior, usually without studying the cause of 'transgressions' such as illness, boredom, or frustration. In most schools rules are expected to be followed, even if, in the process, self-esteem, confidence and responsibility are denied.

The sign in the front on Ms. Frank's room makes a powerful statement: 'It is better to keep your mouth shut and appear stupid than to open it and remove all doubt.' Students in this class are well-advised to keep quiet for fear of humiliation if they speak. This sign implies a rigid rule of silence. When students abide by it, their self-esteem, confidence and responsibility are curtailed, and their opportunities to explore confusing issues are removed. The rule of silence is detrimental to students' intellectual advancement, but it establishes settings which are more easily manipulated.[1]

Trust and respect grow when smaller groups of people work together, sharing the same space. Given the opportunity to decide how to organize the day, the year, the entire kindergarten to twelfth grade experience, or distribute access to resources, individuals may create the very same schedule they are now using. The important difference is that they participate in deciding about their day and thus feel that the day is theirs. When others make these decisions, teachers and students feel that they have no control, that their lives (for the time they are in the building, at least) belong to the organization. The students and teachers sense that they are mere puppets being moved around by others and their perspectives are neither sought nor valued. They remove themselves from being accountable for outcomes when they have little control. In contrast to business organizations which have as their precept: 'Valuable contributions will be forthcoming from people who feel good about themselves', highly bureaucratized schools take little time to consider the contributions of the participants.

Another effect of this situation is that students get little opportunity to take responsibility for personal decisions. They come to rely on others to organize their day and their activities. They are penalized for visualizing alternatives and making decisions. Yet these same activities are essential for becoming independent and self-sufficient. Thus, by restricting students' individual autonomy, schools reward dependency and, in the process, success *at* school is the antithesis of success *outside* of school.

Separating Themselves from Society

Mike teaches a unit on newspapers, one topic listed in the curriculum guide. He assigns readings about newspapers from the textbook. He does not arrange visits to the local newspaper offices, reading from the local newspapers, or creating a class or school paper. He explains this approach as expedient, allowing him to 'expose' students to this topic, and then move along, thereby 'covering the admittedly overstuffed curriculum'. The result is students never really consider their school studies beyond school. Mike considers he has covered this topic in the curriculum. The problem is that his students do not read newspapers. (For an expansive example of this coverage issue, consider Marcia's lesson on *The Three Billy Goats Gruff* where she believed she was covering the classics, but students never studied the themes which are found in stories considered 'classics' — themes which would foster exploration of society's values. Teachers feel pressured to 'cover the curriculum' which is interpreted as a list of topics to be mentioned. The large number of items leaves little opportunity for in-depth analysis and interpretation of issues. Hirsch (1987) Bennett (1988) and Ravitch and Finn (1987) call for cultural literacy which is synonymous with recognizing lists of titles and characters. Their focus on these elements excludes a consideration of the morality of the actions of the troll and the three billy goats, for example. Hirsch and his colleagues' concern for cultural literacy is a superficial name game, bankrupt of any conceptual concerns such as the exploration of different personal values through literary experiences, or a consideration of the values prevailing in a specific historical era. Such isolated learnings only serve well in *Trivial Pursuit* games and short answers to standardized test questions. Schools must engage students' minds to consider crucial issues in our society.

As we enter the school building we implicitly isolate ourselves from the rest of society. School buildings provide only one location where students' learning can be promoted. Students in school buildings are restricted in their access to valuable resources and more expansive experiences. The myth that learning only happens in school buildings is perpetuated when students are only given access to books, but are deprived of direct experiences. We rarely allow the students to engage intellectually in activities. Teachers go over facts and concepts, expecting students will learn them, despite much experience, as well as systematic research, which confirms that learning occurs in purposeful contexts, not in isolated study. (Barnes documented in 1988 that 90 per cent of the facts learned in the traditional first year lecture program at Harvard Medical School are forgotten before the end of that year. The faculty decided to revise the curriculum to contextualize learning by assigning students to authentic patient cases. Breaking down the barriers between school responsibilities and life has created new, more exciting, and more productive experiences for student learning.

Student learning is assumed to be synonymous with being 'taught' or told information. In this typical model, information is 'delivered'. Time is not allocated for integrating experiences or for considering ideas from a broad, philosophical perspective. Thus school becomes an information dispensary with students assigned to 'go home and learn'. School provides little opportunity for developing learning strategies; authentic learning is short-circuited. Students memorize isolated facts with no clear understanding of principles such as how newspaper stories are written, or why stories become 'classics'.

In school the bureaucratic efficiency inherent in restricting individuals to the building takes precedence over educationally sound practices. Permission to 'be released' is suspiciously guarded, confirming the sense of being imprisoned. There is a certain irony here — education which is intended to be a mentally liberating experience becomes its antithesis. It is not difficult to understand why most people are more resolute than joyous on entering school buildings, but a mid-ground in organizing schools for learning seems relatively easy to accomplish, as explained in Chapter 8.

Considering an Alternative

When people know their neighbors, they are more likely to trust and respect them, reducing the need for inflexible rules. The number of people in each educational setting needs to be restricted. Many large buildings have been creatively divided into smaller separate schools, each with their own identities and concerns. The people in each separate school create a 'community' where they get to know and trust each other. In such a setting, flexibility is possible, accommodating the needs of the individual participants while providing places where students learn and get excited about learning.

A more basic issue is deciding what is important for schools to accomplish. This decision needs to be a communal one — not one which is decided bureaucratically. In some settings, acceptance into Harvard is the *sine qua non* of a creditable school. In others, it is 'being on grade level'. A few institutions graduate students who give evidence of their responsibility and proficiency by specific 'performances' or portfolios (Sizer, 1984). These examples do not exhaust the range of explicit or implicit goals for schools. In most cases, they go unexplored.

In place of statements of purpose, there are report cards and standardized tests which implicitly reflect the values and goals of the schools. These artifacts generally go unquestioned, as though they were the only set of goals possible for schools. Most school systems establish goals independent of community discussion and outside the purview of most of the staff. There is no real community in these school settings. They are convenient places to house individuals, they are efficiently run, but they are not cohesive. They do not reflect collaboration among the participants in deciding the goals or strategies for promoting student learning. What do you think schools should accomplish? Are your goals the same as your children's? . . . their teachers? . . . or the school board? We need to discuss these issues at school meetings.

Once there is consensus on the goals and standards, according to Booth Gardner (the current Governor of the State of Washington) then the state legislature, the parents, the professional educators and the community at large 'don't have to worry about how [schools] get them done' (Flax, 1991). Thus, once there is consensus on the educational goals, the larger community is happy to delegate the responsibility to professional educators to establish specific activities and programs which will achieve these goals. The larger community respects the professional judgement of the appointed educational staff and the professional staff respects the concerns and expertise of the larger community. Such stances create communities where authentic learning settings may be realized. In the next chapter we consider the relationship between school and life outside of school buildings.

Note

1 While one reading of this sign suggests the value of judiciously selecting words and timing, students recognize the implicit threat of being ostracized, and become mute. This practice, prudent for the moment, has long-term consequences of restricting students from exploring, risking, and learning.

Why assume that unsuccessful school performance means something is wrong with the children? Why should unsuccessful school performance, particularly when it is widespread, not suggest that something is wrong with the schools?

Mensh and Mensh, 1991, pp. 20–1.

Chapter 7

School and Real Life

'Wait 'til you leave school and face the *real* world — then you'll see how easy you've had it in school!' Some perceive school as separate, not part of the real world, while others stress that school *is* the real world. Isolation from society is potentially as problematic as society itself. Is school a sanctuary, a different world, or is it the same?

School as Separate from Life

Those who see school as separate from the rest of life, believe school serves as a safe haven for students, isolating them from real world problems such as unruly people and rush-hour traffic. Not only are they removed from these elements which are perceived as negative in society, but additional precautions are taken to 'protect' them from problems such as poverty (by providing free meals when needed) and from the cruel, complex and confusing adult world (by guaranteeing each child a place in some school and reducing frustration by simplifying tasks). These are all considered ways to protect children.

From this perspective, removing the stresses of real life 'protects'. Ostrich-like, this sanctuary perspective assumes that if the child does not have to deal with the problems, they do not exist. With such a mindset, safe is synonymous with 'protected'. Schools take responsibility for safety, a practice which is perceived, in some sense as 'helping', but some forms of help may be more beneficial than others.

Help in Its Many Forms

The help we see implemented in most classrooms is what I will call Help-1, where students are carefully apportioned parts of 'the curriculum' and spoon-fed as if they were infants. Students grow to expect others to tell them what

146

they need to learn, when they need to learn it, and how well they have learned it. This process removes all responsibility for learning from the students, placing it all in the hands of 'authorities'. Students are not recognized as important contributors to their own learning, reconstruers of their own worlds (as Kelly, 1955; and Mayher, 1990 discuss) or evaluators of their own growth. It is almost as though a child is systematically fed 'an education' through an intravenous drip-feed with each teacher supplying a separate dose, slowly transfused over the course of twelve years. This view is consistent with students being told they go to school to *get* educated (implicitly by others) or to *get* an education, much like going to the bakery to *get* a loaf of bread.

There is an important difference between helping someone learn to do something (which I call Help-2) and helping someone *by* doing it for them (Help-1). For example, when people take the time to explain how they came to a certain conclusion, they help (Help-2) by sharing their thought processes. In contrast, if I say, 'Just take my word for it' then my 'helping' (Help-1) is depriving that person of the opportunity to understand how I accomplish that task. In such a situation, the individual becomes totally dependent on me. If I do something without providing any explanations for what I have done or why I have made certain decisions or assumptions, I have not shared my personal knowledge. By denying access to that information, I am also denying essential learning opportunities for the individual I am purporting to help.

There is a third use of help (Help-3) wherein people work together, sharing responsibility to get something done (like washing the blackboard or putting a newspaper together). The two people engage in tasks each could do independently, but their joint efforts expedite matters, an example of true collaboration. In our highly competitive world, Help-1 and Help-3 are frequently confused. People who truly collaborate, however, know and value the difference. Schools which seek to educate students to participate in society emphasize both Help-2 and Help-3. Help-3, is crucial in a truly collaborative community. Teachers who handicap students focus on Help-1. (See Mercado's insightful study, 1988, of how different teachers implement 'help' in their classrooms.)

'Help' conveys three different intentions which are important to distinguish:

Help-1 promotes dependency (I'll help you — by doing that task for you).

Help-2 promotes independence (I'll help you — by sharing my strategies with you, and by encouraging you to learn how to do this by yourself).

Help-3 promotes interdependence and collaboration (I'll assist you, allowing you to focus on more specialized acts, or to get on with a new activity, sharing responsibility for completing burdens at which you are proficient, a personally rewarding activity).

Helping Practices

The pervasive practice of grouping students by age or ability is perceived as helping or protecting students. The justification includes such concerns as not frustrating the child (placing her in a setting where others are more proficient), giving her only what she can handle (so she does not feel stupid), placing her with students who have the same problem (so they can muddle along together and not hold others back). None of these reasons actually responds to current knowledge about learning: that people learn in collaboration with others who have different insights, proficiencies and experiences; and that protective strategies negatively impact on work in school (Blase, 1990). While Blase's findings focused on principals and teachers, we can easily relate the same condition to teachers and students.

Typically classes and students are organized from a common-sense perspective, to make school easier for students. Students are grouped by similar birthdates or test scores, despite any evidence to support the assumed benefit for learners. School structures are based upon two unsupported assumptions: students of the same age know the same things and that it is beneficial for learners to be in settings where there are few differences. Frequently this practice is justified by a third assumption: that schools show sensitivity to students' feelings by grouping them 'homogeneously'. The fact that there are no other settings in life where groups are so contrived should cause us to be suspicious of the real reasons for so grouping students. Yet, there is rarely any questioning about the benefits of these practices. Another aspect of help involves removing students from potentially dangerous situations. School buildings are considered sanctuaries in this regard, for example.

What are the outcomes of such protective strategies? Let's consider some situations. A teacher explains to a class why she will not take them on a trip to the museum: 'I don't want to be responsible if you fall off the subway platform, or if you get hit by a car.' Although there is no guarantee that accidents will not happen anywhere, school personnel feel obligated to guard against injury by keeping students within the school building (forgetting that accidents also happen there!).

Instead, students stay inside school buildings in the same way prisoners remain in their cells. Like prisoners, they frequently increase their knowledge of ways to *subvert* the law, but not how to flourish *within* the law. High recidivism rates document former prisoners' difficulties in living within society's rules. Their jail experiences have not helped them deal with life out of jail. Similarly, students who are isolated in school buildings do not learn to live responsibly in society. The 'protection' inherent in such practices has severe negative consequences.

Schools are places where students have restricted responsibility. In the early grades parents tell students they are responsible for bringing their books and cooperating with the teacher. When there are no changed expectations as they get to twelfth grade, students naturally resent the treatment. Schools infrequently consider the needs of maturing students — both to contribute responsibly to the school community and to accept increasing responsibility for larger parts of their lives at school. 'Protecting' truly disables them with the dubious advantage that it makes things easier for bureaucratic organizations.

Those students who have accepted a docile role for twelve years graduate with little evidence of their ability to accept responsibility for their lives. They may have succeeded in the educational system, as documented by their diplomas. But the protective, dependent stance rewarded in school makes graduates dependent upon society and unprepared for independence. The protection that school affords is short lived and therefore of questionable value. If school experiences do not intentionally help students to participate in the larger society, then the 'protection' students experience when in school serves to handicap them once they leave the sanctuary.

Not only is the deferral of responsibility a questionable practice, but the effects of such practice are highly problematic. Given recent events, we know that school buildings are not invulnerable to gun-toters and drug dealers. So the school building itself is not a true sanctuary. Acknowledging this reality makes it difficult to sustain beliefs that it is even possible to isolate society-at-large from schools, even if such a practice were desirable. While some might think it best for students not to have to concern themselves with such matters, experience teaches us differently. In bygone eras, women were 'protected' by staying at home. Fanatics derive their power by isolating and 'protecting' the flock. These helping strategies result in creating dependency (Help-1), the antithesis of democratic education's long-term goals of independence and interdependence.

There are no guarantees in life and least of all is it realistic to guarantee personal safety. Our only protection results from our constant vigilance. Whenever we take our safety for granted, we are most vulnerable. While my intent is not to make us all paranoid that danger lurks at every step, I do feel compelled to remind us that we are all vulnerable, and part of school's responsibility is to prepare students to accept this as a fact of life for which we are each individually and interdependently responsible.

Some parents who choose schools which they consider 'safe', later realize the missed opportunities during the school years for children to learn to participate in different settings. But many choose to censor and 'protect' in the false hope that isolation is a safer course. I, for one, wonder about these issues and think we need to confront them in open forums. These decisions impact on the quality of educational experience students have and the bottom line is, of course, excellence for all.

If students are kept isolated from the rest of the world, they have no advantage over hypothetical Martians who visit Earth for the first time. They will be intimidated by crowds, by people with different experiences and new settings. Students need to gain confidence in their ability to succeed in society. But when school is separated from the rest of the world, this is difficult.

Occasionally students take trips into the adult world. Usually they are bused separately from the larger society, for efficiency and safety, without thinking of the long-term consequences of such isolation. These trips are rewards for having completed significant projects and are usually carefully meted out. Teachers who plan more than two or three trips a year are frequently considered goof-offs who do not take teaching seriously. The trips are viewed suspiciously. At best they are considered a supplement to the learning which occurs in the classroom. Learning is assumed to occur exclusively in the classroom, although there is little evidence to support this assumption (and much to refute it.)

Education is a process which is intended to result in individual independence. 'Protection' results in total dependency. When schools seek to be isolated from the real world, they contribute to this dependent state. The best protection anyone can provide is to gradually introduce students to the real world, sharing strategies for surviving and enjoying life in the process. The world is a complex place, and by denying students access to it, by isolating them from the rest of the world, teachers and parents deny them opportunities to understand how it functions, and how they can enjoy its diversity. Lacking this information, students become fearful of the unknown and dependent on those who know. In life, people make many decisions. We travel in crowded trains, explore new opportunities, or we confine ourselves. Those who venture out get lost, change minds, confirm assumptions or get new perspectives and insights; in other words, learning continues. Those who confine themselves restrict their lifelong learning and active participation in the larger society.

Play in Schools

Schools are frequently perceived as exclusively serious places, where laughter and enjoyment are suspect. Suspicions are aroused when people smile. Learning is considered an important and serious activity, removing any prospect of fun. If it's important, it is serious and therefore cannot be fun, or so folk logic claims. The antithesis of learning, for many people, is play. Humorous stories, satirical role-playing situations, or laughing at one's own mistakes and misinterpretations are considered time wasters. Play, *per se*, is not perceived as a mode for learning, especially not as a school-planned activity within the regular curriculum. This belief prevails despite mounting research studies which find significant benefits to learning when students enjoy what they are doing. The important learnings from playing chess, for example, have been carefully documented (Byrne, 1989; Moffett, 1973). In Great Britain, playtime itself is being reconstructed to make children's experiences more challenging and demanding ([London] *Times Educational Supplement*, 1989). The playground is being taken seriously as a 'powerful former of attitudes and behaviors' (*ibid.* p. 20). Play leads to more mature understandings about people and life (Starratt, 1990).

When play is denigrated, children are denied across to the prime places for learning. Babies play with a rattle, with their toes, with their toys and with their family. While they play, they learn about language, they learn about learning, they learn about themselves, and they learn about the ever-expanding world around them. They experiment with their hypotheses. They increase their awareness of everyday phenomena and become increasingly proficient at participating in the world . . . all this while they are 'playing' (Bruner, 1986; Kagan, 1989; Kegan, 1982; Kelly, 1955; Paley, 1981; Piaget, 1962; Vygotsky, 1978). Once school begins, however, a basic assumption prevails: play must end.

Play in all forms is discouraged. Producing plays for an audience is perceived as disconnected from the curriculum. Rehearsals are held after school to avoid being accused of 'taking time from learning' to rehearse. The educational impact of participating in such productions is denied. Particularly because students enjoy their participation in the rehearsals and the eventual production, adults are suspicious that there must be something wrong. The unquestioned assumption is: It can't be educational if it is also enjoyable, a simplistic and common-sense perspective on schools. When we asked students about the benefits, we get a very different perspective. They explain their increasing understanding of plot and character development, and of the importance of context, for example.

Is it any wonder students feel handicapped by school? Jim Sutton's 'Passing Thoughts' (1989) reflects on such experiences.

Schola Latina Bostonienses, O.

> When I consider how much harm was done
> by setting hurdles none of us cd reach;
> the fears & terrors goading kids to run
> breathless for men who cdn't do or teach;
> the so-called "masters" who igner'd the art
> of building character thru self-esteem
> because they thought no man cd make his mark
> unless the boy before had been demean'd;
> when I consider what they did to me
> and all the rest who'll never be the same
> because of what they taught — anxiety —
> I know I'd never leap that course again.
>   Because it's jumping I'd no longer do,
> I know it's something I won't ask of you.

School as the Real World

School policies frequently establish microcosms of the prejudice and discrimination experienced within our society (McLaren, 1986; Aronowitz and Giroux, 1985). A growing group of people criticize schools for perpetuating society's inequities. Just as people from different ethnic backgrounds are

151

discriminated against in the adult world, they are victims of prejudice in the schools. Racist practices which determine where people can get housing are perpetuated by districting students to schools based on their 'neighbor-hoods'. Students are tracked into specific programs based on their previous achievements — not their interest in exploring specific phenomena, or their desire to learn.

Expectations differ based on ethnic and economic factors. Funding for schools also varies. Affluent neighborhoods (such as Scarsdale, NY, for example) get significantly larger state allocations than poorer ones (Litow, 1990). Sometimes the per student differences in funding between districts within one state are as large as $10,000, with students from comfortable financial settings attending schools that are more highly funded — a clear case of the rich getting richer. These decisions are political and anti-democratic. For example, elected officials representing affluent communities seek to bring back as many dollars as possible, despite the abject poverty of nearby urban communities. The inequities inherent in these practices are not questioned, but are fatalistically are accepted as the facts of life.

Some districts manage to have large, bright classrooms with comfortable space for engaging in a variety of activities. Others are over-crowded. Some have ready access to vast transportation facilities for trips to educational sites while others are virtually locked inside for six hours. These differences can be predicted based on ethnicity and educational background alone (Brause and Mayher, 1991b). Much like the proverbial 'rich getting richer and the poor getting children' phenomenon, the wealthier communities have an abundance of increasing resources and frequently declining enrollments while the poorer ones have fewer facilities and increasing enrollments. These inequities are rarely explicitly addressed. In 1990 New Jersey's newly elected Governor Jim Florio boldly enacted legislation to redistribute the educational budget to account for these inequities. Predictably the wealthy districts complained bitterly. This real world phenomenon is a clear example of how schools are not safe havens. The problems which plague society at large are also plaguing our schools. Believing anything different contradicts reality.

The competition inherent in our 'dog-eat-dog' world is no stranger to the schools. There are few rewards available in schools, typified by the children's game of musical chairs where there is only one winner. Particularly fueled by their parents' enthusiasm for bragging about grades or leading roles in dramatic productions, many students adopt a competitive stance. In this context, parents shout about their child's brilliance based on test scores (believing 'the apple doesn't fall far from the tree' and hinting to others to make the same inference). So we find test-taking 'skills' include copying from peers' papers when unsure of the correct answer, referring to crib notes, buying test answers, and engaging in non-verbal communication with peers as the teacher dictates questions; report writing involves copying from library sources which are then secretly removed from the library shelves; parents 'help' (Help-1) in the writing of papers, or students copy or pay others to write papers. Students do not value academic learning in this context, rather, they are learning how to achieve high grades and the sought-after overt rewards without enhancing their understanding of life. When these students are accepted into prestigious university programs and awarded other distinctions, this perversion of education is explicitly rewarded.

Another World?

Another similarity between school and the real world is people's limited trust of others. The extensive locking up of equipment and restricted access to facilities clearly display this combined mistrust and fear. The secrecy which prevails in the process of assessing student learning, both in terms of the decisions of what to assess and how to interpret student work, reveals a similar lack of trust. The desire of the haves to control others' lives as a way to sustain the differences between the haves and the have-nots, resonates in all these practices.

Students who do not buy into this competition are pleased to get by — to pass. Those who prefer to participate in a collaborative enterprise opt out of situations which pit each person against all others. Such decisions have important ramifications. Such non-competitive personalities get none of the external rewards of the bureaucratic school system. An ideal setting would make it possible for competitive and non-competitive students to flourish — but school, like life, requires individuals to make choices and accept the consequences of those choices. Schools need to be places where we create our ideal worlds while simultaneously promoting student survival in the 'real' world. In the next chapter we will consider how such settings might be established and what they would accomplish.

'I can't believe they pay me to do something I love so much!'

An anonymous teacher

Chapter 8

Schools for Tomorrow/Tomorrow's Schools

Having identified many of the problems with today's schools today, we need to consider how to change our schools for tomorrow. Consistent with all previous chapters, I relate real experiences but go one step further, proposing plans for further reform derived in part from experiences with the Community School, a strong program mounted with grand ideals and enthusiasm. Although it is still in operation, as of 1991 its visions have been much curtailed. My involvement with the Community School allows me to present its origins and consider its inevitable political conflicts. These experiences warn us of many problems inherent in attempting to change enduring schools.

The Evolution of the Community School

Barbara Josephson, (a pseudonym for the principal at PS 7), acting as an agent for some of her teachers invited both my colleague, John Mayher, and me to visit with a group of seven teachers. We have been consulting over fifteen years with Barbara as she engages in program and staff development projects. This invitation, however, came from the teachers who sought to talk with us at a three hour after-school meeting, an activity for which each received credit towards a graduate education program. They were reflecting on and critiquing their current practices, and were particularly struck by students' growing disillusionment and disenchantment with school as they travelled from kindergarten to the eighth grade. These experienced teachers were also personally bored with much of what they were doing. In seeking to regenerate the enthusiasm which accompanied their initial days in teaching they were challenged by the possibility of creating an alternative mini-school within their existing building. Part of the first conversation is recorded below (with names of all participants changed, except for John and me):

> Steve: I'm very concerned because I want kids to stay in school, to graduate, to go to college, and eventually some to

return as teachers in this school. I think we need to find ways to get them more involved in what they do at school. And I think what they do has to have important payoffs — both in terms of their confidence in their own abilities and in their accepting some important responsibility for others — for society. I think that's something we all sort of have agreed to already.

Marty: Yes. And the tests they have to take change the whole focus of schools. I hate those tests. I hate to spend so much time prepping them for the test — and besides which, although most of my students do well on the tests, I think that they're getting the wrong message about what learning is. They are so bored with all this testing — and so am I.

Yvonne: We're all disenfranchised. Our students' personal experiences and concerns are shunted aside to complete exercises in preparation for the tests. I know they know more than their test scores suggest. But the only things that count are those scores.

Barbara: What kinds of changes would you like to make?

Steve: I'd like to stop giving these tests! They are very demoralizing to my students. They trivialize what they're really doing and they do not touch on any of the controversial material we consider. My students are becoming quite adept at participating in debates, yet none of these tests assess their proficiencies with extended discourse and argumentation.

Barbara: Then, are you against *any* tests — or just the ones which are currently used?

Steve: I don't like what we use now. I haven't seen any published tests which address what I'm talking about. So I guess I'm against tests which are created by people who don't know what my students have been doing. I'd be very happy to create a test or at least compile a group of activities which could be used to document their growth during the year. I guess what I'm concerned about is that whatever we use should be consistent with our goals and useful in promoting student learning.

Laura: I think we need to give tests. Somehow, all the parents expect the kids to get tests and their friends in other schools and other classes in this school get tests. I hate them, too, but I think we can't avoid giving them.

Sheila: I really don't have the time to create any new tests. I have so much work to do already. Why can't we just go along with those tests, and then do what we want the rest of the time?

157

John: It seems to me that you've identified many important is-
             sues about tests from the perspective of your students,
             your colleagues in the rest of the school, and your own
             concerns. But I'm not sure why you are starting with
             tests? It seems to me that any assessment needs to be an
             outgrowth of the educational program. Tests shouldn't
             drive the program. It should be the reverse. Maybe we
             should try to focus on the educational program we're
             thinking about here. How would it be different from what's
             happening now?

Kathy: Well, we're talking about having the same students for
             two or three years in a row, rather than just one year.

Marty: And we're thinking of trying to integrate a lot of separate
             subjects . . . like a whole integrated day — expanding the
             idea of whole language programs. Instead of having Read-
             ing from 9:00 to 9:45 and Science from 9:45 to 10:30 for
             example, we thought we might start out by identifying a
             specific focus or activity instead of these isolated subjects.
             We'd hope then the children wouldn't think about school
             as a series of isolated subjects as much as 'enterprises' as
             Frank Smith writes about it.

Yvonne: Some of us were talking about mixing groups so children
             who are 5 or 6 might work with some older kids on
             projects — instead of us giving 'lessons' all the time.

Rita: It seems many of you have a similar general vision about
             your goals for students. This will be really helpful, I think
             as you design your new school. Have you set a schedule
             for planning together?

Steve: That's part of the problem. We have only these meetings
             once a week after school, and we're too exhausted at this
             time to really do what needs doing. We think we need to
             work for an extended time period — but haven't figured
             out how to do that yet. Also, we haven't talked about
             scheduling.

Barbara: And you'll have to make sure you're covering the curric-
             ulum as you plan all of these combinations.

Laura: I'm confused. There seem to be so many different issues
             to deal with. How will we ever get to all of them?

Rita: Maybe we need to consider priorities and then work from
             there. We've gone from testing to students' learning, to
             creating the curriculum, to scheduling, and now to cover-
             ing the curriculum. I'm not sure that this list includes all
             of the issues, but it might be useful to consider which of
             these is *the most important* and start from there.

Steve: Why don't we put the issues on the board — and figure

out how they are related — or how important each one is
to our planning . . .

The meeting continued with the teachers forming two small groups, and then
returning to the large group to pool ideas and plan strategies for subsequent
meetings. There were several major outcomes of that meeting:

- a commitment from several to devote the month of July to conceptualize plans for redesigning the school day;
- John Mayher and I were asked to suggest readings to help formulate
  plans;
- a request for a list of schools, classes, or programs to visit which had
  goals and visions in keeping with the vision of the group;
- a promise from Barbara Josephson for time to visit other schools
  during the school day;
- a decision for each participant to accumulate ideas from readings and
  reflections on classroom practice and site visits.

Barbara volunteered to ask the district office to sponsor summer stipends
for this activity since teachers were giving up part of their vacation to work
on school projects. (While for some, summer was a time to recuperate from
the pressures of the school year and to take graduate courses, others needed
part-time jobs to supplement their teaching salaries.) The principal's offer to
approach the district superintendent sparked their energies. Five of the six
teachers signed up for the summer planning and for the launching of the
unnamed 'mini-school' in September.

In the intervening time, Steve and Laura visited a new alternative K-9
school in a neighboring district. In contrast to teachers initiating change, the
New School had been sponsored by parents who selected their director with
educational goals and visions similar to their own. She in turn, chose four
teacher-leaders to help in the evolution of the program which started with
the early grades (K-3) and gradually extended to cover grades K-9. Laura and
Steve were impressed with the students' enthusiasm and engagement as they
collaborated in small groups to speculate about life in earlier times. The visitors
were each quickly adopted by a group of students to assist them — from
which they freed themselves at lunchtime to eat and chat with other students.
At the end of the day, Jena, the director, invited them to stay for coffee. They
explored much of the history of the project and got a sense of some of the
potential problems. They invited Jena to their next group meeting and shared
some of their experiences with their colleagues on their return.

Yvonne and Kathy read extensively during this time from the suggested
reading list (Identified and updated in Appendix A). They discussed some of
the readings between themselves and talked with us further when we visited
their school. Our conversations focused on many issues, including:

- What is learning?
- How do we know when someone is learning?
- What should students be learning?
- How do we get students to work together?
- What does a teacher do in a student-centered classroom?
- How is 'the curriculum' created?

July finally arrived and the group returned to the empty building, excited and somewhat intimidated by their goals!

Steve: Well, how should we begin?

Laura: How about each of us say something — I'll start. I mentioned this project to my class one day and some of them got all excited. I don't know if it was the prospect of being asked their opinion that attracted their attention or what, but a few of them really stuck with me and came up with some ideas we might consider. I wrote them down:
- School shouldn't be boring. It should be fun, or at least exciting.
- We shouldn't be treated like babies.
- We should be able to make some choices.

Yvonne: Those are great! I didn't even think of telling my students about this project. I thought, I'd hold off telling them until I was ready to invite them in.

Kathy: Well, I was reading some articles and books, and I came up with some ideas:
- We should get more involved with the community.
- We need to have extended time blocks. The forty-five minute periods are creating unnecessary pressures.
- Students can work together without our constant supervision. We need to trust them — just like we're asking Barbara to trust us!

. . . and so the discussion went on for four solid weeks. The teachers shared their visions of alternative structures and constantly questioned how they might initiate them.

The time needed for each individual to develop a clear focus on how the year and the day might be organized was so time consuming they each chose for the first year to establish individual agendas and share resources rather than developing common activities for all the grades. They decided to redesign their classroom activities independently.

Perhaps this decision should have signalled the need for learning to collaborate, or the need for additional time before attempting to implement the program. But at the time, we convinced ourselves that all was in readiness. Predictably, the program faltered. Some of the reasons for this are discussed later in this chapter. Nevertheless, a smaller group of three decided to work together. They agreed to struggle together to create a new program. What follows are descriptions of some projects discussed within the original group, and some which draw on those I've observed in other settings or have dreamed about.

Reflecting on our discussions, the teachers noticed the frequent comments about improving the community, and decided to make this their joint focus. They shared their embarrassment at their limited knowledge of the community despite their daily commutes, and decided to explore it.

They eyed the school yard: an enclosed area with two trees and much garbage. That needed to look better; how could work on the school yard fulfill academic concerns? After some discussion, they realized how easily math and science learnings were at the heart of sustaining the garden. In consultation with the staff at the local botanical garden and the children's science museum they thought of ways to incorporate language, science, math, and social studies goals with a garden project. Suddenly the project seemed so wonderful, yet so academic. Two who were the most excited agree to have major responsibility for that project. They decided to find out how to start a garden and what materials were available. As the teachers roam in the community, they realize the potential value of a list of community resources to local residents, especially those who have recently moved into the neighborhood. The group sketched plans for four specific projects as a way to solidify the community focus:

1   Improving Our Community
2   Gardens in Our Community
3   Directory of Our Community Resources
4   Our Community's History

The community focus might attract students and parents to the program and would give a specific direction for their activities. These projects become vehicles for studying their 'regular' subjects. They could use the products which come out of the project to document each student's progress throughout the year. All of this sounds wonderful, but would it really work? Some teachers met with the parents; others discussed the plans with the principal.

They visualized restructured classrooms and a reorganized curriculum. In the planning process, the teachers identified many issues of professional and personal import which intrigued them. They were all actively invested in this planning, agreeing that nothing was unchangeable, and nothing was ever perfect. They acknowledge that enhancement of students' learning is to be achieved only by hard work, constant reflection and revision. Simultaneously, the teachers experiment with collaborative strategies they hope to use with their students.

They decided they first needed to get students working collaboratively. Eventually, as they and their students became more comfortable and confident

Figure 8.1: *Organization for year one — The Community School*

Class	Student Load	Teacher	Topic
K	25 students	Jane	Community Gardens
1	25 students	Fran	Community Gardens
2	25 students	Cora	Community Directory
3	25 students	Moira	Community History
4	25 students	Pete	Community Improvement

Figure 8.2: *Weekly schedule*

Time	Monday	Tuesday	Wednesday	Thursday	Friday
9–12	Large Class	Small Group	Small Group	Small Group	Whole School
12–1	L ------ U ------ N ------- C ------ H -------				
1–3	Small Group	Small Group	Large Class	Small Group	Whole School

with group work, they sought to move gradually into projects which would involve students from more than one grade group. Topics and schedules for the year were projected (see Figures 8.1 and 8.2).

The overriding focus on the community was common to all grades. The second, third and fourth grades focus on a separate concerns. Kindergarten and the first grade groups were scheduled to work together and to join the upper grades in sharing their information. Each grade had a responsibility to the others. Time is needed both for pursuing their specific responsibilities and for keeping all informed of progress, sharing strategies, information and resources. In this way, the teachers planned together with specific responsibilities for their grade within the overall community focus.

The plan allows for students to work individually on assignments from their group, for groups to plan, share and explore resources and for collaboration with the teacher, peers, guests and other resources. One class which focused on the community's history, for example, might divide into five teams with each team being responsible for one geographical section represented on the community map. The sections, called different names by the residents, made these groupings relatively easy to establish. Some students chose their own neighborhoods, and others explore new sections. Thus each student in one class investigates a specific section in the neighborhood to study eventually to incorporate into one collection of information about how the total community looked fifty years ago.

The students brainstormed about where they might get information and created a list of potential resources including their grandparents, parents and other older residents, the library files, the local historical society, the school archives and the religious centers. From their brainstorming of how they might share their discoveries, they created a wide range of possibilities including: a photographic exhibition with a catalogue, a book, and a theatrical production. The ultimate decision on the presentation was deferred to a later time in the project. There are times when the whole class worked together, creating interview questions, practicing interviewing strategies, exploring the school library's resources, scrutinizing old maps and sharing information. Most of the time was scheduled for group and independent projects. The classroom furniture was organized to promote this combination of activities much like the classroom arrangement presented in Figure 3.3.

With the advent of these new procedures, students need to learn how to work together and how to take responsibility for following through on assignments, particularly on those decided with peers. Teachers evaluate student progress and conceptualize future directions for the program. When students see 'their' plants growing in the garden, and lists of resources expanding on the bulletin board, they realize their productivity. Teachers delight in student learning: a previously shy and withdrawn student accepts responsibility for two interviews; non-readers refer to books for needed information. Community members commend the students on the attractiveness of the garden and request copies of the resource directory.

On a typical day we might see many activities. Mike, the custodian, chatting with several students in the garden. Carol and Janet are raking some leaves, and Tsuneo got the hose ready for watering the grounds. We heard Ephraim explain his desire to dig to China. He'd heard that if he dug deep enough, he'd eventually find China — and he wanted to check this out. He decided to propose this as a project to his teacher. In the interim, the students helped Mike, who is responsible for keeping the garden clean and depends on his team of students to help keep the plants healthy by weeding, watering, and watching. These children live in apartment houses and had no experience maintaining gardens. They took great pride in their school garden. They researched which plants are likely to survive in this setting and establish priorities, assigning some the responsibility of designing the placement of the bulbs, and others strategies for keeping the garden free from litter and straying animals.

The highlight of their day was working in their garden with Mike, but on rainy and cold days, the students used the small room just inside the school entrance to write reports on their plantings. The students enjoy themselves, oblivious to their learning of mathematical concepts as they measure the area available for planting, weigh the rubbish in arranging for its removal, and compute the costs as they create their own budget. They take for granted their increasing language proficiency as they speculate, discuss and explain. They are concerned with keeping their plants healthy and seek alternative strategies for nursing them back to health when they seem to falter. They argue about budget allocations for specific plantings and contemplate organizing a plant sale to raise additional funds for their project. Their comprehension of the botanical life cycle became apparent as the students engaged in all of these activities.

As they plan the year's planting schedule, they consider the weather conditions which will influence both the timing of their activities, and the conditions which will make certain plants more viable than others. Throughout the process of their creation and cultivation of the garden, the students refer to resources — in the school library, from teachers, from local residents, and particularly the staff at the local botanical garden who visit on a regular basis. These resources were identified when students conducted a staff poll, asked their parents for ideas, and explored the map of the community created by another group in the school.

Additional students confered with the garden group. A team of students representing the Improving Our Community Group were concerned with the drug situation in the community. They wanted to know if the gardeners ever found crack vials, or any evidence that drug sales were occurring near the garden. They talked of their common concerns with the gardeners, first individually, and then collectively.

There were many groups visibly active in and around the building. For example there were five students talking as they walked to the library (which occupies 85 per cent of the main floor). Jacques, who is familiar with many resources in the library from his daily visits with his older brother, suggested going there to find books on gardening. He used the computer terminal to find titles listed under 'Gardens'. Others watched as Jacques explained what he was doing. After a while, Agatha suggested just looking through some books. She approached Ms. Barry, the librarian who smiled, listened to her question, and then went with her to the science section. Once Agatha was comfortable with her resources, Ms. Barry returned to the small group at the computer, suggesting they consider exploring other terms within the data base to expand their visions.

These groups of students were all task oriented. They collaborated on identifying assignments and planning how to accomplish their goals. As they engaged in these projects, they acquired, along with the academic content, important social skills which are crucial for academic achievement and success throughout life (Goleman, 1990). They were not bored and while there were no real discipline problems, sometimes the students needed to be reminded to control their enthusiasm by lowering their voices and by sharing materials with others. This situation is a sharp contrast with previous years when students endeavored to avoid schoolwork which translated into tedious and seemingly endless supplies of worksheets. Instead, the students are more confident in their abilities, and they were eager to become more knowledgeable so they could have a greater impact on their own lives and those of others — they feel respected and confident.

The teachers moved from group to group. They listened, offered advice and wrote notes and requests. They then ordered materials appropriate to the students' activities, to find ways to expand students' information base and to challenge them to consider issues of increasing complexity and abstraction; they also created systems for documenting and assessing student progress.

Each student stored work in a portfolio, which serves many purposes: the students could refer back to their previous work; the teacher could respond to work, compare growth over time, or document the range of work accomplished, and plan activities which would increase each student's proficiencies and experiences. The teachers considered their evaluation criteria in new ways, focusing on the content of individual student projects instead of the number of acceptable responses to uniformly administered short answer tests. They are not alone in trying to conceptualize their assessments of student learning; they join a growing group of educators who are seriously contemplating portfolio assessments. These new professional concerns became apparent when they changed their process of assessing progress. The teachers are enacting important professional responsibilities in this process.

The teachers reached out to the community. Many people seem enthusiastic about working with the school project in different ways. A supportive learning community evolves with students, faculty (teachers and administrators), and the community collaborating to help students become more knowledgeable while contributing valued resources to the community. This expanded learning environment includes students' families and other members of the community with both the time and the desire to nurture these youngsters.

The teachers also invited the nearby university to establish a long-term relationship with the program. Teachers participate in university activities and use university resources (with their students) while the local university faculty (with their students) do the same at the school. In the process university faculty have the opportunity to study how individual students and educators learned. This knowledge could serve to restructure the continuum of professional education from the beginning teacher to the learning specialist.

University colleagues promote school-university collaborations at this site for those university students who are starting their professional preparation. Interns enhance the adult-student ratio while participating in exciting, effective programs. These sites enable new teachers and experienced teachers to participate in professional settings that are consistent with current theories and ideals. (This collaboration among professionals is also realized in the Professional Development Schools advocated by the Holmes Group, 1990; and Goodlad, 1990.) The interns become assistant teachers at this school and elsewhere, gradually accepting the same responsibilities as more experienced teachers. In the transition stage, they work closely with experienced colleagues, sharing specific daily activities and plans. Some are more knowledgeable and more effective at promoting student learning; these are identified as

Figure 8.3: Evolution of a learning specialist

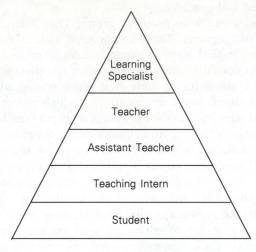

learning specialists. The stages of their evolution from student to learning specialist are presented in Figure 8.3. Learning specialists mentor all administrators, including interns and assistant teachers, while particularly nurturing challenging students. The learning specialists are students as well, constantly seeking to enhance their effectiveness with students and professional colleagues, particularly through reflective inquiry as explained in Brause and Mayher (1991a) and Schön (1987; 1990).

Future Program Plans

The vitality of the staff is much improved over previous years. To sustain the innovative course established, certain accommodations are essential, namely:

Time schedules must be reconceptualized; and
The responsibilities of professional staff need to be reconceptualized.

Teachers and learning specialists need to reorganize the traditional school assignments, allocating time differently and creating different job descriptions, placing teachers and administrators in new roles which will result in increased student learning. These changes in responsibility will influence the school time schedules, particularly planning for students to be actively engaged in learning throughout the day, with assistance from teachers and learning specialists as needed.

Modifications in the program structure are evident in a revised time

Figure 8.4: A student's schedule

	M T W	Th	F
9–12	Cross-grade-collaboration and individual conferences	Community visits	School meeting
12–1	Lunch Lunch Lunch	Lunch	Lunch
1–3	Cross-grade-collaboration and individual conferences	Community visits	Grade meeting

Figure 8.5: A learning specialist's schedule

	M	T	W	Th	F
9–12	Student consult.	Student consult.	Student consult.	Staff mtg.	Student consultations
12–1	Lunch	Lunch	Lunch	Lunch	Lunch
1–3	Student consult.	Student consult.	Student consult.	Staff mtg.	Student consultations

schedule. (Figures 8.4 and 8.5 present a program for students and learning specialists respectively.) With time, the learning specialists expand this program in many ways. They create cross-age groups, and connect with other experts and community members who, on Thursdays, accompany students to their community projects. These Thursday morning community visits to work together free the staff for significant blocks of time. The teachers and learning specialists are thus freed to share their reflections, their problems, their ideas, their insights and their strategies. These sessions also include discussions of current professional issues as well as future dissemination activities. The learning specialists take major responsibility for focusing discussions on specific learning issues. They promote increased inquiry among teachers, and advance specific strategies for encouraging student achievement. They need these sessions to evaluate students' progress, share concerns and create plans for both the short- and long-term.

Another goal is to increase the number of school sites where students and adults collaborate. This decision reflects their realization that expanding the current program will probably jeopardize its effectiveness. But as professionals they feel obligated to increase opportunities for more students to participate in effective educational settings. In addition, attendance and participation at local and national conferences needs to become a regular staff expectation for continued development and expansion of the program.

Reflecting on the Outcomes

The staff at the Community School want to spread the news about their accomplishments, to get supportive feedback and recognition as well as to increase the number of educators who take personal responsibility for their students' learning. They create alternatives to traditional instructional and assessment practices, accommodating the need for external accountability while celebrating the individual student's right to learn. They devote much time to building a learning community. While the teachers acknowledge that it is time consuming, they realize that their commitment is making a difference. They are challenged by their new perspective on themselves as professional educators rejecting external control and accepting responsibility for their decisions, and for their students' learning. The staff seeks to broaden the students' worlds while broadening their own conceptions of how professionals conduct themselves and how students learn most effectively. Time schedules are flexible to accommodate natural learning processes. The teachers expand the learning environment from the four walls of the conventional classroom to the larger community, engaging in frequent field visits. These visits enable both the teachers and the students to form clearer understandings of how and why things happen. Respect, trust, confidence and intellectual engagement are essential to the success of the educational program. Competition is de-emphasized. Cooperation, group activities, knowledge-building and taking leadership are encouraged. They are adopting an uncommon-sense stance, crucial to the creation of settings of educational excellence.

These teachers epitomize qualities of a great teacher identified by Hechinger (1987):

- make education come to life
- use students' experiences
- incorporate dramatic role play
- are unconventional, even controversial
- learn from teaching
- establish a fair, just community
- share with colleagues
- give each student a chance to be a leader and a follower
- develop their own methods without relying on prescribed, or published materials
- work with students to guide student learning
- hold students to their word
- look at student's progress, not grades or others' comments
- convey personal feelings
- have a long-lasting influence.

Hechinger added, 'Anyone who has never had at least one [great] teacher is truly deprived. To expect many is unreasonable.' The intent of the Community

School is for students to experience many great teachers. Instead of enduring school, schooling becomes an enriching experience.

The students become apprentices, working as reporters, scientists, historians, researchers, gardeners, writers, photographers, and teachers. They learn as they work on real projects. Exploring and considering new perspectives are emphasized, replacing the accumulation of facts. As the students mature, the students accept more challenging tasks, consistent with the goals of the Coalition for Essential Schools initiated by Ted Sizer. (See Appendix C for a list of these schools.)[1] Integrating learning and living avoids the isolation of schooling, invigorating children and adults, students and educators.

School becomes integrated into the community and school-sponsored activities expand student opportunities for diverse experiences. Parents collaborate on projects as their time allows. Perhaps most important of all in this process, is the respect which the students are realizing in their work with adults. In the process of working with children, the adults are becoming aware of how complex learning is, and instead of trivializing it, they are celebrating it.

All of these effects of the program lead to students and teachers who are no longer demoralized, who are happy to be together and respect each other's achievements and activities. By organizing time to accommodate the holistic, individualistic and active nature of learning, teachers become resources rather than transmitters of information. Their titles have changed as well; I call them 'learning specialists' conveying both that they have a deep understanding of current theories and research on *how* people learn and they are *lifelong* learners themselves, expert at constantly learning. These learning specialists guide the role transformation for colleagues. Eventually, learning specialists, along with teachers, assistant teachers, interns, and parents consult with the students as they pursue their projects.

In contrast to the bureaucratic organization outlined in Chapter 5, a more integrated and democratic organization results, as presented in Figure 8.6. The hierarchical bureaucratic organization has given way to a more shared structure where responsibilities are identified and assigned as needed. No one person's day is exclusively focused on administrivia. Every individual is responsible for promoting learning. Much of the accountability previously accommodated by test scores is fulfilled by analyzing the contents of students' portfolios, presentations and other shared performances and products. All adults are responsible during each day for being with students. The prime goal of serving students has replaced the bureaucratic goal of efficiently moving papers and people from place to place.

There are five key elements which contribute to this uncommon-sense organization of the Community School:

1   Student learning is at the heart of all school decisions. Good intentions necessitate constant vigilance, reflection on the impact of practice, and revision to improve. Students are trusted and respected in all their

Figure 8.6: School organization

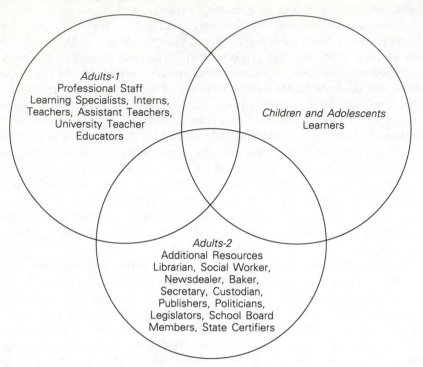

activities. (For useful guidelines on the characteristics of such settings, see The *Rights and Responsibilities of Students and Teachers* in Appendix B.)

2 Students (with parental or other appropriate adult guidance) personally choose educational programs designed to promote students' increasing responsibility as complex decision-makers.

3 Learning is viewed as a complex, personal, lifelong process. Schools are responsible for nurturing individual learners' growth and development as lifelong learners.

4 Schools are collaborative communities where professional educators share goals, concerns and resources with colleagues, parents, students and other members of the community. Professional educators accept increasing responsibility for students' progress, from initial professional preparation as teachers to becoming learning specialists. School activities which enhance the quality of life in the community, diminish barriers between school and the world outside of the school.

5 School-sponsored experiences enrich and increase each individual's knowledge, building on students' and teachers' experiences.

This list responds to many of the criticisms we considered in earlier chapters. Brown and Renyi (1990) identified needed specific curriculum and learning reforms across the disciplines, namely:

- Higher expectations and standards for all students, not just the college-bound; more challenging and interesting content for everyone, based on the assumption that all students can learn whatever they are motivated to learn when they are given adequate opportunities to learn
- More heterogeneous grouping of students and less 'ability grouping' or 'tracking'
- More responsiveness to the diverse needs of an increasingly diverse student body
- More active learning for students and less passivity; more hands-on, direct opportunities to 'make meaning' with language, science, mathematics, writing, and so on and fewer remote, irrelevant, or concocted educational experiences, including textbooks; more primary sources, original documents, 'real life' contexts
- More small-group learning for students and less isolated learning; more time spent working together cooperatively, as people do at work and in civic situations, and less time spent in competitive learning environments
- More performance assessments of students and educators and less emphasis on multiple-choice, norm-referenced testing; more accountability for robust learning experiences and less for test scores
- More critical and creative thinking and problem solving for students and less emphasis on rote knowledge, drill, and memorization
- More learning for understanding and less learning for grades or scores; more learning how to learn throughout life
- More opportunities for teachers to select or tailor learning so students learn a few essential things thoroughly, instead of merely 'covering' a large number of things
- More time organized around student learning and less time organized around adult or bureaucratic needs
- More diverse kinds of teaching and learning opportunities to accomplish the goals listed above; new kinds of preservice and in-service professional-development programs to carry out such an agenda; greater involvement of teachers in designing the curriculum (pp. 2–3).

I am convinced that our schools for tomorrow must be guided by principles similar to those operant in the Community School and those suggested by Mayher (1990) and Brown and Renyi (1990), where students become increasingly independent learners, and increasingly knowledgeable about the world. The teachers see excitement and growth in their students' proficiencies and interests as they engage in the variety of projects and are challenged to constantly consider ways of enhancing understanding. They are mindful of never letting the proverbial 'good' or better prevail when they can strive to become the best. 'Good enough' is neither good nor enough. We need all of our schools to be excellent.

There are many changes from the students' and the professional staff's perspectives. These include learning how to work as a group, how to acknowledge individual accomplishments while encouraging group solidarity, and how to deal with the criticism and jealousy inevitable among staff excluded from the mini-school.

Not only are classrooms restructured, but the whole school context and community need to be changed in tomorrow's schools. Learning specialists will guide the evolution of learner-centered educational programs, seeking alternatives to conventional staffing practices. Teachers and administrators become learning specialists. They work with students, teachers and interns exploring ways to promote learning. These visionaries carry much of the responsibility for the broad implementation of the school goals and constant reconsideration of their effectiveness. They also work closely with the most challenging students. Neophytes (interns, assistant teachers, and beginning teachers) have fewer students and are guided by experienced teachers and learning specialists to develop increasing proficiency as professional educators. These changed staffing responsibilities can do much in reforming contemporary practices in schools. In addition, constant communication and collaboration with the larger community, both in establishing goals and in implementing the educational activities are crucial to the success of this revised perspective on schools.

Two Somber Notes of Caution

There are many factors which handicapped this and similar programs, some of which I consider political. The principal who initially supported the Community School program became increasingly uncomfortable with teacher independence. She questioned why it took some so long to do things, and criticized others for not knowing either how to be efficient, or what they specifically wanted to accomplish. In part, she was reacting to the pressures placed on her by teachers in the same building who were not participating in the innovative program. She was also concerned with her own role in the process — and decided after two years that she was more comfortable when she established the policies. Her confidence in the teachers was waving. She was reluctant to confront her uneasiness and, impatient for change.

Colleagues in the same building who were not part of the program criticized the projects the students were engaged in, and criticized the developing collegial relationships. Reflection on these actions suggests several interpretations. The non-participants felt left out of the project; they were jealous of the attention focused on others; they were threatened by the possibility that they might be either encouraged to rethink their practices or to evaluate their practices in a new light. The Community School became the subject of much school gossip, undermining the initial excitement of the group.

Staff, inexperienced in working intensively together, needed to learn how to work together while they were establishing the program. They needed intensive opportunities to practice their collaborative stance, and there was little time to engage in these activities within the school day. 'Polished results' took longer to present than some people expected. Tensions mounted, and teachers who were initially excited about the prospects of the program, felt discouraged by the lack of support forthcoming from others. Two female faculty members' spouses accepted new positions in different geographic areas, causing them to leave the program unexpectedly. For these reasons, and many more, the alternative programs are struggling to survive.

If you believe, as I do, that we need to make major changes in the schools which students merely endure, and that we can no longer allow expedience to replace excellence, then we need to find ways to encourage innovation of the type which was initiated at the Community School. We need to follow Seletsky's advice (1991) and find the cracks in the strong walls which have endured, and open those cracks to create major inroads for innovation. We need to adopt an uncommon-sense stance and push our ideals to their limit in accord with John Mayher's uncommon-sense perspective on teaching and learning (1990).

This book has presented a macroethnographic perspective on school organization, which highlights some of the central problems in education today. Other crucial issues need more exploration than space provided. These include: the content of instruction; assessment of learning; development and evaluation teachers and teaching; criteria for choosing settings; the change process, and the financing of education. I hope reading this book has aroused your interest, and will result in your continued contemplation of these complex issues.

We need to accept the challenge suggested by Lamar Alexander during the hearings confirming his appointment as US Secretary of Education: 'a nation that could send a missile down a smokestack in Baghdad should be able to lift a disadvantaged child out of ignorance and poverty through a decent education' (DeWitt, 1991, p. A-22). Schools must challenge *all* of our youth, however, not only the 'disadvantaged'. We must find ways to create excellent educational programs. We cannot let commonsense prevail. We need an uncommon-sense perspective to rethink what we are doing. We cannot allow our current schools to endure . . . nor can we continue to make our youth endure schools. With a clearer sense of our problems, we can collectively make major strides towards creating schools of excellence.

Note

1   The Coalition of Essential Schools, started in 1984 as a high school-university partnership established nine common principles which guide their school reform

efforts. In the intervening years the group has enlarged to include elementary as well as secondary schools while retaining the essence of the original principles which are listed below:

1   An Essential school should focus on helping adolescents learn to use their minds well. . . .
2   The school's goals should be simple: that each student master a limited number of essential skills and areas of knowledge. . . .
3   The school's goals should apply to all students, although the means to these goals will vary as those students themselves vary. . . .
4   Teaching and learning should be personalized to the maximum feasible extent. . . .
5   The governing practical metaphor of the school should be student-as-worker, rather than the more familiar metaphor of teacher-as-deliverer-of-instructional-services. . . .
6   Students entering secondary school studies should be those who can show competence in language and elementary mathematics. . . .
7   The tone of the school should stress values of unanxious expectation ("I won't threaten you but I expect much of you"); of trust (until abused); and of decency (the values of fairness, generosity, and tolerance). . . .
8   The principal and teachers should perceive themselves as generalists first (teachers and scholars in general education), and specialists second (experts in one particular discipline). . . .
9   Ultimate administrative and budget targets should include, in addition to total student loads per teacher of 80 or fewer students, substantial time for collective planning by teachers, competitive salaries for staff, and an ultimate per pupil cost not to exceed that at traditional schools by more than 10 percent. . . . (Sizer, 1989b).

While we might take exception to some of the precepts, the identification of clear objectives provides an important document for deliberation in our neverending goal of school excellence.

Appendix A

Suggested Readings

APPLE, M. (1986) *Teachers and Texts: A Political Economy of Class and Gender Relations in Education*, NY, Routledge and Kegan Paul.

ARONOWITZ, S. and GIROUX, H. (1985) *Education Under Seige: The Conservative, Liberal, and Radical Debate over Schooling*, South Hadley, MA, Bergin and Garvey.

ATWELL, N. (1987) *In the Middle: Writing, Reading and Learning with Adolescents*, Portsmouth, NH, Boynton/Cook.

BAYER, A. (1990) *Collaborative-Apprenticeship Learning: Language and Thinking Across the Curriculum, K-12*, Mountain View, CA. Mayfield Publishing.

BISSEX, G. (1980) *GNYS at WRK: A Child Learns to Read and Write*, Cambridge, MA, Harvard University Press.

BOOMER, G. (1987) *Changing Education*, Victoria, Australia, Commonwealth Schools Commision.

BOYER, E. *High School: A Report on Secondary Education in America*, NY, Harper and Row.

BRAUSE, R.S. and MAYHER, J.S. (1991) *Search and Re-Search: What the Inquiring Teacher Needs to Know*, London, England, Falmer Press.

BRITTON, J. (1970) *Language and Learning*, Harmondsworth, England, Penguin.

BRITTON, J. (1982) *Prospect and Retrospect: Selected Essays of James Britton*, G.M. Pradl (Ed.) Portsmouth, NH, Boynton/Cook.

BRUNER, J. (1990) *Acts of Meaning*, Cambridge, MA, Harvard University Press.

CARNEGIE FOUNDATION TASK FORCE ON EDUCATION OF YOUNG ADOLESCENTS (1989) *Turning Points*, Princeton, NJ, Carnegie Foundation Task Force.

COHEN, J. and PRANIS, E. (1991) *GrowLab: Activities for Growing Minds*, Burlington, VT, The National Gardening Association.

CUBAN, L. (1984) *How Teachers Taught: Constancy and Change in American Classrooms, 1890–1980*, NY, Longman.

DEWEY, J. (1938) *Experience and Education*, NY, Macmillan.

DONALDSON, M. (1978) *Children's Minds*, NY, Norton.

DUCKWORTH, E. (1987) *The Having of Wonderful Ideas and Other Essays on Teaching and Learning*, NY, Teachers College Press.

FARNHAM-DIGGORY, S. (1990) *The Developing Child*, Cambridge, MA, Harvard University Press.

FREEDMAN, S.G. (1990) *Small Victories: The Real World of a Teacher, Her Students and their High School*, NY, Harper and Row.

GAMBERG, R., KWAK, W., HUTCHINGS, M., ALTHEIM, J. with EDWARDS, G. (1988) *Learning and Loving It: Theme Studies in the Classroom*, Portsmouth, NH, Heinemann.

GARDNER, H. (1983) *Frames of Mind*, NY, Basic Books.

GOODLAD, J. (1984) *A Place Called School: Prospects for the Future*, NY, McGraw-Hill.

GOODMAN, K., BRIDGES, L. and GOODMAN, Y. (1991) *The Whole Language Catalog*, Santa Rosa, CA, American School Publishers.

HIGH/SCOPE EDUCATIONAL RESEARCH FOUNDATION (1984) *Changed Lives: The Effects of the Perry Preschool Program on Youths Through Age 19*, Ypsilanti, MI, High/Scope Educational Research Foundation.

HOLT, J. (1989) *Learning All the Time*, NY, Addison-Wesley.

KEGAN, R. (1982) *The Evolving Self*, Cambridge, MA, Harvard University Press.

KELLY, G. (1955) *The Psychology of Personal Constructs*, NY, Norton.

KIDDER, T. (1989) *Among Schoolchildren*, Boston, MA, Houghton-Mifflin.

KOHL, H. (1967) *36 Children*, NY, New American Library.

LESTER, N. and ONORE, C. (1990) *Learning Change: One School District Meets Language Across the Curriculum*, Portsmouth, NH, Boynton/Cook.

LINDFORS, J.W. (1987) *Children's Language and Learning*, 2nd ed., Englewood Cliffs, NJ, Prentice-Hall.

MAYHER, J.S. (1990) *Uncommon Sense: Theoretical Practice in Language Education*, Portsmouth, NH, Boynton/Cook.

MCLAREN, P. (1989) *Life in Schools*, NY, Longman.

MCNEIL, L.M. (1986) *Contradictions of Control: School Structure and School Knowledge*, NY, Routledge and Kegan Paul.

METROPOLITAN LIFE INSURANCE AND HARRIS, L. (1988) *The American Teacher 1988: Strengthening the Relationship Between Teachers and Students*, NY, Metropolitan Life.

MOFFETT, J. (1973) *A Student-Centered Language Arts and Reading Curriculum K-13*, Boston, Houghton-Mifflin.

MUNICIPAL ART SOCIETY (1991) *The Livable City*, **15**(1), March.

NATIONAL COMMISSION ON EXCELLENCE IN EDUCATION (1983) *A Nation At Risk*, Washington DC, US Government Printing Office.

New York Times (1991) 'School tries longer classes to deepen learning', March 27, p. B7.

O'NEILL, M. (1991) 'The Restaurant is Small and Intense, and the Chefs and Waiters are, Too,' *New York Times*, May 29, p. C-1.

POWELL, A., FARRAR, E. and COHEN, D. (1985) *The Shopping Mall High School*, Boston, Houghton-Mifflin.

RICHMOND, G.H. (1974) *The Micro-Society School: A Real World in Miniature*, NY, Harper and Row.

SCHÖN, D.A. (Ed.) (1990) *The Reflective Turn*, NY, Teachers College Press.

SEDLAK, M., WHEELER, C. PULLIN, D. and CUSICK, P. (1986) *Selling Students Short*, NY, Teachers College Press.

SIZER, T. (1984) *Horace's Compromise: The Dilemma of the American High School*, Boston, MA, Houghton-Mifflin.

SMITH, F. (1986) *Insult to Intelligence*, NY, Arbor House.

VYGOTSKY, L.S. (1978) *Mind in Society*, Cambridge, MA, Harvard University Press.

WELLS, G. (1986) *The Meaning Makers: Children Learning Language and Using Language to Learn*, Portsmouth, NH, Heinemann.

WILSON, J.L. (1990) *The SimCity Planning Commission Handbook*, NY, McGraw-Hill.

Periodicals

Education Week
Education Leadership
Elementary School Journal
Harvard Education Letter
Harvard Educational Review
Kappan
Rethinking Schools
School Library Journal
School Voices
Teachers College Record

Rights and Responsibities of Students and Teachers

(From Lloyd-Jones, R. and Lunsford, A.A., (Eds) (1989) pp. 45–48.)

Preamble

In order to work productively, students and teachers in all subject areas should enjoy the following rights and privileges, which represent not luxuries but *necessary conditions* for effective learning and teaching. Because of the intensive student/teacher interaction in language arts classes, these conditions are particularly important to English teachers from elementary school through college. This list of rights covers all levels of education, although some items apply specifically to one institutional setting and not to others. The 'responsibilities' in this list form the reverse side of the 'rights'. For example, the right of students to well-planned, productive classtime is a responsibility of teachers; the right of teachers to reciprocal evaluation is a responsibility to carry out such evaluation.

Rights of Students

Place

- A safe place to keep private possessions
- Safe and clean hallways, gymnasiums, and lunchrooms
- Sanitary bathrooms where doors are on stalls
- Private times
- Adequate public telephones to make personal phone calls at appropriate times
- Clean and cheerful classrooms
- A comfortable place to spend free time and to eat meals
- A well-equipped library, staffed by a professional librarian who also has training in learning

- An adequate supply of quality, up-to-date textbooks, resources, and materials
- Classroom libraries of quality literature

Time

- Times when teachers are available to meet with students
- Humane spacing of tests and homework
- Homework and assignments returned within a reasonable amount of time
- A reasonable, consistent, and public policy regarding absences, tardiness, and attendance
- Adequate time for breaks, including recess, lunch, and passing between classes
- Few or no classroom interruptions
- Classroom time that is planned and spent productively

Staff/Student Relations

- Substitute teachers who deal with students in a professional manner
- Teachers who are up-to-date on current teaching methods and their subject areas
- Teachers who treat students with a humane and caring attitude
- Administrators and counselors who are accessible to students and parents
- Teachers who make goals, expectations, and classroom guidelines clear from the beginning of the school year or semester
- Teachers who are not habitually late or absent
- A person to see (administrator, department head, counselor, ombudsperson, or community liaison) to appeal alleged unfair or abusive behavior
- Flexibility about use of language or dialect in journals or private writing or writing not directed to a specified audience
- Classroom free of racial and sexual discrimination, especially including such discrimination in the setting of standards
- Teachers who are committed to students' personal as well as intellectual growth and who see students regularly

Rights of Teachers

Place

- A private classroom for elementary and secondary school; an appropriate classroom (size, configuration, equipment) for college

- Sufficient supplies of appropriate materials, including texts, to carry out the curriculum
- A private, comfortable place in which to meet with students, parents, or other teachers
- A place to be alone
- A safe place in which to keep private possessions
- A telephone in a department office or classroom, or any other arrangement that assures immediate and private contact with the outside world
- A clean, appealing lounge and private restrooms
- A large, up-to-date professional library
- An adequate number of functioning typewriters, word processors, copiers, and telecommunications equipment

Time

The items under this heading are primarily directed to elementary and secondary schools. Although some of these items are concerns at the college level, different circumstances pertain there.

- Some adjustable periods or segments in the school week for the purpose of meeting with students and parents
- Time for private planning (recommended: at least one hour every school day for K-12)
- Time each week during school for meeting and planning with other teachers (recommended: at least two hours each week for K-12)
- Time to be alone every school day
- A reasonable lunch period with no supervisory duties (recommended: forty-five uninterrupted minutes)
- Paid days to attend professional meetings and conferences
- An opportunity for teachers with outside professional duties and responsibilities — such as holding office in local, state, regional, national, and international groups — to engage in these activities without penalty
- Few or no classroom interruptions
- Sufficiently long class periods for the achievement of educational objectives
- No more than four classes per day with a maximum of 100 students at the secondary level; no more than twenty students for elementary teachers
- Opportunity to spend time with exemplary professionals and projects

Staff Status

- A decisive voice in the curriculum and all other matters that affect the teacher's professional life

- A voice in the hiring of new teachers in one's department
- Individual conferences with administrators, set at convenient and appropriate times, to discuss mutual concerns
- Evaluation only by persons with current knowledge about . . . learning and teaching . . .
- Evaluation aimed at improving instruction rather than at judging the person
- Reciprocal evaluation: teachers evaluate all those who evaluate them
- Representation on the school board or board of trustees by a teacher elected by the faculty
- Regular, frequent provisions for growth and learning within the school
- A salary commensurate with the teacher's professional standing
- Opportunities for new teachers to be oriented by their colleagues to their new academic institution

Coalition of Essential Schools

Arkansas
Sheridan Junior High School
Springdale High School

California
Rancho San Joaquin Middle School (Irvine)
Mid-Peninsula High School (Palo Alto)

Connecticut
Avon High School
Watkinson School (Hartford)
Weaver High School (Hartford)

Florida
The Nova Complex Schools
• Blanche Forman School (Davie)
• Eisenhower School (Davie)
• Nova Middle School (Ft. Lauderdale)
• Nova High School (Ft. Lauderdale)

Illinois
Anna-Jonesboro High School
Carpentersville Middle School
Calumet High School (Chicago)
Sullivan High School (Chicago)
Elmwood Community School
North Middle School (Godfrey)
Malta Junior/Senior High School
Broadmoor Junior High School (Pekin)
Sparta High School
Lake Park High School (Roselle)

Iowa
Metro High School (Cedar Rapids)

Kentucky
Jefferson County Public Schools
- Ballard High School
- Brown School
- Doss High School
- Eastern High School
- Fairdale High School
- Iroquois High School
- Seneca High School
- Western High School
- Pleasure Ridge Park High School
- Mayme Waggener High School (St. Matthews)
- Valley High School

Maine
Portland High School

Maryland
Bryn Mawr School (Baltimore)
Park Heights Street Academy (Baltimore)
Walbrook High School (Baltimore)

Massachusetts
Andover High School
Brimmer and May School (Chestnut Hill)

Missouri
Parkway South High School (Manchester)
The Whitfield School (St. Louis)

New Hampshire
Thayer High School (Winchester)

New York
Fox Lane High School (Bedford)
Bronxville High School
Croton-Harmon High School
Alternative Community School (Ithaca)
John Jay High School (Katonah)
Adelphi Academy (Brooklyn)
Central Park East Secondary School (Manhattan)
Satellite Academy — Forsyth Site (Manhattan)

Urban Academy — Manhattan
University Heights High School (Bronx)
Irondequoit High School (Rochester)
School Without Walls (Rochester)
Scarsdale Alternative

Pennsylvania
Elizabethtown Area High School
Alternative for the Middle Years (Philadelphia)
The Crefeld School (Philadelphia)

Rhode Island
St. Xavier Academy (Coventry)
The Gordon School (East Providence)
Narragansett Elementary School
Narragansett Pier Middle School
Narragansett High School
Hope High School (Providence)
School One (Povidence)
Mary Quirk Junior High School (Warren)

South Carolina
Heathwood Hall (Columbia)

Tennessee
Hixson High School (Chattanooga)
St. Andrew's Sewanee

Texas
Paschal High School (Fort Worth)
Westbury High School (Houston)
Judson Montessori (San Antonio)

Vermont
The Putney School

Washington
Finn Hill Junior High School (Kirkland)

Wisconson
Lincoln High School (Manitowoc)
Walden III (Racine)

Canada — Alberta
Bishop Carroll High School (Calgary)

References

AMERICAN ASSOCIATION FOR TEACHER EDUCATION (1990) *Teacher Education Policy in the States: A 50-State Survey of Legislative and Administrative Actions*, Washington, DC, American Association for Teacher Education.

ANDERSON, G.L. (1989) 'Critical Ethnography: Origins, Current Status, and New Directions', *Review of Educational Research*, **50**(3) pp. 249–70.

ANDERSON-LEVITT, K. (1989) 'Degrees of Distance between Teachers and Parents in Urban France', *Anthropology and Education Quarterly*, **20**(2) pp. 97–117.

APPLE, M. and JUNGCK, S. (1990) ' "You Don't Have to Be a Teacher to Teach This Unit": Teaching, Technology, and Gender in the Classroom', *American Educational Research Journal*, **27**(2) pp. 227–55.

ARONOWITZ, S. and GIROUX, H.A. (1985) *Education Under Seige: The Conservative, Liberal and Radical Debate Over Schooling*, South Hadley, MA, Bergin and Garvey.

ATWELL, N. (1987) *In The Middle: Writing, Reading and Learning with Adolescents*, Portsmouth, NH, Boynton/Cook.

AYERS, W. (1990) 'Classroom Spaces, Teacher Choices', *Rethinking Schools*, October–November, pp. 3, 16.

BARNES, M. (1988) *Can We Make A Better Doctor?* Boston, MA, WGBH Educational Foundation and NOVA.

BARNES, D., BRITTON, J.N. and TORBE, M. (1986) *Language, The Learner, and the Schools*, Third Edition, New York, NY, Penguin.

BARRON, J. (1990) 'Fernandez Removes Principal in Inquiry on Politics', *The New York Times*, May 22, p. B-9.

BENNETT, W. (1988) *James Madison High School Curriculum*, Washington, DC, US Department of Education.

BERGER, J. (1990) 'A Parent Representative Feels His Way', *The New York Times*, December 1, pp. 27–8.

BERNSTEIN, B. (1975) *Class, Codes and Control*, London, UK, Routledge and Kegan Paul.

BLASE, J.J. (1990) 'Some Negative Effects of Principals' Control-Oriented and

Protective Political Behavior', *American Educational Research Journal*, **27**(4) Winter, pp. 727–53.

BRADLEY, A. (1989) 'Teaching Board Says Professional Degree is not Requirement', *Education Week*, August 2, p. 1.

BRADLEY, A. (1990) 'Study Notes Lack of Policy Activity on Principalship', *Education Week*, May 2, p. 5.

BRADY, M. (1989) *What's Worth Teaching?* Albany, NY, SUNY Press.

BRAUSE, R.S. (1987) 'School Days: Then and Now', *Anthropology and Education Quarterly*, **18**(1).

BRAUSE, R.S. and BRAUSE, R.C. (1989) *Report to the Center for Workplace Literacy*, New York.

BRAUSE, R.S. and HODGE, G. (1987) *Hispanic High School Drop Outs*, Report to The Ford Foundation, New York, NY.

BRAUSE, R.S. and MAYHER, J.S. (1982) 'Teachers, Students, and Classroom Organizations', *Research in the Teaching of English*, **16**(2).

BRAUSE, R.S. and MAYHER, J.S. (1983) 'The Classroom Teacher as Researcher', *Language Arts*, **60**(6).

BRAUSE, R.S. and MAYHER, J.S. (1984) 'Asking the Right Questions', *Language Arts*, **61**(5).

BRAUSE, R.S. and MAYHER, J.S. (1985) 'Language at Home and at School', *Language Arts*, **62**(8).

BRAUSE, R.S. and MAYHER, J.S. (1989) *Project A DEPT [Achieving and Developing English Proficiency with Technology]*, Report to US Department of Education, Washington, DC.

BRAUSE, R.S. and MAYHER, J.S. (Eds) (1991a) *Search and Re-Search: What the Inquiring Teacher Needs to Know*, London, UK, Falmer Press.

BRAUSE, R.S. and MAYHER, J.S. (1991b) 'Our Students', in *The Handbook of Research in the Teaching of English Language Arts*, J. FLOOD, J. JENSEN, D. LAPP and J. SQUIRE (Eds) NY, Macmillan.

BRAUSE, R.S. and MAYHER, J.S. and BRUNO, J. (1982) *An Investigation into Bilingual Students' Classroom Communicative Competence*, Rosslyn, VA, National Clearinghouse on Bilingual Education.

BRITTON, J. (1970) *Language and Learning*, Harmondsworth, England, Penguin.

BRITTON, J. (1982) *Prospect and Retrospect: Selected Essays of James Britton*, G.M. PRADL (Ed.) Portsmouth, NH, Boynton/Cook.

BRITTON, J., BURGESS, T., MARTIN, N., McLEOD, A. and ROSEN, H. (1975) *The Development of Writing Abilities (11–18)* London, Macmillan Education and Urbana, IL, National Council of Teachers of English.

BROWN, R. and RENYI, J. (1990) The First Curriculum Congress, Unpublished report cited in Franklin, P. 1990, Editor's Column, *MLA Newsletter*, **22**(4) p. 4.

BRUNER, J.S. (1990) *Acts of Meaning*, Cambridge, MA, Harvard University Press.

BRUNER, J.S. (1986) *Actual Minds, Possible Worlds*. Cambridge, MA, Harvard University Press.

BRUNER, J.S. and HASTE, H. (Eds) (1987) *Making Sense: The Child's Construction of the World*, NY, Methuen.

BYRNE, R. (1989) 'Chess Seen As Aid in the Classroom', *New York Times*, July 19, B-7.

CAMPBELL, J. (1982) *Grammatical Man: Information, Entropy, Language and Life*, NY, Simon and Schuster.

CAMPBELL, J. (1989) *The Improbable Machine: What the Upheavals in Artificial Intelligence Research Reveal About How the Mind Really Works*, NY, Simon and Schuster.

CARMODY, D. (1989) 'Teachers Taking More Pride in Profession, Survey Finds', *New York Times*, September 22, A-14.

CARNEGIE FOUNDATION FOR THE ADVANCEMENT OF TEACHING (1988a) *The Condition of Teaching: A State-by-State Analysis*, Princeton, NJ: Carnegie Foundation for the Advancement of Teaching.

CARNEGIE FOUNDATION FOR THE ADVANCEMENT OF TEACHING (1988b) *Teacher Involvement in Decisionmaking: A State-by-State Profile*, Princeton, NJ, Carnegie Foundation for the Advancement of Teaching.

CHIRA, S. (1989) 'Governors and Experts Are Divided on Setting Nation's Education Goals', *New York Times*, December 6, p. B-3.

CHIRA, S. (1989) 'Support Grows for National Education Standards', *New York Times*, December 26, p. A-1.

CHOMSKY, N. (1989) *Necessary Illusions*, Boston, MA, South End Press.

CHOMSKY, N. (1987) *The Chomsky Reader*, J. PECK (Ed.) NY, Pantheon Books.

CHOMSKY, N. (1972) *Language and Mind*, (Enlarged Ed.) NY, Harcourt, Brace, Jovanovich.

CHUBB, J.E. and MOE, T.M. (1990) *Politics, Markets and America's Schools*, Washington, DC, Brookings Institute.

CLAIN, E. (1990) 'Letter to the Editor', *New York Times*, September 2, p. 21.

CLARKE, M.A. (1987) 'Don't Blame the System: Constraints on "Whole Language Reform"', *Language Arts*, **64**(4) pp. 384–96.

COLEMAN, J. and HOFFER, T. (1987) *Public and Private High Schools: The Impact of Communities*, NY, Basic Books.

COMMISSION ON THE SKILLS OF THE AMERICAN WORKFORCE (1990) *America's Choice: High Skills or Low Wages!* Rochester, NY, National Center on Education and the Economy.

CORCORAN, T.B., WALKER, L.J. and WHITE, H.L. (1988) *Working in Urban Schools*, Washington, DC, Institute for Educational Leadership.

COUNCIL OF CHIEF STATE SCHOOL OFFICERS (1989) *Success for All in a New Century*, A Report by the Council of Chief State Officers on Restructuring Education, Washington, DC.

CUBAN, L. (1984) *How Teachers Taught: Constancy and Change in American Classrooms: 1890–1980*, NY, Longman.

DALEY, J. (1990) 'Besieged Urban School Chief are Dropping Out', *New York Times*, December 26, p. A1.

DARLING-HAMMOND, L., GENDLER, T. and WISE, A.E. (1990) *The Teaching*

Internship: Practical Preparation for a Licensed Profession, Santa Monica, CA, RAND Center for the Study of the Teaching Profession.

DEVISE, P. (1989) *The Geography of Wealth and Poverty in Suburban America: 1979 to 1987*, Chicago, IL, Roosevelt University.

DEWEY, J. (1934) *Art as Experience*, NY, Minton, Balch.

DEWEY, J. (1963) *Experience and Education*, NY, Macmillan.

DEWITT, K. (1991) 'Nominee Criticizes Scholarship Move', *New York Times*, February 7, p. A22.

DONALDSON, M. (1978) *Children's Minds*, NY, Norton.

DUCKWORTH, E. (1987) *'The Having of Wonderful Ideas' and other Essays on Teaching and Learning*, NY, Teachers College Press.

DURKIN, D. (1978–79) 'What Classroom Observations Reveal about Reading Comprehension Instruction', *Reading Research Quarterly*, **14**(4) pp. 481–533.

EDUCATION WEEK (1989) 'Across the Nation', September 2, p. 2.

EDUCATIONAL TESTING SERVICE (1990) *America's Challenge: Accelerating Academic Achievement: A Summary of Findings from 20 of Years N[ational] A[ssessment] of E[ducational] P[rogress]*, Princeton, NJ: Educational Testing Service.

ENGLISH MAGAZINE (British) (1989) 'Leaving English', Summer, 22, pp. 21–2.

ERICKSON, F. (1989) 'The Meaning of Validity in Qualitative Research', Paper presented at the annual meeting of the American Educational Research Association, San Francisco CA.

FERNANDEZ, H. (1985) *Parents Organizing to Improve Schools*, Columbia, MD, National Committee for Citizens in Education.

FILLION, B. and BRAUSE R.S. (1987) 'Research into Classroom Practices', in *Dynamics of Language Learning*, J. SQUIRE (Ed.) Urbana, IL, National Conference on Research in English and ERIC Clearinghouse on Reading and Communication.

FINE, M. (1989) 'Silencing and Nurturing Voice in an Improbable Context: Urban Adolescents in Public Schools', in *Critical Pedagogy, the State and the Cultural Struggle*, H.A. GIROUX and P.L. MCLAREN (Eds) Albany, NY, State University Press, pp. 152–73.

FINE, M. (1991) *Framing Dropouts: Notes on the Politics of an Urban High School*, Albany, NY, SUNY Press.

FISKE, E.B. (1990) 'Lessons: More and More Educators Agree that Grouping Students by Ability is Misguided', *New York Times*, January 3, p. B-6.

FLAX, E. (1991) 'Proposal Calls for Students to Show Mastery of Skills: Washington Governor Urges Overhaul of Standards', *Education Week*, January 9, p. 1.

GAMBERG, R., KWAK, W., HUTCHINGS, M., ALTHEIM, J. with EDWARDS, G. (1988) *Learning and Loving It: Theme Studies in the Classroom*, Portsmouth, NH, Heinemann.

GARDNER, H. (1983) *Frames of Mind: The Theory of Multiple Intelligences*, NY, Basic Books.

GIROUX, H.A. (Ed.) (1991) *Postmodernism, Feminism, and Cultural Politics: Redrawing Educational Boundaries*, Albany, NY, SUNY Press.

GIROUX, H.A. (1988) *Teachers as Intellectuals: Towards a Critical Pedagogy of Learning*, Granby, MA, Bergin and Garvey.

GOLEMAN, D. (1990) 'Study of Play Yields Clues to Success', *New York Times*, October 2, p. C-1.

GOODLAD, J. (1984) *A Place Called School*, NY, McGraw-Hill.

GOODLAD, J. (1990) *Teachers for Our Nation's Schools*, San Francisco, CA, Jossey-Bass.

GREEN, J. (1983) 'Exploring Classroom Discourse: Linguistic Perspectives on Teaching-Learning Processes', *Educational Psychologist*, **18**(3) pp. 180–99.

HANLEY, R. (1989) 'New Jersey Governor Offers Plan to Teach 4 "Core Values"', *New York Times*, April 5, p. B-5.

HECHINGER, F.M. (1987) 'About Education', *New York Times*, November 10, p. C-8.

HECHINGER, F.M. (1990) 'Why Is College Tuition So High?' *New York Times*, April 25, p. B-9.

HIRSCH, E.D. JR. (1987) *Cultural Literacy: What Every American Needs to Know*. Boston, Houghton-Mifflin.

HOLMES GROUP (1986) *Tomorrow's Teachers: A Report of the Holmes Group*, East Lansing, MI: The Holmes Group.

HOLMES GROUP (1990) *Tomorrow's Schools: Principles for the Design of Professional Development Schools*, East Lansing, MI.

JENSEN, J. (Ed.) (1988) *Stories to Grow On*, Portsmouth, NH, Heinemann.

JOHNSON, S.M. (1990a) *Teachers at Work*, NY, Basic Books.

JOHNSON, S.M. (1990b) 'Making Schools Work for Teachers', *Harvard Education Letter*, **VI**(6) Nov/Dec. p. 1.

JOHNSTONE, B. (1990) *Stories, Community and Place*, Bloomington, IN, Indiana University Press.

KAGAN, J. (1989) *Unstable Ideas: Temperament, Cognition and Self*, Cambridge MA, Harvard University Press.

KAPLAN, G.R. (1989) *Who Runs Our Schools?* Washington DC, Institute for Educational Leadership.

KEGAN, R. (1982) *The Evolving Self: Problems and Process in Human Development*, Cambridge MA, Harvard University Press.

KELLY, G. (1955) *The Psychology of Personal Constructs*, NY, Norton.

KIDDER, T. (1988) *Among Schoolchildren*, Boston, MA, Houghton-Mifflin.

LAMBERT, L. (1989) 'The End of an Era of Staff Development', *Educational Leadership*, September, **47**(1) pp. 78–81.

LANZONE, S. and BRAUSE, R.S. (1990) 'Report on a high school reading program'. Submitted to Morris High School, New York City Board of Education.

LEE, F.R. (1989) 'These Kids are Better than that Ranking, A School Gripes', *New York Times*, December 20, p. B-1.

LESTER, N. and ONORE, C. (1990) *Learning Change*, Portsmouth, NH, Boynton/Cook.

LITOW, S. (1990) Speech to the New York Community Trust. New York, October.

LLOYD-JONES, R. and LUNSFORD, A.A. (Eds) (1989) *The English Coalition Conference: Democracy through Language*, Urbana, IL, National Council of Teachers of English.

[LONDON] *TIMES EDUCATIONAL SUPPLEMENT* (1989) 'The State of Play', July 14, pp. 20–21.

LOUNSBURY, J.H. and CLARK, D.C. (1990) *Inside Grade Eight:From Apathy to Excitement*, Reston, VA, National Association of Secondary School Principals.

LYONS, R.D. (1989) '100,000 sq. ft. Hunter Addition', *New York Times*, December 31, Section 10, p. 1.

MAEROFF, G.I. (1991) 'Class Size as an Empowerment Issue', *Education Week*, January 9, p. 56.

MAHARIDGE, D. and WILLIAMSON, M. (1989) *And Their Children After Them*, NY, Pantheon.

MARION, R. (1989) *The Intern Blues: The Private Ordeals of Three Young Doctors*, NY, William Morrow.

MARCUS, G.E. and FISCHER, J.M. (1986) *Anthropology as Cultural Critique*, Chicago, IL, University of Chicago Press.

MAYHER, J.S. (1990) *Uncommon Sense: Theoretical Practice in Language Education*, Portsmouth, NH, Boynton/Cook.

MAYHER, J.S. and BRAUSE, RITA, S. (1976) *An Evaluation of Bilingual Early-Start*, Report to the US Department of Education, Washington, DC.

MAYHER, J.S. and BRAUSE, R.S. (1977) *An Evaluation of the Bilingual School, 1976–77*, (1977) Report to the US Department of Education, Washington, DC.

MAYHER, J.S. and BRAUSE, R.S. (1980) *Assessments of Bilingual Students' Comprehension of School Language*, Report to the US Department of Education, Washington, DC.

MAYHER, J.S. and BRAUSE, R.S. (1984) 'Lessons from a First Grade', *Language Arts*, **61**(3).

MAYHER, J.S. and BRAUSE, R.S. (1985) 'A Structure for Inquiry and Change', *Language Arts*, **62**(3).

MAYHER, J.S. and BRAUSE, R.S. (1986) 'Is Your Classroom Like Your Grandmother's?' *Language Arts*, **63**(6).

McLAREN, P. (1989) *Life in Schools: An Introduction to Critical Pedagogy in the Foundation of Education*, NY, Longman.

McLAREN, P. (1986) *Schooling as a Ritual Performance: Towards a Political Economy of Education*, NY, Longman.

McNEIL, L.M. (1986) *Contradictions of Control: School Structure and School Knowledge*, NY, Routledge, Chapman and Hall.

MEHAN, H. (1979) *Learning Lessons*, Cambridge, MA, Harvard University Press.

MENSH, E. and MENSH, H. (1991) *The IQ Mythology: Class, Race, Gender and Inequality*, Carbondale, IL, Southern Illinois University Press.

MERCADO, C.I. (1988) 'An Ethnographic Study of Classroom Help With Language Minority Students', Dissertation completed at Fordham University.

METROPOLITAN LIFE SURVEY (1990) *The American Teacher, 1990: New Teachers: Expectations and Ideals — Part I: Entering the Classroom*, NY, Metropolitan Life Insurance Co. and Louis Harris and Associates.

MOFFETT, J. (1973) *A Student-Centered Language Arts and Reading Curriculum, K-13*, Boston, MA, Houghton-Mifflin.

MOFFETT, J. (1988) *Storm in the Mountains: A Case Study of Censorship, Conflict, and Consciousness*, Carbondale, IL, Southern Illinois University Press.

MULLIS, I. (1990) *Learning to Write in our Nation's Schools*. Princeton, NJ, National Assessment of Educational Progress, Educational Testing Service.

NATIONAL CENTER FOR EDUCATIONAL STATISTICS (1990) *National Longitudinal Survey*, Washington DC.

NATIONAL COMMISSION ON EXCELLENCE IN EDUCATION (1983) *A Nation At Risk*, Washington DC.

NEW YORK TIMES (1989) 'Boston to Close or Consolidate 9 Schools', August 26, p. 7.

NEW YORK TIMES (1990a) 'US is Said to Lag in School Spending', January 16, p. A-23.

NEW YORK TIMES (1990b) 'Equivalency Degrees Down', May 16, p. B-7.

OAKES, J. (1985) *Keeping Track*. New Haven, CT, Yale University Press.

OLSON, L. and RODMAN, B. (1988) 'In the Urban Crucible: Teachers and Students Struggle with an Indifferent System that "Grinds Them Up"', *Education Week*, June 22, pp. 27–33.

OSBORN, A.B. (1989) 'Insiders and Outsiders: Cultural Membership and the Micropolitics of Education Among the Zuni', *Anthropology and Education Quarterly*, **20**(3) pp. 196–215.

PALEY, V. (1981) *Wally's Stories: Conversations in the Kindergarten*, Cambridge, MA, Harvard University Press.

PIAGET, J. (1962) *Language and Thought of the Child*, 3rd Ed, NY, Humanities Press.

POLNER, R. (1990) 'Thousands of JHS Students Dropping Out of School', *New York Post*, October 27, pp. 5, 8.

POLANYI, M. (1958) *Personal Knowledge*, Chicago, IL, University of Chicago Press.

POLANYI, M. (1966) *The Tacit Dimension*, NY, Doubleday.

PORTER, A. (1989) 'A Curriculum, Out of Balance: The Case of Elementary School Mathematics', *Educational Researcher*, **18**(5) pp. 9–15.

PRUD'HOMME, A. (1989) 'Design for Learning', *New York*, August 28, p. 25.

RASELL, M.E. (1990) *Short Changing Education*, Washington DC, Economics Policy Institute.

RAVITCH, D. and FINN, C. (1987) *What do our 17-Year-Olds Know? A Report of the First National Assessment of History and Literature*, NY, Harper and Row.

ROSE, M. (1989) *Lives on the Boundary: The Struggles and Achievements of America's Underprepared*, NY, Free Press.

ROSENTHAL, R. and JACOBSON, L. (1968) *Pygmalion in the Classroom: Teacher Expectation and Pupils' Intellectual Development*, NY, Holt.

ROSOW, L. (1989) 'Arthur: A Tale of Disempowerment', *Phi Delta Kappan*, November, pp. 194–9.

ROTHMAN, R. (1991) 'Group unveils plan for national test for all high-school seniors', *Education Week*, February 6, p. 5.

RUTTER, M., MAUGHAN, B., MORTIMORE, P., and OUSTON, J. (1979) *Fifteen Thousand Hours: Secondary Schools and Their Effects on Children*, Cambridge, MA, Harvard University Press.

SCHÖN, D. (1983) *The Reflective Practitioner*, New York, Basic Books.

SCHÖN, D. (Ed.) (1990) *The Reflective Turn*, New York, Teachers College Press.

SELETSKY, A. (1991) 'Look for the Cracks', *Connections*, **2**(1) p. 8.

SHANKER, A. (1990) 'Twenty Years (and 1000 Columns) Later', *New York Times*, December 16, Section 4, p. 7.

SHEFFIELD, A. and FRANKEL, B. (1989) *When I was Young I Loved School: Dropping Out and Hanging In*, NY, Children's Express.

SHULMAN, L.S. (1987) 'Knowledge and Teaching: Foundations of the New Reform', *Harvard Educational Review*, **57**(1) pp. 1–22.

SIZER, T. (1984) *Horace's Compromise: The Dilemma of the American High School*, Boston, Houghton-Mifflin.

SIZER, T. (1989a) 'Education Today and Tomorrow', Presentation at the Harvard Club, New York City, September 20.

SIZER, T. (1989b) 'Diverse Practice, Shared Ideas: The Essential School', In *Organizing for Learning*, WALBERG, H.J. and LANE, J.J. (Eds), Reston, VA, National Association of Secondary School Principals, pp. 1–8.

SMITH, F. (1986) *Insult to Intelligence*, NY, Arbor House.

SMITH, F. (1990) *To Think*, NY, Teachers College Press.

SOBOL, T. (1990) 'A New Compact for Learning', Paper presented to the Center for Educational Innovation, New York, October, 25.

STANLEY, J. (1989) *Marks on the Memory: Experiencing School*, Philadelphia, Open University Press.

STARRATT, R.J. (1990) *The Drama of Schooling/The Schooling of Drama*, London, UK, Falmer Press.

STEFFENSEN, J.P. (1991) 'The Privatization of Teacher Education', *Education Week*, January 31, p. 40.

STEWART, D.C. (1989) 'What Is an English Major, and What Should It Be?' *College Composition and Communication*, **40**(2) pp. 188–202.

STONE, M. (1989) 'What Really Happened in Central Park?' *New York*, August 14, pp. 30–3.

SUNDAY WORLD HERALD (1984) 'Dealing With Discouragement: Classes Help Teachers Understand "Burnout"', April 29, p. 2-S.

SUTTON, J. (1989) 'Passing Thoughts', *Phi Delta Kappan*, November, p. 235.

TINTO, V. (1987) *Leaving College: Rethinking the Causes and Cures of Student Attrition*, Chicago, IL, University of Chicago Press.

TOMPKINS, J. (1990) 'Pedagogy of the Distressed', *College English*, **52**(6) pp. 653–60.

US BUREAU OF THE CENSUS (1983) *Characteristics of the Population: General Social and Economic Characteristics: A US Summary* (PC80-1-c1) Washington, DC, Government Printing Office.

VERHOVEK, S.H. (1990) 'New York Education Chief Seeks New Stress on Nonwhite Cultures', *New York Times*, February 7, p. A-1.

VINING, E.G. (1952) *Windows for the Crown Prince*, NY, Philadelphia, Lippincott.

VIORST, J. (1972) *Alexander and the Terrible, Horrible, No Good, Very Bad Day*, NY, Atheneum.

VONOECH, R. (1989) *Creative Whack Pack*, Stamford, CT, US Games Systems.

VYGOTSKY, L.S. (1978) *Mind in Society: The Development of Higher Psychological Processes*, M. COLE, S. SCRIBNER, V. JOHN-STEINER and M. SOUBERMAN (Eds) Cambridge, MA, Harvard University Press.

VYGOTSKY, L.S. (1986) *Thought and Language* (Ed.) A. Kozulin, Cambridge, MA, MIT Press.

WALLER, W. (1932) *The Sociology of Teaching*, NY, Russell and Russell.

WELLS, G. (1986) *The Meaning Makers*, Portsmouth, NH, Heinemann.

WELLS, G., CHANG, G.L.M. and MAHER, A. (1990) Creating Classroom Communities of Literate Thinkers, In S. SHARAN, Ed. *Cooperative Learning: Theory and Research*, NY, Prager.

WERTSCH, J.V. (1991) *Voices of the Mind*, Cambridge, MA, Harvard University Press.

WHITE, J.J. (1989) 'Student Teaching as a Rite of Passage', *Anthropology and Education Quarterly*, **20**(3) pp. 177–95.

WILLIAMS, P. (1988) *Gathering Threads — Clues to Children's Language Tapestries*, Australia, Riverina-Murray Institute of Higher Education.

YARROW, A.L. (1991) 'Teacher Corps May Feel Weight of NYC Budget Crisis', *New York Times*, January 19, pp. 33, 35.

ZILL, N. and WINGLEE, M. (1990) *Who Reads Literature?: The Future of The US as a Nation of Readers*, Cabin John, MD, Seven Locks Press.

Index